Über dieses Buch: Niemand, auch kein Politiker, hat sich so frühzeitig und so beharrlich, so eindringlich und entschieden zur Frage nach der »Wiedervereinigung« geäußert wie Günter Grass.

Dieser Band enthält die grundlegenden Reden, Aufsätze und Gespräche des Autors zum Thema: ein klares Konzept, ein präzise formuliertes Denkmodell, ein gewichtiger Beitrag zur politischen Debatte über »Wiedervereinigung« oder Konföderation, über eine deutsche Kulturnation.

»Lernen wir von unseren Landsleuten in der DDR, denen nicht, wie den Bürgern der Bundesrepublik, Freiheit geschenkt wurde, die sich vielmehr gegen den Widerstand des allumfassenden Systems ihre Freiheit erkämpfen mußten; eine drüben erstrittene Leistung, vor der wir hier, umstellt von Reichtum, arm dastehen.«

Über den Autor: Günter Grass wurde 1927 in Danzig geboren und lebt in Berlin.

Günter Grass
Deutscher Lastenausgleich
Wider das dumpfe
Einheitsgebot
Reden und Gespräche

Luchterhand
Literaturverlag

Originalausgabe
Sammlung Luchterhand, Januar 1990
Lektorat: Klaus Roehler
Luchterhand Literaturverlag GmbH, Frankfurt am Main. Copyright ©
1990 by Luchterhand Literaturverlag GmbH, Frankfurt am Main. Alle
Rechte vorbehalten. Umschlagentwurf: Max Bartholl, unter Verwendung
eines Motivs von Günter Grass. Satz: Uhl + Massopust, Aalen. Druck:
Ebner Ulm. Printed in Germany.
ISBN 3-630-61921-5

2   3   4   5   6   94 93 92 91 90

Inhalt

Lastenausgleich

Gustav Heinemann sprach vor zwanzig Jahren von »schwierigen Vaterländern«, eines nannte er beim Namen: Deutschland. Diese Feineinschätzung bestätigt sich gegenwärtig. Wieder einmal sieht es so aus, als werde vernunftbestimmtes Nationalbewußtsein von diffusem Nationalgefühl überschwemmt; beklommen bis verschreckt nehmen unsere Nachbarn den rücksichtslos herbeigeredeten Einheitswillen der Deutschen zur Kenntnis.

Das wirkliche Geschehen jedoch, wie sich das Volk der DDR von Tag zu Tag mehr Freiheiten erkämpft und dabei gewaltlos die Bastionen des verhaßten Systems schleift, dieser in der deutschen Geschichte einzigartige, weil revolutionäre und dennoch erfolgreiche Vorgang, droht in den Hintergrund zu geraten. Anderes, Zweitrangiges drängt sich vor. Einige westdeutsche Politiker beanspruchen die Rampe und selbstverständlich Rampenlicht. Während die Bundesregierung, vorneweg der Finanzminister, den Früchtekorb, drapiert mit glitzernden Versprechungen, immer höher hält und so den Revolutionären drüben immer gewagtere Sprünge abverlangt, versucht der Bundeskanzler, die Aufmerksamkeit der Welt auf sich und sein Zehn-Punkte-Programm zu lenken.

Und jenes staatsmännisch vorgetragene Flickwerk fand Beifall. Einige vernünftige Ansätze täuschten hinweg über Widersprüche und wahltaktische Auslassungen: wieder einmal wurde die uneingeschränkte Anerkennung der polnischen Westgrenze verweigert.

Tags drauf folgte die Ernüchterung. Der faule Zauber wich. Die Wirklichkeit, das heißt, berechtigte und auf Erfahrung gründende Sorgen der Nachbarn, holten den Deutschen Bundestag ein. Die Wortblase »Wiedervereinigung« platzte, weil niemand, der bei Verstand und geschlagen mit Gedächtnis ist, zulassen kann, daß es abermals zu einer Machtballung in der Mitte Europas kommt: Die Großmächte, nun wieder betont als Siegermächte, gewiß nicht, die Polen nicht, die Franzosen nicht, nicht die Holländer, nicht die Dänen. Aber auch wir Deutsche nicht, denn jener Einheitsstaat, dessen wechselnde Vollstrecker während nur knapp fünfundsiebzig Jahren anderen und uns Leid, Trümmer, Niederlagen, Millionen Flüchtlinge, Millionen Tote und die Last nicht zu bewältigender Verbrechen ins Geschichtsbuch geschrieben haben, verlangt nach keiner Neuauflage und sollte – so gutwillig wir uns mittlerweile zu geben verstehen – nie wieder politischen Willen entzünden.

Lernen wir vielmehr von unseren Landsleuten in der DDR, denen nicht, wie den Bürgern der Bundesrepublik, Freiheit geschenkt wurde, die sich vielmehr gegen den Widerstand des allumfassenden Systems ihre Freiheit erkämpfen mußten; eine drüben erstrittene Leistung, vor der wir hier, umstellt von Reichtum, arm dastehen.

Was soll also dieser Hochmut, der mit Glashausfassaden und Exportüberschüssen prahlt. Was soll dieses Besserwissen in Sachen Demokratie, deren erste Lektionen wir selbst allenfalls »ausreichend« begriffen haben. Was soll der Triumph über Skandale drüben, wenn unsere Skandale von der Neuen Heimat, über Flick und Barschel bis zum Celler Loch ihren Gestank nicht loswerden. Und was soll – gemessen an den bescheidenen Wünschen der angeblichen Habenichtse da drüben – jene, in Gestalt von Helmut Kohl, hier fleischgewordene Selbstherrlichkeit! Haben wir vergessen, wollen wir, geübt im Verdrängen, nun auch verdrängen,

daß auf dem kleineren deutschen Staat die Last des verlorenen Krieges weit mehr, als gerecht sein kann, drückte?

So sahen die Möglichkeiten der DDR nach 1945 aus, und
so wirken sie nach bis heute: kaum hatte das großdeutsche
Zwangssystem seine Macht verloren, da griff schon mit
neuen und gleichwohl altbekannten Zwängen das stalinistische System zu. Wirtschaftlich ausgebeutet von einer Sowjetunion, die zuvor vom Großdeutschen Reich ausgebeutet und zerstört worden war, beim Arbeiteraufstand im Juni
1953 sogleich sowjetischen Panzern konfrontiert, schließlich eingemauert, haben die Bürger der Deutschen Demokratischen Republik bezahlen müssen, auch stellvertretend
für die Bürger der Bundesrepublik zahlen und draufzahlen
müssen. Nach ungerechtem Maß haben nicht wir für sie,
nein, sie für uns die Hauptlast des von allen Deutschen
verlorenen Zweiten Weltkrieges getragen.

Also sind wir ihnen ziemlich viel schuldig. Nicht gönner-
haftes »Mal-kurz-unter-die-Arme-greifen« oder flinkes
Aufkaufen der »Konkursmasse DDR« ist gefragt, vielmehr
ein weitreichender Lastenausgleich, fällig ab sofort und
ohne weitere Vorbedingungen. Die Kürzung der Militär-
ausgaben und eine Sondersteuer, die, je nach Vermögen,
jeden Bundesbürger betrifft, können diese Bringschuld finanzieren.

Ich erwarte von meiner Partei, der Sozialdemokratischen
Partei Deutschlands, daß sie sich diesen gerechten, überfäl-
ligen und selbstverständlichen Lastenausgleich zueigen
macht und als Forderung ersten Ranges in den Bundestag
einbringt.

Erst dann, wenn unseren Landsleuten in der DDR, die
erschöpft sind, denen das Wasser bis zum Hals steht, die
sich dennoch Stück für Stück ihre Freiheit erkämpfen, auch

von unserer Seite Gerechtigkeit widerfährt, erst dann können sie gleichberechtigt mit uns und wir mit ihnen über Deutschland und Deutschland, über zwei Staaten einer Geschichte und einer Kulturnation, über zwei konföderierte Staaten im europäischen Haus sprechen und verhandeln. Selbstbestimmung setzt umfassende, also auch ökonomische Unabhängigkeit voraus.

Das Blendwerk der zwar verführerischen, doch auf Dauer nichtsnutzenden Wiedervereinigungsrhetorik beiseite geräumt, wird deutlich, daß die vom DDR-Ministerpräsidenten Hans Modrow vorgeschlagene Vertragsgemeinschaft der wirklichen Lage und ihren ferneren Möglichkeiten entspricht. So könnten paritätisch besetzte Ausschüsse neben naheliegenden Aufgaben im Verkehrs-, Energie- und Postbereich den in der Bundesrepublik fälligen und der DDR zustehenden Lastenausgleich regeln; sie könnten sich den schrittweisen Abbau des Verteidigungsetats zur friedenssichernden Aufgabe machen; sie könnten sodann in gemeinsamer deutscher Verantwortung die Entwicklungspolitik zugunsten der Dritten Welt koordinieren; auch den von Johann Gottfried Herder geprägten Begriff der Kulturnation mit neuen Inhalten anreichern; sie könnten – nicht zuletzt – der ohnehin grenzüberschreitenden Umweltzerstörung Halt gebieten.

Diese und mehr Anstrengungen werden, wenn sie erfolgreich sind, Raum schaffen für weitere deutsch-deutsche Annäherungen und so den Weg zu einer Konföderation beider Staaten ebnen; diese freilich, wenn sie gewollt wird, setzt Verzicht auf den Einheitsstaat im Sinne von Wiedervereinigung voraus.

Vereinigung als Einverleibung der DDR hätte Verluste zur Folge, die nicht auszugleichen wären: denn nichts bliebe den Bürgern des anderen, nunmehr vereinnahmten Staates von ihrer leidvollen, zum Schluß beispiellos erkämpften Identität; ihre Geschichte unterläge dem dumpfen Einheitsgebot. Nichts wäre gewonnen außer einer beängstigenden Machtfülle, gebläht vom Gelüst nach mehr und mehr Macht. Allen Beteuerungen, selbst den gutgemeinten zum Trotz, wären wir Deutschen wieder zum Fürchten. Weil von unseren Nachbarn mit berechtigtem Mißtrauen aus zunehmender Distanz gesehen, könnte bald wieder einmal das Gefühl des Isoliertseins und mit ihm jene gemeingefährliche Mentalität aufkommen, die sich aus Selbstmitleid als »von Feinden umringt« begreift. Ein wiedervereinigtes Deutschland wäre ein komplexgeladener Koloß, der sich selbst und der Einigung Europas im Wege stände.

Hingegen würde eine Konföderation der beiden deutschen Staaten und deren erklärter Verzicht auf den Einheitsstaat der europäischen Einigung entgegenkommen, zumal diese, gleich dem neuen deutschen Selbstverständnis, eine konföderative sein wird.

Als Schriftsteller, dem die deutsche Sprache ein grenzüberschreitendes Vermögen ist, bin ich, solange ich Sätze kritisch abklopfe, dem Entweder-Oder, dieser unheilvollen Alles-oder-nichts-Sentenz konfrontiert. Noch steht uns eine dritte Möglichkeit als Antwort auf die Deutsche Frage offen. Ich erwarte von meiner Partei, daß sie diese Möglichkeit erkennt und in Politik umsetzt.

Die SPD ist seit Jahrzehnten Schrittmacher und Baumeister einer friedfertigen, weil geschichtsbewußten Deutschlandpolitik. Wenn nicht schon zuvor, dann läßt sich jetzt, nach dem Bankrott des kommunistischen Dogmas, erkennen, daß der Demokratische Sozialismus weltweit Zukunft hat. Ich bekenne: die Rückkehr Alexander Dubceks auf die politische Bühne hat mich ergriffen, aber auch in meinen politischen Vorstellungen bestätigt. Uns Sozialdemokraten sollte der Wandel in Ost- und Mitteleuropa Impulse geben. Wir brauchen sie. Zu viele Bedenkenträger haben oft genug unsere geforderte Tatkraft gehemmt. Die neunziger Jahre werden uns politischen Gestaltungswillen abverlangen. Im Verlauf der Geschichte haben die deutschen Sozialdemokraten diesen Willen manchmal unter Hausarrest gestellt, doch oft genug bewiesen: von August Bebel bis Willy Brandt; jetzt, Hans-Jochen Vogel, bist du an der Reihe.

Viel Gefühl, wenig Bewußtsein

Ein SPIEGEL-*Gespräch, geführt von Willi Winkler*

SPIEGEL Herr Grass, vor 28 Jahren haben Sie am Tag nach dem Mauerbau einen offenen Brief an Ihre Kollegin Anna Seghers in der DDR geschrieben, in dem Sie von Ihrem Schock beim Anblick der Vopos berichteten: Ich »ging zum Brandenburger Tor und sah mich den unverkennbaren Attributen der nackten und dennoch nach Schweinsleder stinkenden Gewalt gegenüber«. Welche Gefühle haben Sie am 9. November 1989 bewegt?

GRASS Ich dachte, hier hat eine deutsche Revolution stattgefunden: unblutig, mit klarem Kopf und offenbar erfolgreich. Das hat es in unserer Geschichte noch nie gegeben.

SPIEGEL Diese Revolution wurde der SED-Regierung ja durch die Ausreisewelle über Ungarn und die Belagerung der Botschaften in Prag und Warschau abgetrotzt. Ohne diesen Druck hätte sie nicht stattgefunden.

GRASS Es war ein doppelter Druck. Ein Druck der Auswanderung und ein Druck der Protestveranstaltungen, die sich zur Revolution ausgeweitet haben. Das sind Massen gewesen, wie es sie noch nie auf den Straßen der DDR gegeben hat. Am 16./17. Juni 1953, der kein Volksaufstand war, vielmehr ein Arbeiteraufstand, aber in beiden Teilen Deutschlands verfälscht worden ist, dort zur Konterrevolution und hier nach Adenauers Sprachregelung zum Volksaufstand, waren nur 350 000 Menschen auf den Straßen.

SPIEGEL So ganz glücklich scheinen Sie mit dieser Revolution trotzdem nicht zu sein.

GRASS Die Reihenfolge der Änderungen war falsch. Es hätte die innere Demokratisierung weiter vorangetrieben, die Öffnung der Grenzen angekündigt werden müssen. Die Kommunalwahl hätte wiederholt werden müssen. Das wiederum hätte zu einer Umstrukturierung der DDR auf der höheren Ebene führen können und auch den Oppositionsgruppen mehr Spielraum gegeben. Sie hätten die politische Praxis gewinnen können, die vielen fehlt.

SPIEGEL Ihre Gefühle sind also durchaus zwiespältig?

GRASS Zwiespältig heißt, daß ich mir Sorgen mache, ob dieser kleinere deutsche Staat in dem Zustand, in dem er sich befindet, die offene Grenze aushalten wird. Und die weitere Sorge ist, daß in der Bundesrepublik in Ermangelung realisierbarer Konzepte das Wiedervereinigungsgeschrei wieder losgeht.

SPIEGEL Nun ist es aber so, daß nach konservativer Auslegung das Grundgesetz die Wiedervereinigung zwingend vorschreibt.

GRASS Im Grundgesetz steht nichts von Wiedervereinigung; in der Präambel ist die Rede von der Einheit der Deutschen, und für die bin ich auch.

SPIEGEL Dann werfen Sie jedem, der vom Wiedervereinigungsgebot der Verfassung redet, vor, daß er die Verfassung nicht kennt.

GRASS ... die Verfassung nicht kennt oder, wenn er sie kennt, wider besseres Wissen redet.

SPIEGEL Was würden Sie bei Helmut Kohl annehmen?

GRASS Ich glaube, der Bundeskanzler kennt sie gar nicht. Aber schon ein rascher Blick würde ihn lehren, daß dieser Begriff Einheit vieles erlaubt, vieles möglich macht. Mehr erlaubt als diese Entweder-oder-Forderungen, die in Deutschland schon viel kaputtgemacht haben. Da hält sich die eine Seite faul an den Status quo und sagt: Aus Gründen der Sicherheit in Mitteleuropa muß es bei der Zweistaatlichkeit bleiben. Dann gibt es die andere Liga, die sich immer zur Zeit oder zur Unzeit auf Wiedervereinigung verständigt. Dazwischen aber liegt die Möglichkeit, eine Einigung zwischen den beiden deutschen Staaten herbeizuführen. Das käme dem deutschen Bedürfnis und Selbstverständnis entgegen, und auch unsere Nachbarn könnten es akzeptieren. Also keine Machtballung im Sinne von Wiedervereinigung, keine weitere Unsicherheit im Sinne von Zweistaatlichkeit, Ausland zu Ausland, sondern vielmehr eine Konföderation zweier Staaten, die sich neu definieren müßte. Da hilft kein Rückblick auf das Deutsche Reich, sei es in den Grenzen von 1945, sei es in den Grenzen von 1937; das ist alles weg. Wir müssen uns neu definieren.

SPIEGEL Aber die deutsche Einigung seit den Befreiungskriegen lief doch immer auf eine Nation, einen gemeinsamen Staat hinaus.

GRASS Keineswegs. Damals in der Paulskirche 1848 wurde ein Vielzahl von Konzepten diskutiert. Ich beziehe mich lieber auf den Herderschen Begriff der Kulturnation.

SPIEGEL Nun ist der Begriff der Konföderation ja nicht ganz unbelastet...

GRASS Wieso?

SPIEGEL Die Ulbrichtschen Konföderationspläne der fünfziger und sechziger Jahre sind für die junge Bundesrepublik immer ein Schreckgespenst gewesen.

GRASS Es hieße Ulbricht zuviel Ehre antun, wenn man ihm nachträglich erlaubte, einen praktikablen Begriff aus dem Verkehr zu ziehen. Konföderation gibt es in vielen demokratischen Staaten. Die beiden deutschen Staaten kommen einer solchen Konföderation auch noch aus anderen Gründen entgegen. Das föderalistische Prinzip in der Bundesrepublik hat uns eigentlich trotz gewisser Erschwernisse nur Gutes gebracht, und ich wünschte mir, daß auch in der DDR im Laufe der nächsten Jahre die alten Länder wieder zum Vorschein kommen.

SPIEGEL Müßte der Vorwurf der Faulheit nicht auch Ihrem Parteifreund Egon Bahr gelten, der doch gesagt hat: Laßt uns bei Gott nicht an diesen beiden Staaten rütteln?

GRASS Also, Faulheit wäre das letzte, was ich Egon Bahr vorwerfen würde, denn er ist einer der beweglichsten Köpfe *gewesen*. Da fängt meine Kritik an. Ich glaube, daß Egon Bahr auch von dieser plötzlichen Entwicklung überrascht worden ist – das spricht nicht gegen ihn – und daß er bei seiner Politik der kleinen Schritte immer sorgfältig darauf bedacht gewesen ist, den Erfolg der kleinen Schritte abzusichern. Deshalb wird er nicht rütteln an der gegebenen Zweistaatlichkeit. Selbst bei besten Absichten würde die Wiedervereinigung dazu beitragen, uns zu isolieren. Und wenn Deutschland sich isoliert fühlt, kennen wir die oft panikartige Reaktion.

SPIEGEL Aber würde eine durch Konföderation angebundene DDR nicht zu einem Trabanten der EG werden?

GRASS Ich weigere mich, das Ganze in Schwarzweiß zu sehen. Hier die völlig runtergewirtschaftete sozialistisch-kommunistische Wirtschaft, und da wie ein festgefügter Block der Kapitalismus. Auch der Kapitalismus erfährt von Land zu Land verschiedene Ausprägungen. Also kann man auch hier differenzieren von kapitalistischer Seite und Methoden anwenden, die für die DDR akzeptierbar sind, die nicht zur Verformung und zur Verwerfung führen, die nicht zu neuen sozialen Unruhen führen, womöglich auch mit einem Rechtsruck, wie wir ihn hier aufgrund verfehlter kapitalistischer Politik haben.

SPIEGEL Was kann denn eigentlich die DDR in eine wie

auch immer geartete Zweisamkeit der beiden deutschen Staaten einbringen?

GRASS Etwas, das vielleicht jedem aufgefallen ist, der mehrmals in der DDR gewesen ist, etwas, das uns hier fehlt: ein langsameres Lebenstempo, entsprechend mehr Zeit für Gespräche. Eine interne Nischengesellschaft (ich glaube, der Ausdruck geht auf Günter Gaus zurück) ist da entstanden, etwas Biedermeierliches wie zu Metternichs Zeiten. Etwas, von dem ich nicht weiß, ob es mit der Öffnung zur Straße und zur Demokratie hin nicht schon wieder vorbei ist.

SPIEGEL Sie glauben im Ernst, dieses Spätbiedermeier könnte der geballten Wirtschaftsmacht des Westens widerstehen?

GRASS Wir vergessen, daß bei dieser notwendigen Hinwendung zum deutsch-deutschen Thema die eigentlichen Problematiken der Gegenwart verdeckt sind, aber in wenigen Wochen und Monaten sind sie wieder da: eine um sich greifende Umweltzerstörung. Das Ozonloch wird durch die Annäherung der Deutschen nicht kleiner.

SPIEGEL Wenn wir noch mal auf Ihre Gefühle zurückkommen dürfen: Hätten Sie denn vorletzte Woche im Bundestag beim Deutschlandlied mitgesungen?

GRASS Wahrscheinlich ja. Ganz gewiß aber mit anderen Gedanken als diejenigen, die es angestimmt haben. Ich vermute mal, daß sie die Wiedervereinigung im Auge hatten. Inzwischen findet schon eine Inflationierung dieser Hymne statt, und vor der ist zu warnen, gerade auch mit Rücksicht auf den doch bedeutsamen Inhalt.

SPIEGEL Der dritten Strophe?

GRASS Ja. Einigkeit und Recht und Freiheit, das sind Inhalte, die beide Staaten betreffen. Die DDR kann uns etwas geben, ja, einen Impuls. Sieht es bei uns denn so blendend aus? Ist denn bei uns das, was in der Verfassung steht, so deckungsgleich mit dem, was Verfassungswirklichkeit bedeutet? Ist bei uns der arme Mann oder der nicht betuchte Mann in der Lage, vor unseren Gerichten seinen Rechtsstandpunkt, sein Recht durchzukämpfen? Gehört nicht Geld dazu, gehören nicht hochdotierte Anwälte dazu, um Recht durchzusetzen in der Bundesrepublik? Gibt es diese Art von Ungleichheit nicht in einem skandalös großen Maß in einem reichen Land? Hätten wir nicht allen Anlaß, den neuen, den gewaltlos revolutionären Impuls, der von der DDR ausgeht, auf uns zu übertragen?

SPIEGEL Wie das? Von der DDR lernen heißt siegen lernen?

GRASS Ich habe am 4. November auf dem Alexanderplatz eine Vielzahl von treffenden Transparenten gesehen, die meisten betrafen die Situation in der DDR. Aber ein Transparent war darunter, das nicht nur für die DDR gilt: »Sägt die Bonzen ab, schützt die Bäume«. Diese Bonzen gibt es auch bei uns in der Bundesrepublik. Und die Bäume die zu schützen sind, gleichfalls. Eine, wenn Sie so wollen, gesamtdeutsche Parole: ich habe selten die Doppel-Problematik unserer Existenzlage so knapp formuliert gesehen.

SPIEGEL Fürchten Sie denn, daß die Bonzen in der Bundesrepublik in dem Maß selbstgefälliger und gefestigter werden, wie es denen in der DDR schlechter geht?

GRASS Ich will beispielhaft einen einzigen Fall nennen: den Herrn Lambsdorff, einen Mann, der einiges am Stekken hat, Vorsitzender einer demokratischen Partei und von keinem Selbstzweifel angekränkelt ist. Der erst mal die großen Reformen in der DDR sehen will, bevor er Geld lockermacht. Dieser Mann mit seiner Vergangenheit und seiner Selbstgefälligkeit wäre, auf unsere Verhältnisse übertragen, der Bonze, der abgesägt werden muß, damit die Bäume geschützt werden können.

SPIEGEL Die DDR war bisher der einzige deutsche Staat, in dem der Sozialismus probiert worden ist. Dieses Experiment scheint jetzt zu Ende zu gehen.

GRASS Doch unter welchen Bedingungen fand dies statt: dieser kleine Staat hat die Hauptlast des verlorenen Krieges tragen müssen. All die Jahre hindurch bis heute. Allein das wäre Verpflichtung für uns, möglichst selbstlos zu helfen. Die DDR hat unter weit schwierigeren Bedingungen etwas aufbauen müssen, unter einem wirtschaftsunfähigen, zentralistischen Bürokratismus, unter der Last des Stalinismus und ohne Marshall-Plan, auch mit weit größeren Reparationsleistungen. Das Experiment ist auch aus diesen Gründen gescheitert.

Doch gibt es bei der DDR-Opposition und zwar nicht nur bei der neugegründeten Sozialdemokratischen Partei, sondern auch beim Neuen Forum und bei der Gruppe Demokratie Jetzt Versuche, einen demokratischen Sozialismus zu entwickeln. Denn es ist mit keinem Satz bewiesen, daß der Niedergang dieses Wirtschaftssystems, das sich zu Unrecht sozialistisch genannt hat, auch das Experiment eines demokratischen Sozialismus in Deutschland beendet hat. Diese abenteuerliche These, die auf nichts gründet, zielt natürlich hauptsächlich gegen die Sozialdemokraten.

SPIEGEL Hat der Sozialdemokrat Günter Grass eigentlich eine Erklärung dafür, warum gerade die Sozialdemokraten dieser Entwicklung so sprachlos gegenüberstehen?

GRASS Ich glaube, daß sich die Sozialdemokraten von ihrer erfolgreichen »Politik der kleinen Schritte« den Blick haben verstellen lassen auf Entwicklungen, die sprunghafter sind und schneller gehen. Doch sprachlos sind die Sozialdemokraten jetzt nicht mehr. Daß sie es eine Zeitlang gewesen sind, war oft ein Ärgernis. Zum Beispiel löste die Ankündigung einer Neugründung der Sozialdemokratischen Partei in der DDR zunächst einmal Verwirrung aus, stieß auch auf Unverständnis wie »Muß das jetzt sein?« und »Ist das der richtige Zeitpunkt?« – lauter Bedenkenträger meldeten sich zu Wort.

SPIEGEL Wie kann es denn sein, daß eine Partei wie die SPD, die doch so viele Deutschlandpolitiker hohen Kalibers hat, so leidenschaftlich auf das falsche Pferd, nämlich auf ihre SED-Kontakte gesetzt hat?

GRASS So sehe ich das nicht. Es ist ja kein Fehler, wenn man SED-Kontakte hat, nur halte ich es für falsch, daß man ausschließlich sich auf SED-Kontakte konzentriert und nicht gleichzeitig das im Auge behält und, wo es angemessen ist, mit Sympathie und Solidarität unterstützt, was sich in einem Land tut und entwickelt.

SPIEGEL Norbert Gansel hat offenbar unter Schock am Ende der Honecker-Ära den Spruch geprägt: Wandel durch Abstand.

GRASS Ich glaube, daß er das heute nicht mehr so formulieren würde. Aber seine Kritik war begründet.

SPIEGEL Also bleibt es doch dabei: Die SPD hat keine klare Linie in der Deutschlandpolitik.

GRASS Man kann immerhin darauf verweisen, daß man zum richtigen Zeitpunkt Kontakte mit offiziellen Stellen geknüpft, dann etwas erarbeitet hat, was nicht nur die Beziehung SPD und SED, sondern die Bevölkerung insgesamt betrifft. Und auf der Grundlage dieses damals erarbeiteten gemeinsamen Papiers war es für die Opposition leichter, zu einem eigenen Selbstverständnis zu finden und zu dem zu kommen, was sie heute ist.

SPIEGEL Helmut Kohl hat gesagt, die Verfassung in der Bundesrepublik erlaube ihm nicht, für Gesamtdeutschland zu sprechen, erlaube ihm also auch nicht, die polnische Westgrenze anzuerkennen.

GRASS Aber damit spricht er ja dem damaligen Bundeskanzler Willy Brandt das Recht ab, die Warschauer Verträge unter Dach und Fach gebracht zu haben, auf die Kohl sich gleichzeitig beruft. Es ist seine Rücksichtnahme auf die CDU, auf den rechten Flügel der Union, es ist die Angst vor den Republikanern, die Kohl hindert, dieses erlösende, befreiende und notwendige, schon längst überfällige Wort zu sprechen. Und das ist der eigentliche Skandal, denn diese Gelegenheit wird sich ihm nicht mehr bieten.

Man muß jetzt auch noch über die Peinlichkeiten der Polenreise des Kanzlers sprechen. Über die Engstirnigkeit dieses Mannes, die Unbelehrbarkeit, die penetrante Besserwisserei und das schier Unerträgliche dieses Mannes als Bundeskanzler. Ich weiß nicht, wer ihm zum Annaberg geraten hat, das einzig Positive daran ist, daß die jüngere Generation durch Nachfragen, was war denn da los auf dem Annaberg, eine nachträgliche Geschichtslektion bekommen hat. Wie dort Polen von deutschen Freikorps, die auch an anderen Stellen tätig waren, zusammengeschossen worden sind. Ich weiß nicht, welche Geschmacklosigkeiten, Instinktlosigkeiten Herrn Kohl noch einfallen werden in Zukunft. Seine Amtstätigkeit ist in dieser Beziehung konsequent.

SPIEGEL Wie kommt es eigentlich, daß den Intellektuellen in der Bundesrepublik so wenig zur deutschen Frage einfällt?

GRASS Das ist nicht pauschal zu beantworten. Da mögen viele Dinge eine Rolle spielen: der Kulturbetrieb in der Bundesrepublik absorbiert sehr viel, es ist ein hochdotierter Betrieb, der zur Beschäftigung mit sich selbst reizt. Dann gibt es einige Trends, die besonders von der Kritik gewürdigt werden. Etwa eine Literatur, die sich sehr stark mit sich selbst beschäftigt, was sicher auch seine Berechtigung hat. Doch das ist nicht gerade eine Position, die Schriftsteller dazu bringen könnte, von sich abzusehen und sich innerhalb einer Gesellschaft oder einer geschichtlichen Entwicklung zu begreifen, als Zeitgenossen zu begreifen. Das ist zum Beispiel meine Position, die des Zeitgenossen. Und die hat mich, ob ich's wollte oder nicht, immer wieder dazu gebracht, Stellung zu beziehen.

Mir ist gerade in diesen Tagen eine Rede eingefallen, die ich auf Einladung des Presseclubs Bonn Ende der sechziger Jahre oder Anfang der siebziger Jahre gehalten habe und die damals viel Widerspruch fand. Sie hieß: »Von der kommunizierenden Mehrzahl«. Und damals habe ich, mit anderen Worten als heute, ein Nebeneinander und Miteinander, DDR mit BRD, zu formulieren versucht. In den »Kopfgeburten« komme ich neben dem Thema Dritte Welt immer wieder auf das, was vor der eigenen Haustür liegt, zurück; in diesem Buch ist auch der Begriff der Kulturnation zum erstenmal vorformuliert.

SPIEGEL Nur Ihr Kollege Martin Walser wird durch das Thema Deutschland um den Schlaf gebracht. Da kommt er dann mächtig ins Grübeln: »Wenn mir Königsberg einfällt, gerate ich in einen Geschichtswirbel, der mich dreht und hinunterschlingt.«

GRASS Das ist zuviel Gefühl und zuwenig Bewußtsein.

SPIEGEL Er meint, das sei Geschichtsgefühl.

GRASS Aber natürlich, es ist ein Schmerz, den auch ich ein Leben lang mit mir herumtrage. Geschichtsbewußtsein zu haben oder sich zu erarbeiten heißt ja nicht, daß man ohne Gefühl ist. Wenn ich nach Gdańsk fahre, um Spuren von Danzig zu suchen, bin ich nie frei von Gefühlen. Das führt oft zu Streitgesprächen, weil ich mich, wie gegen den deutschen Chauvinismus, auch gegen den polnischen Chauvinismus ausspreche.

Ich bin aber auch stolz, daß von meiner Heimatstadt etwas ausgeht. Als ich im Jahr 1981 wieder einmal in Gdańsk war und in einer Ausstellung meine Grafiken gezeigt wurden, hielt der Bürgermeister dort eine kleine Rede auf deutsch und sagte sinngemäß: Ein Sohn unserer Stadt ist zu internationalem Ruhm gekommen. Wir sind stolz auf ihn. Diese Gefühle sind auch bei mir da, aber das verführt mich nicht dazu, in Gefühligkeit auszubrechen. Und hier beginnt meine Kritik an Walser. Ich finde es sehr gut, daß er sich – auch wenn ich anderer Meinung bin – äußert, sich in dieses Gespräch einmischt und zum Widerspruch reizt. Mir ist das lieber als das mufflige Nichtsagen vieler anderer, die sich dauernd an dem Thema vorbeidrücken.

SPIEGEL Aber das hat ihm eine Einladung zur Klausurtagung der CSU nach Wildbad Kreuth eingebracht, wo er mit Theo Waigel, der auf den Grenzen von 1937 besteht, Schafkopf gespielt hat.

GRASS Das muß Walser mit sich abmachen. Was ich eher als problematisch ansehe, ist, daß ein Schriftsteller mit Gedächtnis – das ist bei einem Schriftsteller Voraussetzung –, der 1967 während der letzten Tagung der Gruppe 47 in der Pulvermühle den Boykott der Springer-Zeitungen gefordert und betrieben hat, als einer der ersten diesen Boykott durchbricht. Das hat mir weh getan.

Es sei Martin Walser unbenommen, seine Meinung zu ändern. Als ich ihn kennenlernte, war er ein aufgeklärter Konservativer vom Bodensee, mit einer gewissen vorsichtigen Neigung zur SPD hin, die sich über den Studentenprotest zur DKP-Nähe hin entwickelte, dann wieder Abstand nahm, jetzt plaudert er mit Waigel – da sind ein paar unerklärte Drehungen zuviel dabei, die mir nicht gefallen. Da bleibt auch vom so herrlich beredten Widerspruchsgeist Walsers zuviel auf der Strecke, es wird flach und endet, wie immer, wenn Intellektuelle sentimental werden, in Rührseligkeiten.

SPIEGEL Das fehlende Interesse an Deutschlandpolitik ist natürlich kein gutes Vorzeichen für Ihre Kulturnation.

GRASS Na, in der DDR ist das doch anders. Ich denke zum Beispiel an Christoph Hein. Außerdem gibt es die Autoren, die mittlerweile in der Bundesrepublik leben wie etwa Erich Loest. Ich könnte eine Vielzahl von Schriftstellern aufzählen, die aufgrund ihrer Biographie, ihrer Erfahrungen, die sie entweder in dem einen oder dem anderen oder in beiden Staaten gemacht haben, durchaus in der Lage sind, diesen Begriff Kulturnation mit Inhalt auszufüllen.

SPIEGEL Peter Schneider stellt sich für die Zeit nach der Mauer die Frage: »Können wir ohne Feind existieren?«

GRASS Ich glaube, daß zur Zeit der Westen Schwierigkeiten hat, ohne Feindbild zu leben. Daß die westliche Industrie große Schwierigkeiten hat, vom Rüstungskonzept Abschied zu nehmen. Jahrzehntelang hat man, zum Teil aus guten Gründen, das Rüstungspotential der Sowjetunion und der, damals konnte man sagen: Satellitenstaaten, als Gefahr empfunden und hat Rüstung so begründet – so hat sich das hochgeschaukelt. Aber nun, nachdem dort die Abrüstung begonnen hat, fehlen entsprechende Reaktionen auf unserer Seite. Da wird also im Wörnerstil nach wie vor die Notwendigkeit der Nato in der bestehenden Form beteuert – ein Wandel findet nicht statt. Hier trifft auch das Gorbatschow-Wort zu: »Wer sich verspätet, den bestraft das Leben.«

Die Zwiemacht aus Zwietracht

Die Zwiemacht aus Zwietracht.
Zwiefach die eine Lüge getischt.
Hier und da auf alte Zeitung
neue Tapeten geleimt.
Was gemeinsam lastet, hebt sich
Als Zahlenspiel auf, ist von statistischem Wert;
die Endsummen abgerundet.

Hausputz im Doppelhaus.
Ein wenig Scham für besonderen Anlaß
und schnell die Straßenschilder vertauscht.
Was ins Gedächtnis ragt, wird planiert.
Haltbar verpackt die Schuld
und als Erbe den Kindern vermacht.
Nur was ist, soll sein und nicht mehr, was war.

So trägt sich ins Handelsregister
doppelte Unschuld ein, denn selbst der Gegensatz
taugt zum Geschäft. Über die Grenze
spiegelt die Fälschung sich: täuschend vertuscht,
echter als echt und Überschüsse zuhauf.
Für uns, sagt die Rättin, von der mir träumt,
war Deutschland nie zwiegeteilt,
sondern als Ganzes gefundenes Fressen.

Scham und Schande

Zum 50. Jahrestag des Kriegsausbruchs

Wer sich erinnert, stößt auf Banalitäten, die auf den Schutthalden der Vergangenheit in der Regel obenauf liegen. Am 1. September 1939 suchte ich als Elfjähriger Bombensplitter im benachbarten Hafenvorort Neufahrwasser. Und als ich keine fand, tauschte ich – weiß nicht mehr, was – gegen solch ein zackiges Stück Metall. Es waren versprengte Splitter jener Bomben, die deutsche Sturzkampfflugzeuge über die Westerplatte, der polnischen Militär-Enklave im Gebiet des Freistaates Danzig, abgeworfen hatten.

So begann bei mir zu Hause der Krieg. Ich erinnere mich an spätsommerliches Badewetter, das auch anhielt, wenngleich die Ostseestrände, solange auf der Halbinsel Hela gekämpft wurde, gesperrt blieben. Der Krieg kam plötzlich, wortwörtlich von heiterem Himmel herab, war bald zu Ende und wurde später »Polenfeldzug« genannt. Ach ja, ein Onkel, der zu den Verteidigern der Polnischen Post gehört hatte, wurde standrechtlich erschossen; doch darüber sprach man in der Familie nicht.

Diesen kurzen Krieg, wie später weitere, nicht mehr so kurze Feldzüge, erfuhr ich eindringlich einseitig mit Hilfe der Deutschen Wochenschau. Nach endlosen Gefangenenkolonnen und Pferdekadavern inmitten zerbombter Artilleriestellungen belieferte sie mein Unverständnis mit Ausschnitten einer später nie wieder gezeigten Siegesparade: da marschierten Einheiten der Wehrmacht und der Roten Armee nacheinander vor einem deutschen und einem sowjetrussischen General vorbei; beide Generäle salutierten.

Polen war doppelt geschlagen: ein schwacher Staat unter

unzulänglicher Führung und eine zwar traditionsbeflissene, doch kümmerlich ausgerüstete Armee zerbrachen unter den Schlägen zweier moderner Militärmächte, indem die Wehrmacht überfallartig zuerst zuschlug und die Rote Armee den Rest besorgte. Danach entwickelte sich, wie vorgeplant, die Vernichtung der polnischen Eliten und schließlich des polnischen Volkes zum Alltagsprogramm. Von 1939 bis 1946 ging die Bevölkerung von rund 35 Millionen auf rund 24 Millionen zurück. Auf annähernd sieben Millionen wird die Zahl der im Krieg gefallenen, ermordeten und verhungerten Polen und polnischen Juden geschätzt. Und dennoch hat der Mordversuch an einem Volk, das doch besiegt, geschlagen zu sein schien, nicht verhindern können, daß sich sogleich nach dem September 1939 der polnische Widerstand zu organisieren begann. Bald erfaßte er weite Teile des Landes und wurde, als der Warschauer Aufstand zusammengebrochen war, dennoch fortgesetzt.

Wenn wir uns heute, nach fünfzig Jahren, des polnischen Leids und der deutschen Schande erinnern, bleibt, so hart wir bestraft wurden – und trotz verstrichener Zeit nicht gemildert –, Schuld genug, dieser nicht wegzuredende Bodensatz. Und sollte mit neuer Anstrengung unsere Schuld eines Tags beglichen sein, wird Scham bleiben.

Scham und Trauer. Denn das von uns Deutschen in die Welt gesetzte Verbrechen hatte weiteres Leid, abermaliges Unrecht und den Verlust von Heimat zur Folge. Millionen Ost- und Westpreußen, Pommern und Schlesier mußten ihren Ort verlassen. Diese Last war nicht auszugleichen. Dauerhafter als auf andere Deutsche schlug auf diese Vertriebenen der verlorene Krieg zurück. Solch ungleiches Maß hat viele der älteren Generationen bitter gemacht; einige sind es heute noch.

Auch ich verlor 1945 einen durch nichts zu ersetzenden Teil meiner Herkunft, meine Heimatstadt Danzig. Auch ich konnte diesen Verlust nicht leichtnehmen. Immer wieder mußte ich mir sagen lassen, wo unveränderlich die Ursachen für diesen Verlust zu finden sind: in deutscher Anmaßung und Menschenverachtung, in der Unbedenklichkeit deutschen Gehorsams, in jener Hybris, die, jedem Gesetz zuwider, das Alles-oder-Nichts zum deutschen Willen erklärte und schließlich, als alles unter Leid verschüttet lag, das Nichts nicht wahrhaben wollte.

Und das bis heute. Deshalb diese Rede über Scham und Schande. Denn zusätzlich schändlich ist es, wenn bundesdeutsche Politiker die Stirn haben, vor geneigtem Publikum die Grenzen des Deutschen Reiches von 1937 zu beschwören. So erhofft man, rechtsradikale Wähler beschwichtigen zu können. Und so wird Polens Westgrenze leichtfertig ins Gerede gebracht. Als sei Polen gegenwärtig nicht verunsichert genug. Als wolle man aus Polens Schwäche einen Vorteil herausschinden. Als müsse Polen immer wieder aufs neue von Deutschen gedemütigt werden. Als dürfe ein Bundesminister und Parteivorsitzender, bei Verzicht auf Scham, die Schande in Kauf nehmen.

Solche Sonntagsreden, gehalten mit Kalkül vor landsmannschaftlichen Versammlungen, haben ihre Vorgeschichte: während der fünfziger und sechziger Jahre gehörten sie zum Ritual einer Politik, die – abseits jeder Verantwortung – die Ursachen und Konsequenzen des begonnenen und verlorenen Krieges nicht wahrnehmen oder akzeptieren wollte. »Friedliche Rückgewinnung« und »Recht auf Heimat« hießen die durch Wiederholung leergedroschenen Floskeln. Jene Millionen Polen, die nach dem Verlust der polnischen Ostprovinzen an die Sowjetunion

Wilna und Lemberg verlassen mußten und in Danzig und Breslau angesiedelt wurden, durften ihr »Recht auf Heimat« in den Wind schreiben; nicht zu reden von der deutschen Sandkastenoffensive einer »friedlichen Rückgewinnung«.

Keine Aufklärung, kein Hinweis auf die Beschlüsse der Siegermächte in Jalta und Potsdam half. Unbelehrbar und trotzig hieß es auf Transparenten: »Schlesien bleibt deutsch!« Als sei diese im Verlauf der Geschichte zwischen Preußen und Österreich blutig umkämpfte Provinz nicht immer wieder wechselnden Herrschern untertan gewesen; als sei Danzig, bevor es durch die dritte Teilung Polens an Preußen fiel, nicht 300 Jahre unter polnischer Herrschaft reich geworden und hansisch geprägt geblieben. Das geschah alles, bevor sich Europa in Nationalstaaten organisierte und somit Anlässe für neue, vom allseitigen Nationalismus entfesselte Kriege schuf. Dieser Bazillus ist, als Widerpart der gegenwärtigen Europa-Euphorie, immer noch virulent, wie in Frankreich und Deutschland, so auch in Polen; weshalb sich polnische Nationalisten, denen ihr Polentum zum gottgefälligen Mysterium mißrät, nach wie vor einreden, es seien die ehemaligen ostdeutschen Provinzen zurückgewonnenes, urpolnisches Land. Jene Borniertheit, welche die Mißachtung geschichtlicher Tatsachen zur Tugend erklärt hat, ist offenbar in Polen wie in Deutschland seßhaft geblieben.

Dennoch fand gegen erbitterten Widerstand dieses unwirkliche Gezänk – so durfte gehofft werden – im Dezember 1970 ein Ende: in Warschau wurde durch die Unterzeichnung des deutsch-polnischen Vertrages Polens Westgrenze anerkannt. Und weil sich der damalige Bundeskanzler Willy Brandt der geschichtlichen Anerkennung von Tatsachen bewußt war, gehörten damals, neben anderen, zwei Schriftsteller zu seinem Reisegefolge. Siegfried Lenz und ich waren dabei, als durch ein völkerrechtlich gültiges Dokument der Verlust unserer Heimat besiegelt wurde. Schon lange war uns dieser Verlust gewiß gewesen; wir hatten lernen müssen, mit ihm zu leben. Mehr noch: viele unserer Bücher handelten von diesem Verlust und seinen Ursachen. Dennoch sind wir nicht reiselustig, wohl eher mit Blei in den Sohlen nach Warschau geflogen. Und erst als Willy Brandt dort auf die Knie fiel, wo unter deutscher Herrschaft das jüdische Getto gewesen ist, und deutlich wurde, daß die von Deutschen geplante und vollzogene Ermordung von sechs Millionen Juden, daß dieses Verbrechen und die Vernichtungslager Ghelno, Treblinka, Auschwitz, Birkenau, Sobibor, Belzec und Majdanek nicht zu bewältigen sind, wog der Verlust von Heimat gering.

Wenige Tage nach der Unterzeichnung des deutsch-polnischen Vertrages streikten zum ersten Male die Hafenarbeiter in den polnischen Ostseestädten. Die Miliz schoß auf Arbeiter. Die Anfänge jener ein Jahrzehnt später »Solidarnocz« genannten Gewerkschaftsbewegung sind im Dezember 1970 zu finden.

Seitdem ist Polen nicht zur Ruhe gekommen. Hoffnungen wurden unter dem Kriegsrecht zunichte. Regierungen kamen und gingen. Allein der Mangel blieb. Er begleitet auch gegenwärtig den Niedergang des alten Systems und die verzweifelten Anstrengungen der neuen, halbwegs demokratisch gewählten Regierung.

Polen braucht Hilfe, unsere Hilfe, denn noch immer sind wir in Polens Schuld. Hilfe freilich, die nicht Bedingungen diktiert, die nicht der polnischen Schwäche deutsche Stärke zu kosten gibt, die nicht auftrumpft mit schändlichen Reden wie jener, die kürzlich der bayerische Politiker Theo Waigel gehalten hat. Der 1. September sollte für ihn Anlaß genug sein, seine nur Unheil stiftenden Sätze zurückzunehmen. Wer Polens Westgrenze in Frage stellt, ruft zum Vertragsbruch auf. Wer so redet, heute so redet, noch immer so redet, handelt schamlos und macht uns Schande.

Nachdenken über Deutschland

Aus einem Gespräch mit Stefan Heym in Brüssel 1984

[...] GÜNTER GRASS Die Deutschen haben beim Suchen einer Eigendefinition als Nation lange Zeit Schwierigkeiten gehabt. Aber es gab ja, bevor Bismarck zum Zuge kam und die politische Einigung des Staates und damit auch den Nationbegriff geschaffen hat, in der Paulskirche lange und erschöpfende Debatten, darunter, wenn man es nachliest, interessante Gedanken zum Teil von deutschen Schriftstellern formuliert, von Uhland zum Beispiel, die den Begriff der Kulturnation in den Vordergrund stellten und nicht den der politischen Einigung. Sicher, die Zeiten haben sich geändert und damit auch der Kulturbegriff. Aber wenn wir davon ausgehen, daß wir in Deutschland zweimal mit unserem *politischen* Nationbegriff gescheitert sind, zu unserem Nachteil und zum Nachteil unserer Nachbarn, dann böte sich doch ein Rückgriff auf diesen nichtgemachten Versuch an.

Zumal sich gezeigt hat, daß man alles teilen konnte, geographisch, politisch, wirtschaftlich, und ausgerechnet die Kultur, der sensible Bereich, hat sich am zähesten dem Teilungsprozeß widersetzt. Wenn ich nur das Beispiel Literatur nehme, läßt sich zu meiner eigenen Überraschung nachweisen, daß es in der DDR eben nicht gelungen ist, eine Nationalliteratur zu schaffen. Und es ist trotz der Ignoranz im Westen, dem langen Abblocken der DDR-Literatur, nicht gelungen, das Interesse an der Entwicklung drüben zu stoppen. Es gibt seit einem Jahrzehnt und länger deutlich nachprüfbar ein Miteinander-Reden von Buch zu Buch, ohne daß es eine Absprache, ohne daß es Verlagsprogramme gibt, geschweige denn eine gemeinsame Kulturpolitik. Vorbei an der jeweils herrschenden Kulturpolitik sind die Autoren miteinander ins Gespräch gekommen.

Deswegen ist die Tatsache, daß wir beide heute hier sitzen, in diesem Zusammenhang kein Wunder. Vergleichbare Ministerialbeamte aus dem einen oder anderen Staat hätten größere Schwierigkeiten, bis in die Sprache hinein, miteinander umzugehen. Wir gehen immerhin davon aus, daß es eine deutsche Literatur gegeben hat, bevor es die Bundesrepublik und die DDR gab. Im Grunde ein Gemeinplatz, den aber viele Politiker, die jeweils ihren Staat für das A und O halten, nicht einsehen wollen. Und so glaube ich, daß der Kulturbegriff, erweitert um unseren gemeinsamen Geschichtsbegriff, eine tragfähige Grundlage wäre für den Versuch, den Begriff Nation neu zu definieren, bis ins Praktische hinein.

Es wird hier nicht so bekannt sein, daß es seit Jahren einen Streit zwischen beiden deutschen Staaten um den sogenannten Preußischen Kulturbesitz gibt. Was spricht dagegen, diesen Preußischen Kulturbesitz gemeinsam zu verwalten? So könnte von Punkt zu Punkt etwas Gemeinsames, etwas Gesamtdeutsches entstehen, ohne daß es zu einer Machtzusammenballung wirtschaftlicher oder gar militärischer Art in der Mitte Europas käme.

Wenn es dann noch gelingen sollte – was Stefan Heym sagte und dachte – daß die beiden Staaten auch ihre politische Aufgabe wahrnehmen könnten, in der Mitte Europas und ihren Nachbarn gegenüber, wäre das für mich eigentlich schon als Definition eines neuen Nationbegriffes genug. Gemeinsame Aufgabe heißt: nach der Erfahrung zweier von Deutschland ausgelöster Weltkriege gehört es zu den Aufgaben beider Staaten, weitere Kriege zu verhindern, mehr als andere Länder dazu beizutragen, Spannungen abzubauen, also erst einmal Spannungen im eigenen Haus, zwischen den Deutschen. Und ich könnte mir einen beginnenden Dialog zwischen den beiden Staaten, sei es erst einmal im Bereich der Kultur, als eine Art Entspannung vorstellen, so daß unsere Nachbarn nicht – wie gegenwärtig – Angst haben müßten vor einer neuen Machtzusammenballung in der Mitte Europas. [...]

STEFAN HEYM Ich glaube nicht, Günter Grass, daß sich die deutsche Frage von der Kultur her aufdröseln läßt. Und zwar glaube ich das deshalb nicht, weil bei uns in der DDR die Kultur als ein Teil des ideologischen Überbaus und der Ideologie angesehen wird, die bekanntlich das Monopol der Leute ist, die bei uns die Macht haben. Und da werden die Blockierungen auftreten, wenn Sie da kommen und wollen, daß von der Kultur her eine gewisse Einheit oder Vereinheitlichung geschaffen wird. Natürlich soll man dafür arbeiten, natürlich soll man gemeinsame Veranstaltungen haben, gemeinsame Veröffentlichungen von Büchern. Ich freue mich, von Ihnen zu erfahren, daß jetzt endlich zwei Bücher von Ihnen bei uns gedruckt werden, und ich freue mich, daß unsere führenden Leute erkannt haben, daß dadurch nicht die DDR stürzen wird. Und wenn sie eines Tages erkennen werden, daß auch die Bücher von Heym die DDR nicht stürzen werden, dann werden sie die vielleicht auch veröffentlichen. [...]

Grass hat etwas sehr Wichtiges angesprochen, nämlich die Frage von Krieg und Frieden und was das mit den beiden deutschen Staaten zu tun hat. Eines ist sicher, und hier gebe ich jenem Franzosen recht, der gesagt hat, er liebt Deutschland so sehr, daß er froh ist, daß es zwei davon gibt. [...] Es ist so: keiner der beiden deutschen Staaten allein und für sich gesehen ist in der Lage, heute einen Krieg anzufangen. Aber beide deutsche Staaten zusammen können darauf hinwirken, daß der Frieden erhalten bleibt. Und hier möchte ich einmal, und das ist selten, etwas zum Lobe unserer DDR und ihrer Führung sagen. Nämlich, Honecker hat erklärt, daß er die Raketen auf dem Boden der DDR durchaus nicht liebt. Und Honecker hat erklärt, daß er bereit ist, das Gebiet der DDR einzubringen in eine atomwaffenfreie Zone. Diese beiden Erklärungen fehlen mir noch aus dem Munde von Helmut Kohl. Und wenn sich das erreichen ließe, dann wären wir einen großen Schritt weiter. Und ich glaube, daß damit auch ein Anfang gemacht wäre zum Abbau des Mißtrauens, des durchaus berechtigten Mißtrauens gegen die Deutschen und gegen die vereinigten Deutschen erst recht. Denn was sind das eigentlich für Leute?

Ich habe etwas mitgebracht – das ist das einzige, was ich vorlesen werde –, was Thomas Mann über die Deutschen geschrieben hat:

»Der deutsche Freiheitsbegriff war immer nur nach außen gerichtet. Dieser Freiheitsbegriff meinte das Recht, deutsch zu sein, nur deutsch und nichts anderes, nichts darüber hinaus. Er war ein protestierender Begriff selbstzentrierter Abwehr gegen alles, was den völkischen Egoismus bedingen und einschränken, ihn zähmen und zum Dienst an der Gemeinschaft, zum Menschheitsdienst anhalten wollte. Ein vertrotzter Individualismus nach außen, vertrug er sich im Inneren mit einem befremdenden Maß von Unfreiheit, Unmündigkeit, dumpfer Untertänigkeit.«

Ich möchte, daß Sie diese drei letzten Begriffe im Gedächtnis behalten, denn nur allzuoft, bei uns in der DDR wie in der Bundesrepublik, gilt das heute noch. Und diese Menschen, diese Menschen müssen wir versuchen zu ändern, diese Menschen müssen frei werden, kritisch werden, und wenn das der Fall ist, wird ein zweiter Block weggenommen werden von dem großen Mißtrauen gegen die Deutschen, die man immer nur kennt mit den Händen an der Hosennaht.

Ich möchte noch erzählen, daß ich vor wenigen Tagen in dem Schaufenster einer Bahnhofsbuchhandlung in Göttingen eine Serie von sehr schönen Bildbänden gesehen habe, »Aus deutschen Landschaften«, und alle diese deutschen Landschaften waren gar nicht mehr deutsch. Und zwar waren sie verloren worden durch Hitler. Einer dieser Bildbände trug den Titel »Breslau, eine deutsche Stadt«. Solange es so etwas noch gibt, kann man sich nicht beschweren, wenn man den Deutschen nicht viel Vertrauen entgegenbringt. [...]

GÜNTER GRASS Ich glaube, daß nur jemand, der durch diese deutsche Schuld seine Heimatstadt oder seine Heimat verloren hat, genau darüber sprechen kann. Denn das Ganze ist und bleibt ein Verlust. Aber ein Verlust, der akzeptiert werden muß. Für mich ist es mit ein Grund gewesen, neben der Schreibarbeit, neben der Bildhauerei und der Grafik, mich in die Politik hineinzubegeben und die SPD zu unterstützen, und zwar zu einem Zeitpunkt, als diese Partei bereit war, in diese Richtung hin zu wirken. Für mich war es mit ein Grund, im Dezember 1970 zusammen mit Siegfried Lenz nach Warschau zu reisen, als der deutsch-polnische Vertrag unterschrieben wurde; Siegfried Lenz aus Ostpreußen, ich aus Danzig. Wir sind dafür beschimpft worden, das gehört sicher dazu.

Aber wenn heute schon wieder Politiker, nicht zurückgerufen von dem derzeitigen Bundeskanzler, Töne in diese Richtung riskieren: Das sei noch gar nicht gesagt, daß diese Grenze für alle Zeit anerkannt sei, darüber müsse noch gesprochen werden, dann fallen wieder diese verlogenen Floskeln der fünfziger und sechziger Jahre, »friedliche Wiedervereinigung in den Grenzen von 1937«, das schließt also Ostpreußen, Schlesien und Pommern ein, dann wird es gefährlich. Ich kann verstehen, wenn man in Polen heute wieder neu beunruhigt ist durch Äußerungen dieser Art.

Es hat ja eine Reihe von Politikern gegeben, die frühzeitig erkannt haben, daß wir auch in der deutsch-deutschen Sache nur weiterkommen, wenn wir den Polen gegenüber das Selbstverständliche tun. Es sind Deutsche und die Sowjetunion gewesen, das Dritte Reich unter Hitler und die Sowjetunion, die einen Pakt zuungunsten Polens geschlossen haben. Polen hat seine Ostprovinzen verloren, es ist insgesamt nach Westen gerückt worden, dadurch haben die Deutschen ihre Ostprovinzen verloren. Das sind die geographischen Fakten mit schrecklichen Folgen, bis in eine Vertreibung hinein, die grausam war, mit unnötigen Grausamkeiten, die man vielleicht zum Teil verstehen kann, aber die dennoch Grausamkeiten bleiben. Es ist ein Faktum, daß Polen durch unser Verschulden seine Ostprovinzen verlor und daß dadurch auch chauvinistische Bewegungen in Polen Auftrieb bekamen, die lange Zeit davon gesprochen haben – ähnlich chauvinistisch wie deutsche das in die umgekehrte Richtung taten – die Grenze Polens liege an der Elbe, so weit gingen die sogar. Diese Fakten haben wir geschaffen, wir müssen sie anerkennen, und wir haben sie durch Vertrag anerkannt.

Aber ich wollte noch ein Wort zu Ihren berechtigten Zweifeln sagen, ob über die Kultur ein Nationbegriff definiert werden könnte.

STEFAN HEYM Definieren sicher, ja, aber ist es politisch wirksam?

GÜNTER GRASS Es liegt sicher auch daran, daß beide deutsche Staaten in ihrer Art der Neugründung nach 1945 in erster Linie vulgär-materialistisch sind. Die Kultur spielt entweder eine bestätigende oder eine schmückende Rolle oder soll jeweils diese Rolle spielen, sie ist in ihrer Brisanz nicht erfaßt worden. Es kann allerdings sein, daß wir durch eine ganz andere Entwicklung noch einmal auf die Kultur zurückgreifen müssen. Das betrifft übrigens nicht nur die beiden deutschen Staaten. Wenn wir sehen, daß sich menschliche Existenz bei zunehmender Arbeitslosigkeit aus einem Strukturwandel heraus nicht mehr ausschließlich durch Arbeit definieren läßt, als sei nur die Arbeit dazu geeignet, den Menschen zu realisieren, dann wird die Frage nach dem zweiten Bein gestellt werden müssen. Und es könnte sich herausstellen, daß die Kultur in einem neuen Verständnis dieses Bein sein könnte, und somit also ein neues Kulturverständnis entstünde, das jenseits von diesen schmückenden oder bestätigenden Postulaten in Deutschland vertreten wird.

Ich meinte auch nicht, als ich sagte, es gäbe eine Annäherung, einen Dialog zwischen den beiden deutschen Literaturen, daß nun durch einen Nation-Kultur-Begriff eine Vereinheitlichung stattfinden sollte. Ich glaube, daß die deutsche Kultur ihre Stärke immer aus der Vielfalt bezogen hat. Wie ja auch der Föderalismus in Deutschland eine politische Tradition ist, die man nicht einebnen sollte. Sicher, das macht manches Verhandeln schwierig, aber der Kulturföderalismus in der Bundesrepublik hat auch seine Vorteile. Und wenn es einen solchen in der DDR gäbe, wäre das zum Vorteil der DDR. Dort hat man auf preußische Art und

Weise vereinfacht, sicher nicht zum Nutzen der Kultur. Und wenn es hier dann zwischen den vielen Vielfalten beider Staaten, aber auch den Unterschieden zwischen den einzelnen Regionen zu einem Konzert käme, kultureller Art, wäre auch für die Kultur viel gewonnen.

Es gibt auch Unterschiede, rein vom Herkommen oder von der Struktur her, zwischen nord- und süddeutscher Literatur. Es gibt Unterscheidungen politischer Art bis heute – die Main-Linie etwa –, die in manchen Bereichen tiefer wurzeln als im Vergleich die Teilung zwischen DDR und Bundesrepublik. Also, wir haben verschiedene politische Stränge, die ihre Wirkungen und Nachwirkungen haben, und ich glaube, daß man mit einem so offen diskutierten Kulturbegriff zu einem Nationverständnis käme, das Vielfalt erlaubte und nicht unbedingt Einigung zur Folge hätte. [...]

STEFAN HEYM Ich glaube nicht, daß wir von der Kultur her allein die Sache lösen können. Kollege Grass, Sie haben auch von diesen Kräften in der Bundesrepublik gesprochen, die den Drall nach Osten haben. Das kommt natürlich auch daher, daß bei Ihnen eine Gesellschaftsordnung herrscht, die einen solchen Drall nach Osten nicht nur duldet, sondern auch noch fördert.

Sie sprachen von 1945, von der Vergangenheitsbewältigung. Das war bei mir etwas anders, ich habe meine Heimat 1933 überhaupt verloren und kam dann 1945 in einer ganz anderen Rolle zurück, nämlich als Eroberer, und sah die ganze Sache von einer anderen Seite her und auch die Gefahr.

Die Frage ist: wo ist denn diese Spaltung hergekommen? Wie hat sich denn das ergeben? Grass und ich sprachen heute nachmittag darüber, und Grass sagte, das gehe zurück auf 1945. Ich würde sagen, es geht noch ein Stückchen weiter zurück; im Jahre '44 schon hatte ich als amerikanischer

Offizier Verhöre durchzuführen mit deutschen Offizieren. Und da sprach ich mit einem Stabsmajor, der mir sagte, Ihr Amerikaner seid ja völlig verblödet, warum zerschlagt Ihr unsere Armee? Ihr braucht uns doch, und in allernächster Zeit, gegen die Russen. Hier war also bereits eine politische Konzeption, die dann in einer etwas anderen Form in der deutschen Spaltung ihren Ausdruck fand.

So ist die Sache leider entstanden. Und wir müssen uns heute mit der Situation auseinandersetzen. Und da ist die Frage: wie? Wie soll das geschehen, wie sollen diese Gesellschaftsordnungen – lassen Sie mich diesen Ausdruck gebrauchen, denn ich will nicht wieder von Staaten reden – aussehen, die es dann ermöglichen werden, eine wirkliche Klammer zu schaffen zwischen den beiden deutschen Teilvölkern?

Es ist völlig klar: weder der real existierende Kapitalismus in der Bundesrepublik – ich benutze die Worte »real existierende«, Sie werden wissen warum – mit seiner Arbeitslosigkeit, seinem Rauschgift, seinen Barzels und und und, ist etwas, was man dem gesamten deutschen Volke zumuten kann. Aber ebensowenig ist der real existierende Sozialismus zumutbar, mit seiner Mauer und mit seinen Frustrationen und und und. Wir werden etwas finden müssen, was von beiden vielleicht ausgehen und Elemente benutzen kann von beiden: das Gute im Sozialismus, und da ist allerhand Gutes drin, und auch im Westen gibt es Dinge, die durchaus erhaltenswert sind und die von unserer Seite aus immer als kapitalistisch dargestellt worden sind, die einfach auch menschlich sind, nicht? Die Initiative, die einer entwickeln möchte, die Freiheit zu reisen und so weiter und so fort. Das alles muß bleiben.

Es wäre vermessen von mir, irgendwelche Rezepte zu

geben. Ich habe nur angefangen nachzudenken: wie sollte so ein Deutschland aussehen? Und ich weiß, daß mit mir zusammen viele Leute darüber nachdenken. Im Herbst 1983 gab es in München eine Reihe von Reden, in denen diese Fragen angeschnitten wurden. Es ist eine merkwürdige Sache, daß sich das gerade in diesen Jahren entwickelt. Es kommt sicher auch daher, daß sich eben – wie wir vorhin schon sagten – die beiden deutschen Bevölkerungen gleicherweise bedroht sehen und sagen, also wiedervereinigt werden möchten wir nicht im Tode. [...]

Eine letzte Frage in diesem Zusammenhang: Wenn ich sage, was für ein Deutschland? Ja, soll das zum Beispiel ein Deutschland sein, das keine Wälder mehr hat? Soll das ein Deutschland sein, das völlig verkarstet ist? Ein Deutschland, in dem es sich gar nicht mehr zu leben lohnt? Das ist auch eine Frage, die eine Rolle spielt und die im Zusammenhang damit gesehen werden muß. Denn die Wälder gehen natürlich kaputt, weil im Sozialismus – ich war im Erzgebirge, ich möchte niemandem diese Ansicht zumuten. Ich bin über eine Brücke bei Bernburg gefahren, der ganze Fluß hat ausgesehen wie Rasierschaum. Aber Rasierschaum ist noch etwas Edles im Vergleich zu dem, was da herumgeschwommen ist. Also, die Wirtschaft im Sozialismus schafft ebenso viel Umweltdreck und Vernichtung – was sie nicht tun sollte, dafür haben wir den Sozialismus nicht – wie die Wirtschaft im Kapitalismus, und auch das muß weg, wenn wir ein gesundes Deutschland wollen, ein einheitliches eines Tages, das man mit Stolz seinen Kindern und Kindeskindern hinterlassen kann. Gepredigt habe ich wieder, scheußlich. [...]

GÜNTER GRASS Wenn wir jetzt von Möglichkeiten sprechen, möchte ich eigentlich das Wort Wiedervereinigung vermeiden, weil es ja einschließt, daß etwas geschieht, was es schon einmal gegeben hat. Und ein politisch wiedervereinigtes Deutschland, einmal abgesehen von den Grenzen von 1937, aber auch selbst ohne diese Grenzen, halte ich nicht für wünschenswert. Es würde wieder, selbst wenn es keine Bedrohung sein wollte, so aufgefaßt werden und unter entsprechendem Druck und entsprechender Beobachtung stehen.

Wenn wir aber von einer Föderation sprechen würden in der Mitte Europas und damit auch die Möglichkeit hätten, innerhalb eines föderierten Europas eine Variante zu bilden, gäbe ich diesem Modell mehr Zukunft. Dieses föderierte Verhältnis zwischen den beiden deutschen Staaten würde auch ein Verhältnis zum Beispiel zu Österreich erlauben, das nichts an dem Zustand Österreichs ändert. Vielleicht kommen wir verspätet auf die Idee zu sagen, na so schlecht beraten waren die Österreicher nicht mit ihrem Staatsvertrag, vielleicht sollten wir etwas, nicht Ähnliches, etwas Vergleichbares, spät aber dennoch versuchen. Ich habe keine Angst vor dem Wort »Finnlandisierung«, ich habe vor diesem finnischen Volk einen ungeheuren Respekt und finde es schäbig, wenn gerade in der Bundesrepublik das Wort »Finnlandisierung« als Schimpfwort benutzt wird, als diffamierendes Wort, der will »finnlandisieren«. Dieses kleine Land mit einer sehr langen Grenze zur Sowjetunion hat seine Selbständigkeit bewahrt und legt eine Demokratie an den Tag, tagtäglich, von der sich manche Demokraten in der Bundesrepublik eine Scheibe abschneiden könnten. Mit anderen Worten: man muß, glaube ich, von alten Vorschlägen ausgehen, beim Rapacki-Plan angefangen bis zum Palme-Plan, das atomwaffenfreie Europa, das sich immer wieder erweitern ließe, und für Deutschland eine Lösung erarbeiten, die kann man nicht einfach vorschlagen, in der – meiner Meinung nach – auf der vorhandenen Grundlage der Kultur ein Nationbegriff geschaffen wird, der die politische Einheit nicht mehr nötig hat. Der durchaus auch im Sinne eines Wandels durch Annäherung – nennen wir es einmal so, wie Egon Bahr es genannt hat – die Föderation zweier deutscher Staaten erlaubte, die mittlerweile auch ihre eigene Geschichte haben, die wir auch nicht wegstreichen können, auch wenn sie kurz ist. Aber die andere Geschichte ist länger, und sie könnte dann auch die Grundlage der beiden Staaten im Verhältnis zueinander sein.

Also, um es zusammenzufassen: Nicht Wiedervereinigung, weil das sofort zu Recht Befürchtungen erweckt, falsche Inhalte provoziert, aber doch Föderation der deutschen Staaten und deutschen Länder. Das wäre eine Möglichkeit, die für die Deutschen befriedigend sein könnte und unseren Nachbarn keine Angst machen müßte. [...]

STEFAN HEYM Hier ist eine Möglichkeit angegeben, die ich übrigens für eine sehr gute halte und die – jetzt, bitte lachen Sie nicht und werten Sie damit den Grass'schen Vorschlag nicht ab – von Ulbricht stammt. Der Genosse Ulbricht hat zuerst von der Föderation gesprochen, schon vor vielen, vielen Jahren, und es ist damals abgetan worden; wie sollte der etwas sagen, was für uns Gültigkeit hat. Vielleicht hat es damals auch gar keine Möglichkeit dafür gegeben, und Ulbricht hat es in die Diskussion geworfen, wie er es oft getan hat; wenn er es aufgreift, dann weiß er, es ist verloren, und darum macht er es, nicht? Er war ein sehr listiger Politiker.

GÜNTER GRASS Wie Adenauer...

STEFAN HEYM Ja, die beiden haben sich sehr gut auf dem Gebiet ergänzt. [...] Und es ist vielleicht auch einmal gut, wenn Deutschland zwei gescheite Köpfe zugleich hat, auch wenn sie nicht immer die richtige Politik gemacht haben; das nebenbei. Ich meine, was Günter Grass vorgeschlagen hat, ist durchaus diskussionswürdig, und man sollte diese Diskussion, die dadurch angeregt worden ist, nicht abbrechen lassen – ich meine nicht heute abend, irgendwann müssen wir nach Hause –, sie sollte weitergeführt werden an anderem Orte und nicht unbedingt nur von Schriftstellern.

Das ist ja überhaupt das Komische, daß die Schriftsteller in dieser Zeit in Westdeutschland wie bei uns immer dazu aufgerufen werden, irgend etwas zu vertreten und plötzlich zu Leitfiguren werden, die wir gar nicht sein wollen oder sein können; denn was tun wir eigentlich, wir schreiben Romane, und ich hoffe, daß diese Romane gut gefunden werden... ich mache wieder einmal Schleichpropaganda. Aber wir haben doch durchaus gar kein Recht, uns irgendwie größer aufzuspielen als die anderen Bürger, und doch werden wir immer wieder dazu aufgerufen. Ich wünschte, daß uns die Politiker, die eigentlich dafür bezahlt werden, die Aufgabe abnähmen, einmal über neue Entwicklungen nachzudenken, einmal über Grundsätzliches nachzudenken und das auch in der Öffentlichkeit zu sagen, anstatt sich immer nur opportunistisch von einem Tag auf den anderen durchzuwinden. Das wäre vielleicht eine Sache. Nicht, daß wir uns deshalb aus dem öffentlichen Leben zurückziehen sollten, aber man soll nicht mehr von uns fordern, als wir liefern können. [...]

GÜNTER GRASS Es kommt noch eins hinzu: es klingt jetzt so, als sei das so eine Idee von mir, die ich nun wiederholt geäußert habe, aber ich sehe mich da in Tradition, ich sehe uns beide auch in Tradition. Die deutschen Schriftsteller der

Aufklärung befanden sich zu ihren Landesfürsten ja nicht nur aus Gründen der Aufklärung im Gegensatz, sondern auch als Patrioten. Das patriotisch aufgeklärte Verständnis von Deutschland ging zum Beispiel auf Kultur und auf eine gewisse Einigkeit aus und widersprach dem Separatismus-Wunsch der Landesfürsten. Diese Tradition hat angehalten, sie geht über Lessing und Heine, ja bis hin zu Biermann, der mir in seiner Zeit in der Chaussee-Straße, wenn ich ihn gelegentlich besuchte, wie ein direkter Nachfahre genau dieser Richtung vorkam. Und so ist es mir auch ergangen bei den Gesprächen, die wir in den siebziger Jahren in Ost-Berlin geführt haben. Einige Autoren aus West-Berlin fuhren so alle sechs, acht Wochen dorthin, wir trafen uns dann in wechselnden Privatwohnungen, lasen uns aus Manuskripten vor und führten unter anderem Gespräche über die unterschiedliche Entwicklung der Lyrik in beiden deutschen Staaten und über das, was die Manuskripte hergaben oder nicht, mit harter Kritik zum Teil.

Sicher, es stimmt, daß wir kein geschriebenes Mandat haben, uns in politischer Sache wie Wortführer aufzuführen. Aber es stimmt auch, daß wir als Autoren in Deutschland Erfahrungen gemacht haben, und es waren immer zuallererst die Autoren, die außer Landes getrieben wurden, die Schriftsteller. Das waren auch in der Regel Autoren, die sehr früh Entwicklungen zum Schlimmen vorausgesagt haben und denen niemand zugehört hat. [...]

Und vielleicht noch eine kleine Korrektur: aufgrund der Teilung Europas reden wir immer so gerne von West- und Ost-Europa, am liebsten reden wir von Europa und meinen nur West-Europa und machen uns – glaube ich – keine Vorstellungen davon, wie bitter das in der Tschechoslowakkei, in Ungarn, in Polen aufgenommen wird.

STEFAN HEYM Auch in der Sowjetunion.

GÜNTER GRASS Auch in der Sowjetunion, natürlich. Auch das ist Europa und gehört dazu. Und in Prag versteht man sich nicht in Ost-Europa, nach wie vor nicht, sondern in Mittel-Europa. Vielleicht ist das in einer Stadt wie Brüssel ganz nützlich zu sagen. [...]

Nationalstiftung

Denn wenn ich nun vor den Deutschen Reichtum ausbreite, von den deutschen Literaturen spreche und sie das Wunder nenne, das wir vollbracht haben, kann ich zwar, vergleichend mit anderen, schon bröckelnden Wundern, dessen Bestand nachweisen, aber die Deutschen wissen sich nicht, wollen sich so nicht wissen.

Immer müssen sie schrecklich mehr oder dürftig weniger sein als sie sind. Nichts wächst ihnen unbeschadet. Auf ihrem Hauklotz spaltet sich alles. Körper und Seele, Praxis und Theorie, Inhalt und Form, Geist und Macht sind Kleinholz, das sich schichten läßt. Auch Leben und Tod klaftern sie säuberlich: ihre lebenden Schriftsteller vertreiben sie gerne (oder unter Bedauern); ihren toten Dichtern sind sie fleißige Kranzbinder und Trauerdarsteller. Denkmalpflegende Hinterbliebene, solange die Kosten vertretbar bleiben.

Aber wir Schriftsteller sind nicht totzukriegen. Ratten und Schmeißfliegen, die am Konsens nagen und die Weißwäsche sprenkeln. Nehmt sie alle, wenn ihr am Sonntagnachmittag (und sei es beim Puzzle) Deutschland sucht: den toten Heine und den lebenden Biermann, Christa Wolf drüben, Heinrich Böll hier, Logau und Lessing, Kunert und Walser, stellt Goethe neben Thomas und Schiller neben Heinrich Mann, laßt Büchner in Bautzen und Grabbe in Stammheim einsitzen, hört Bettina, wenn ihr Sarah Kirsch hört, lernt Klopstock bei Rühmkorf, Luther bei Johnson, beim toten Born des Gryphius Jammertal und bei Jean Paul meine Idyllen kennen. Und wen ich noch durch die Zeiten wüßte. Laßt keinen aus. Von Herder bis Hebel, von Trakl bis Storm. Pfeift auf die Grenzen. Wünscht nur die Sprache geräumig. Seid anders reich. Schöpft ab den Profit. Denn Besseres (über die Drahtverhaue hinweg) haben wir nicht. Einzig die Literatur (und ihr Unterfutter: Geschichte, Mythen, Schuld und andere Rückstände) überwölbt die beiden sich grämlich abgrenzenden Staaten. Laßt sie gegeneinander bestehen – sie können nicht anders –, doch zwingt ihnen, damit wir nicht weiterhin blöde im Regen stehen, dieses gemeinsame Dach, unsere nicht teilbare Kultur auf.

Sie werden sich sträuben, die beiden Staaten, weil sie vom Gegensatz leben. Sie wollen nicht klug wie Österreich sein. Immerfort müssen sie ihren Beethoven gegen unseren Beethoven (der in Wien liegt) abgrenzen. Ihren unseren: täglich bürgern sie Hölderlin aus.

Ich werde davon im Wahlkampf reden: an Strauß vorbei, doch fordernd gegen Schmidt, damit er es hört, der Macher, damit er macht, was zu machen uns bleibt.

Zum Beispiel die Nationalstiftung. Brandt hat sie '72 in seiner Regierungserklärung angekündigt. Darauf ist sie zum Ländergezänk geworden: nichtig inzwischen, ein lästiger Posten im Haushalt. Der Opposition war einzig die Standortfrage, der Regierung feige das »Niedrigerhängen« wichtig. Wirtschaft ging vor, Tarifabschlüsse, die Radikalenhatz. Anfragen der Künstler und ihrer Verbände hatten nur Reisespesen zur Folge. Die sich fortschreibende Ignoranz. Ins nächste Jahrzehnt das Unvermögen verschleppt.

Heute weiß ich, daß die Bundesrepublik vor dieser Aufgabe dürftig aussieht – wie auch die DDR alleine ihr nicht gewachsen wäre. Nur gemeinsam – wie sie ihr Veterinärabkommen schließen, ihre Straßengebühren regeln, mühselig also nach Gausschem Gesetz und immer wieder vom Katastrophenspiel der Weltpolitik gefoppt – könnten sie einer

49

Nationalstiftung deutscher Kultur das Fundament legen, damit wir uns endlich begreifen, damit uns die Welt anders und nicht mehr als fürchterlich begreift.

In dieser Nationalstiftung hätte viel Platz. Der von beiden Staaten zänkisch beanspruchte preußische Kulturbesitz fände seinen Ort. Die planlos verstreuten Kulturreste der verlorenen Ostprovinzen könnten uns dort die Ursachen unserer Verluste erkennen lehren. Raum böte sich den Widersprüchen der gegenwärtigen Künste. Es ließe sich aus dem vielschichtigen Reichtum deutscher Regionen Beispielhaftes zusammentragen. Nicht daß die beiden Staaten und in ihnen die Länder, eifersüchtig, wie sie ihren Besitz halten, deshalb verarmen müßten. Es soll ja kein museales Monstrum, sondern ein Ort geschaffen werden, der jedem Deutschen geeignet wäre, sich selbst, seine Herkunft zu suchen und Fragwürdigkeiten zu finden. Kein Mausoleum, vielmehr eine begehbare, von mir aus durch zwei Eingänge begehbare (und deutschartig um die Ausgänge besorgte) Hauptstätte sollte – Ja wo? rufen die Schlauberger – ihre Adresse finden. Von mir aus im Niemandsland zwischen Ost und West, auf dem Potsdamer Platz. Dort könnte die Nationalstiftung den Widerpart aller Kulturen, die Mauer, an einer, einer einzigen Stelle aufheben.

Aber das geht doch nicht! höre ich rufen. Die wollen wie wir für sich bleiben. Das machen die drüben nie mit. Und wenn ja, zu welchem Preis. Was, gleichberechtigte Mitsprache sollen die haben? Die sind doch viel kleiner und keine echte Demokratie! Und anerkennen sollen wir die, endlich, als souveränen Staat anerkennen? Und was genau kriegen wir dafür? Lächerlich, zwei Staaten einer Nation. Auch noch Kulturnation. Was kann man sich dafür schon kaufen?!

Ich weiß. Es ist nur ein hellwacher Tagtraum. (Eine Kopf-geburt mehr.) Mir ist bekannt, daß ich in einer kulturbe-triebsamen Barbarei lebe. Mit traurigen Zahlen läßt sich belegen, daß in beiden deutschen Staaten nach dem Krieg mehr kulturelle Substanz in Trümmer ging, als während des Krieges zerstört wurde. Hier und drüben wird Kultur allen-falls subventioniert. Drüben fürchtet man die Eigengesetz-lichkeit der Künste, hier wird uns der »Kunstvorbehalt« als Narrenkappe verpaßt. Als Helmut Schmidt am 4. Dezem-ber in Berlin vor dem Parteitag der SPD zwei Stunden lang umsichtig und auch mich beeindruckend sprach, fand in seiner Rede, die sonst nichts ausließ, Kultur nur als Aufzäh-lung europäischer Zentren und Industrierevere Platz; und wenn sich Erich Honecker in seinen Reden für Planungs-ziele abmüht, muß jedesmal befürchtet werden, daß er sich auch auf die Kulturschaffenden und deren Planungsrück-stände einläßt.

Warum spreche ich hier (und demnächst im Wahlkampf) dennoch aus, was nur wenige juckt, obgleich so viele, so-bald sie von Deutschland und deutscher Kultur sprechen, den Mund bis zur Maulsperre voll nehmen? Weil ich es besser weiß. Weil die Tradition unserer Literatur diesen ohnmächtigen Trotz fordert. Weil es gesagt sein soll. Weil Nicolas Born tot ist. Weil ich mich schäme. Weil unser Mangel kein materieller und sozialer, sondern geistiger Notstand ist.

Sieben Thesen zum demokratischen Sozialismus

Vor fünfeinhalb Jahren wurde nicht nur die Tschechoslowakei durch die Armeen der Warschauer-Pakt-Mächte besetzt, sondern wohl auch der erste Versuch, den sowjetischen Staatskommunismus zu reformieren, gewaltsam unterbunden.

Zwar glückte die Unterdrückung auf altbekannte Weise, doch den Schaden hat, wie sich zeigt, nicht nur die Tschechoslowakei zu tragen; in erster Linie beraubte sich die Sowjetunion der einzigen Möglichkeit, die Fehlentwicklung ihres Systems grundlegend zu ändern.

Der Versuch, die undemokratische Struktur und die zentrale Alleinherrschaft der Parteispitze zu korrigieren, ist so alt wie die Sowjetunion selbst: Als erste warnte Rosa Luxemburg mit den Austromarxisten vor der fehlenden Toleranz dem Andersdenkenden gegenüber, vor der Gefahr des Bürokratismus und vor den Terrormethoden Lenins, die weiteren Terror zur Folge haben müßten und im Gegensatz stünden zu einem befreienden, freiheitlichen Sozialismus.

Diese Warnungen wurden überhört oder hämisch abgetan. Als drei Jahre nach der Oktoberrevolution die Arbeiter und Matrosen in Petrograd und Kronstadt gegen die Alleinherrschaft der Parteielite, gegen die Entmachtung der Arbeiter- und Soldatenräte und den zunehmenden zentralistischen Bürokratismus rebellierten, wurde ihr Aufstand von Lenin und Trotzki, von Leuten also, denen sie drei Jahre zuvor revolutionär zur Macht verholfen hatten, blutig niedergeschlagen.

Was in Kronstadt und Petrograd parteioffiziell zur Konterrevolution verfälscht wurde, wiederholte sich nach dem Tod Stalins in mehreren Ostblockstaaten und – nach dem unterdrückten Reformversuch in der Tschechoslowakei – zum letztenmal im Dezember 1970 in den polnischen Hafenstädten.

Die Forderungen der aufständischen sozialistischen Arbeiter sind gleich geblieben: Sie wollen einen Sozialismus der Basis. Sie sind dagegen, daß man den Privatkapitalismus nur in einen genauso unkontrollierten Staatskapitalismus verwandelt hat; sie wollen ihre Konflikte mit Hilfe unabhängiger Gewerkschaften lösen; sie wollen mitbestimmen und nicht bevormundet werden.

Diese – um es deutlich zu sagen – ursozialdemokratischen Forderungen sind als Revisionismus verketzert worden: unter Berufung auf Marx, doch seit Lenin im Widerspruch zu Marx. Und weil nicht Marxsche Theorie, sondern die durch Lenin eingesetzte Parteidiktatur zwangsläufig Stalin und dessen Methoden produziert hat, ist es falsch und irreführend, den Leninismus als folgerichtige Weiterentwicklung des Marxismus zu begreifen.

Daraus ergibt sich meine

1. These: Wer den demokratischen Sozialismus anstrebt, sollte nach den gemachten Erfahrungen die verfälschende Klitterung Marxismus/Leninismus ablehnen und, der geschichtlichen Entwicklung entsprechend, vom Leninismus/Stalinismus sprechen.

Den letzten Anstoß dazu mag Alexander Solschenizyn mit seinem Buch *Archipel Gulag* gegeben haben; denn Solschenizyn wurde nicht aus der Sowjetunion ausgewiesen, weil er den Stalinismus kritisiert hat, sondern weil er belegen konnte, daß es Lenin gewesen ist, der mit seinem zentralistischen System den Stalinismus möglich gemacht hat.

Diese Erkenntnis dämmert mittlerweile wohl auch den westeuropäischen Kommunisten; doch scheut man die harte Konsequenz, nicht nur vom Stalinismus, sondern auch von seiner Voraussetzung, dem Leninismus, Abschied zu nehmen; der Papst soll unfehlbar bleiben. Hieraus folgert sich meine

2. These: Wer den demokratischen Sozialismus will, kann nicht mit Kommunisten zusammenarbeiten, denen nach wie vor die leninistische Parteihierarchie sakrosant und damit jederzeit der Umschlag in den Stalinismus möglich ist.

Keine Volksfrontseligkeit kann diesen unlösbaren Widerspruch aufheben. Wer bis jetzt nicht erkannt hat, daß die Theorie des Marxismus und die noch ältere Idee eines freiheitlichen Sozialismus durch Lenin zu einem autoritären Staatskapitalismus verfälscht worden ist, und wer die Tatsache ignoriert, daß das leninistisch-stalinistische System keiner Reform mehr fähig ist und, gefangen von seiner eigenen Ideologie, nur noch imperiale Ansprüche erhebt, dem ist verborgen geblieben, daß sich die Sowjetunion an den imperialen Ansprüchen der USA mißt.

Auch die zweite Weltmacht besteht auf einem rechten System; beide Weltmächte sichern ihren Bestand durch militärische Gewalt und Unterdrückung der Menschenrechte. Ob vor mehr als fünf Jahren der demokratische Sozialismus in der Tschechoslowakei niedergewalzt wurde, ob im vergangenen Jahr in Chile die demokratisch gewählte Regierung Allende gestürzt wurde, in beiden Fällen hat die Reaktion, die staatskapitalistische und die privatkapitalistische, ihr Machtwort gesprochen. Dazu meine

3. These: Wer den demokratischen Sozialismus will, dem bedeutet der Staatskapitalismus keine Alternative zum Pri-

vatkapitalismus. Denn beide Machtgefüge entziehen sich der demokratischen Kontrolle und lehnen die Mitbestimmung der Arbeiter zwar ideologisch-spiegelverkehrt, doch, genau gelesen, aus einer Absicht ab: Sie wollen die Macht nicht teilen.

Diese doppelte Anfeindung und Gegnerschaft profiliert den demokratischen Sozialismus. Als Alternative zum überkommenen Privatkapitalismus mit seinen übermächtigen, weil jeder demokratischen Kontrolle entzogenen Konzernen und als Alternative zum in der Sowjetunion pervertierten Sozialismus mit seinen gleichfalls unkontrollierten Staatskonzernen fällt ihm die Aufgabe zu, Demokratie und Sozialismus als wechselseitige Entsprechungen zu definieren. Hierzu meine

4. These: Wer den demokratischen Sozialismus will, der toleriert seine politischen Gegner, verlangt ihnen allerdings gleichfalls Toleranz als Selbstverständnis der Demokratie ab; ihr Elixier sind nicht die zeitweilig machtausübenden, sondern die opponierenden Parteien. Eine Gesellschaft, die Opposition nicht zuläßt, verhindert alternatives Denken und verarmt schließlich unter der dogmatischen Herrschaft einer widerspruchslosen und deshalb alleinherrschenden Partei.

Doch um das Selbstbewußtsein der westeuropäischen sozialistischen, sozialdemokratischen und linksliberalen Parteien ist es schlecht bestellt. Dort, wo sie regieren, werden sie durch den altbekannten Wankelmut ihrer zumeist liberalen Koalitionspartner gehemmt; dort, wo sie sich in Opposition befinden, scheitert der Versuch, eine linke Mehrheit zu bilden, jeweils am Unvermögen gleichfalls opponierender kommunistischer Blöcke, sich von der leninistischen Zwangsjacke zu befreien.

Es mag sein, daß sich die Kommunistische Partei Italiens als erste von Lenins hierarchischer Elitestruktur emanzipieren wird; doch ob dieser emanzipatorische Vorgang auch der kommunistischen Partei Frankreichs möglich sein wird, ist anzuzweifeln. Daraus ergibt sich meine

5. These: Der demokratische Sozialismus definiert, kontrolliert und baut sich von unten nach oben auf; deshalb lehnt er die Vorherrschaft eines Zentralkomitees ab. Sein Ziel ist eine sozial bestimmte Demokratie der Basis in allen Bereichen der Gesellschaft. Ein bloß formaler Demokratiebegriff kann ihm nicht genug sein; denn die Glanzstücke der formalen Demokratie – mögen sie Presse- und Meinungsfreiheit, mögen sie freie Marktwirtschaft heißen – haben ihre Fragwürdigkeit bewiesen und sich selbst widerlegt, indem Großkonzerne den angeblich freien Markt beherrschen und marktbeherrschende Pressekonzerne Meinung und Information zunehmend manipulieren.

Doch wie, so fragen wir uns, definiert der demokratische Sozialismus eine nicht nur freie, sondern auch soziale Marktwirtschaft? Wird sie sich nur durch zentrale, wenn auch demokratisch kontrollierte Lenkung realisieren lassen? Und weiter gefragt: Wenn, wie bewiesen ist, die Verstaatlichung von privatwirtschaftlichen Großkonzernen nur neue und unkontrollierte Abhängigkeit schafft, welche Eigentumsform strebt dann der demokratische Sozialismus an?

Gewiß bietet die paritätische Mitbestimmung dort, wo sie Gesetz wird, zum erstenmal die Möglichkeit, privatwirtschaftliche und staatliche Großkonzerne unter Kontrolle zu bringen; und gewiß hat die Praxis gezeigt, daß die Kontrolle der Macht wichtiger ist als ihr Besitz, und dennoch bleibt die alternative Frage zu den privatkapitalistischen und staatskapitalistischen Besitzverhältnissen offen. Daraus ergibt sich meine

6. These: Der demokratische Sozialismus ist nur in Ansätzen definiert. Das Bedürfnis, ihn definiert zu sehen, wird immer größer, seitdem der moralische Bankrott und der politische Systemverfall der beiden Weltmachtblöcke offenbar sind.

Ich meine: Es sollte Aufgabe dieses Colloquiums sein, den demokratischen Sozialismus und seine Ziele, seine Chance und Herausforderung, seine immer noch vage Hoffnung frei von dogmatischen Festlegungen zu diskutieren, damit der tschechoslowakische Versuch, dem Sozialismus ein menschliches Gesicht zu geben, nicht in Vergessenheit gerät, sondern fortgesetzt wird. Hieraus leitet sich ab meine letzte und

7. These: Der demokratische Sozialismus ist kein Dogma. Da er kein Endziel beschreibt und da die Ziele von gestern morgen schon Hemmschuh sein können, muß er sich immer wieder neu definieren. Weder blindlings-pragmatisches Wurschteln noch Ausflüge und Ausflüchte in utopisches Gelände sind ihm gemäß, sondern die Einheit von Theorie und Praxis. Mit ihm könnte sich die europäische Aufklärung und ihr Kampf gegen Dogmatismus und Intoleranz erneuern. Keine kommunistischen Kirchenheiligen und keine kapitalistischen Ölgötzen dürfen ihm heilig sein; denn der demokratische Sozialismus verlangt die permanente Revision des Bestehenden. Dem jahrtausendealten Verlangen der Völker nach Freiheit und Gerechtigkeit entspricht die Synthese aus Demokratie und Sozialismus; an ihr zu arbeiten sollte uns Aufgabe sein.

Deutschland
– zwei Staaten – eine Nation?

Wenn ich mir das Thema meines Vortrages als Fragesatz gestellt habe: *Deutschland – zwei Staaten – eine Nation?*, dann möchte ich Sie bitten, vorauszusetzen, daß die Frage nach der Nation in Deutschland älter ist als die Geschichte der beiden Staaten deutscher Nation. Die deutsche Geschichte, soweit wir sie zurückverfolgen mögen, hat sich immer schon schwer getan, wenn es darum ging, die Begriffe »Vaterland« und »Nation« oder den Staatsbegriff Deutschlands konkret zu formulieren.

Da ich nicht vorhabe, historisch den Krebsgang zu üben, also beim Heiligen Römischen Reich Deutscher Nation zu beginnen, auch weil mein Vortrag afterlastig werden müßte, wenn ich die Geschichte des deutschen Separatismus als Spiegelkabinett des Absurden schildern wollte, muß ich mich damit begnügen, auf meine Rede *Die kommunizierende Mehrzahl* hinzuweisen, die ich im Mai 1967 vor dem Presseclub in Bonn gehalten habe.

Damals ging es mir darum, nachzuweisen, wie unfähig die Deutschen gewesen sind, sich als Nation zu verstehen, und wie verkrampft sie dem Nationalismus verfielen, als sie sich endlich die Nation als Mythos wie einen kultischen Zwang auferlegten. Damals ging es mir darum, nachzuweisen, daß die föderalistische Struktur Deutschlands mit ihrer Tendenz zum Separatismus Grundlage aller Überlegungen sein sollte, die dem Begriff »Deutsche Nation« einen neuen, doch nicht abermals mystifizierenden Inhalt geben wollen. Ich sah die beiden Staaten deutscher Nation, möglicherweise, in einem konföderierten Verhältnis zueinander. Ich machte einen Unterschied zwischen deutscher Einheit und deutscher Einigung. Deutsche Einheit, so lehrt die Geschichte, hat, in der Mitte Europas und bis in die Welt hinein wirksam, immer wieder landläufige Krisen zum überregionalen Konflikt auswuchern lassen. Deutsche Einheit hat sich zu oft als Bedrohung für unsere Nachbarn erwiesen, als daß wir sie uns und unseren Nachbarn weiterhin – und sei es auch nur als Zielvorstellung – zumuten dürften. Hingegen ist deutsche Einigung dann möglich, wenn sie sich der Projektion Einheit enthält, ja, weitergehend, wenn sie Verzicht auf Einheit als Voraussetzung für die Einigung begreift.

Die Notizen für diese Überlegungen entstanden unterwegs: auf dem Bundesparteitag der SPD in Saarbrücken, danach auf einer Reise nach Prag, also konfrontiert mit den Sorgen der tschechoslowakischen Nation.

Dort, angesichts zunehmender zentralistisch gelenkter Gewalt, wurde mir deutlich, daß auch den tschechoslowakischen Völkern in ihrer Vielzahl und Eigenständigkeit gerade in dem Moment eine gleichmachende Einheit aufgezwungen worden ist, in dem sich zwischen Tschechen und Slowaken wie zwischen diesen beiden Völkern und der Vielzahl der Minderheiten eine demokratische Einigung vorzubereiten begann.

Gelegentlich ist es notwendig, das ganz in sich verstrickte und sich allzu leicht absolut verstehende Deutschland von außen zu betrachten: Der melancholisch eingefärbte Prager Frühling erwies sich als geeignet, Gustav Heinemanns Wort – »Es gibt schwierige Vaterländer. Eins davon ist Deutschland« – mit Randnotizen zu versehen und begründete Skepsis zu Wort kommen zu lassen.

Die Rückreise nach Berlin über Zinnwald und Dresden

bot, weil sie in ihrer bürokratischen Akkuratesse Wartepausen vorsah, genug Gelegenheit, uniformierten wie nicht uniformierten Bürgern der DDR Fragen zu stellen: Denn was in Erfurt begann, stand in Kassel bevor.

Meine bei Hochwasser in Saarbrücken, zwischen pfingstlichen Touristen in Prag und zwischen Zinnwald und Berlin gesammelten Reiseeindrücke vermittelten das Bild einer mäßig besorgten und nur unterschwellig hoffnungsvollen Nation. Oft wollte es mir vorkommen, als werde aus mehreren Perspektiven ein laubgrüner Wetterfrosch beobachtet, wobei sich alle darin einig waren, daß weder mit Schönwetter noch mit einem Wettersturz zu rechnen sei. Wie immer, wenn die Politik an die Grenzen ihrer Möglichkeiten stößt, beginnen die Orakel zu sprechen.

Am 21. Mai wurde im Fernsehen weniger im Stil der Wettervoraussage, dafür eindeutig in der Tonlage der Verkehrsspezialisten orakelt: Kassel – Sackgasse oder Zwischenstation? Und auch wir werden uns mutmaßend fragen, welches Ereignis das Kasseler Treffen mehr bestimmen wird: Willy Brandts zwanzig Punkte oder die Schlagzeilentat jener drei Oberschüler, deren fragwürdige Kühnheit sich am nationalen Symbol vergriff. Immerhin besteht Anlaß zu befürchten, es könnten die Oberschüler auf fatale Weise Politik gemacht haben; denn die Fahnen und der Streit um Nationalflaggen haben bei uns immer schon mehr Gewicht gehabt als nüchterne Versuche, mit Hilfe der beiden deutschen Staaten eine mitteleuropäische Entspannungspolitik einzuleiten.

Das in Deutschland mangelnde nationale Bewußtsein war selbst durch ein Übermaß an verschwommenem Nationalgefühl nicht zu kompensieren; jetzt richten sich die Komplexe gesamtdeutsch an Fahnenmasten auf.

Wir können gewiß sein, daß das Haus Springer dererlei Hysterie auflagenstark füttern und bei Laune halten wird; wir können gleichfalls gewiß sein, daß die Presse der DDR jener in Kassel zerschnittenen Fahne Reliquienwert zusprechen wird. Kein Irrationalismus, der nicht sein Echo fände, indem er sich fortpflanzt. Der Vernunft hingegen mangelt es an Hallräumen und fotogener Symbolkraft.

Dennoch sind die Verhandlungen in Kassel nicht durch einen x-beliebigen und deshalb entschuldbaren Bubenstreich erschwert worden. Vielmehr haben drei Schüler genau das getan, was die Unionspolitiker Barzel und Strauß als Nationalpolitik verstanden wissen wollten. Wenn immer die Regierung Brandt/Scheel versucht hat, auf dem Verhandlungsweg jenes Maß an Entspannung zu erreichen, das die Erschießung von DDR-Flüchtlingen beenden könnte, wurden Strauß und Barzel nicht müde, die Tatsache, daß nach wie vor an der Grenze geschossen wird, als Verhandlungsbarriere aufzubauen. Drei Schüler haben zwei Unionspolitiker in Kassel beim Wort genommen. Der SED-Politiker Honecker hat Grund, den drei Schülern und ihren Vorsprechern dankbar zu sein. Und umgekehrt dürfen sich Strauß und Barzel bei Honecker und Norden für den Aufmarsch der DKP-Jugend bedanken. Die Dogmatiker des Kalten Krieges wissen, was sie sich und einander schuldig sind.

Sie werden sich fragen, warum ich den Kasseler Episoden so breiten Raum gewähre, zumal Schlagzeilentaten kurzlebig sind und in der Regel rasch genug von anderen Schlagzeilentaten verdrängt werden. Meine Antwort versucht zu klären, inwieweit das Niederholen und Zerschneiden der DDR-Flagge Ausdruck einer Politik ist, die in beiden deutschen Staaten dem Nationalismus das Wort geredet und gleichzeitig altdeutsch-überlieferten Separatismus betrieben hat.

So begrenzt die Möglichkeiten europäischer Entspannungspolitik in Mitteleuropa während der letzten zwanzig Jahre gewesen sein mögen, die bundesdeutsche Außen- und Deutschlandpolitik hat sich, besonders unter Bundeskanzler Konrad Adenauer, mit Vorzug an Unmöglichkeiten orientiert, indem sie mit dem vagen Versprechen einer Wiedervereinigung des Deutschen Reiches in den Grenzen von 1937 ein solches Übermaß an Hybris, Ansprüchen und Illusionen gespeichert hat, daß jede zukünftige Politik, also auch die zur Zeit von der Regierung Brandt/Scheel praktizierte, nur dann erfolgreich sein kann, wenn der diffamierende Terminus »Verzichtpolitiker« keine breite Öffentlichkeit mehr findet.

Es gilt, aus dem Katalog politischer Unmöglichkeiten den Anspruch auf Wiedervereinigung in den Grenzen von 1937 ersatzlos zu streichen. Da selbst die Unionsparteien diesen verbalen Anspruch Konrad Adenauers nur noch unterschwellig aufrechterhalten, beginnen die eigentlichen Schwierigkeiten beim zwar territorial reduzierten und doch unmöglichen Anspruch auf eine Wiedervereinigung der beiden deutschen Staaten, wie sie nach 1949 – einander ausschließend – entstanden sind.

Es wird keine Vereinigung der DDR und der Bundesrepublik unter westdeutschem Vorzeichen geben; es wird keine Vereinigung der DDR und der Bundesrepublik unter ostdeutschem Vorzeichen geben. Nicht nur der Einspruch unserer west- wie osteuropäischen Nachbarn stünde einer solchen Vereinigung, sprich: Machtballung, entgegen; zudem schließen zwei grundsätzlich verschiedene Gesellschaftssysteme einander aus. Und selbst wenn sich das kapitalistische Gesellschaftssystem im Westen, bei anhaltend sozialdemokratisch bestimmter Politik, im Sinne der Mitbestimmung wandeln sollte, stünde der sich demokratisch mitbestimmende Sozialismus westlicher Prägung unvereinbar dem demokratisch nicht kontrollierten Staatskapitalismus des östlichen Sozialismus gegenüber. Eher ließe sich eine wirtschaftlich-technokratische Übereinkunft zwischen überliefertem Privatkapitalismus und überliefertem Staatskapitalismus denken als ein Ausgleich zwischen der Sozialdemokratie und dem Kommunismus.

Als vor zwei Jahren in der Tschechoslowakei zum ersten Mal versucht wurde, dem zentralistischen Kommunismus eine demokratische Basis und Legitimation nachzuliefern, machte der Einmarsch der fünf Warschauer-Pakt-Mächte, neben dem Führungsanspruch der Sowjetunion, auch die Grenzen des kommunistischen Selbstverständnisses deutlich. Der zentralistische Kommunismus, wie ihn Lenin entworfen und Stalin folgerichtig weiterentwickelt hat, erlaubt keine Demokratisierung; es sei denn, er stellt sein Dogma und damit seine Macht in Frage.

Mit andern Worten: Wenn wir heute von zwei deutschen Staaten deutscher Nation sprechen, werden wir neben der territorialen und staatlichen Trennung auch die Unvereinbarkeit zweier deutscher gesellschaftlicher Gegebenheiten zur Kenntnis nehmen müssen.

Wäre dann nicht, so mag zu Recht gefragt werden, die völkerrechtliche Anerkennung und also das Verhältnis von Ausland zu Ausland die genaueste Konsequenz solcher Überlegungen? Und wozu bedarf es weiterhin eines hierzulande so gefährlichen Begriffs wie Nation, wenn diese Nation doch territorial, staatlich und gesellschaftlich getrennt lebt?

Ich gehe davon aus, daß die überlieferte Form der völkerrechtlichen Anerkennung, also die Verwandlung der geteilten Nation in ein Verhältnis von Ausland zu Ausland, nur zur Verfestigung des Krisenzustandes in Mitteleuropa führen kann, indem sie den latenten Konflikt zwischen den beiden Machtblöcken durch überholtes nationalstaatliches Denken verlängert, den deutschen Nationalismus verdoppelt und der notwendigen europäischen Entspannungspolitik den Boden entzieht; denn zwiefacher Nationalismus zeugt zwiefache Unruhe, zwiefachen Anspruch auf Einheit und eine permanente Krise in der Mitte Europas. Die völkerrechtliche Anerkennung der DDR, also der Verzicht auf das inländische Verhältnis zweier deutscher Staaten zueinander, könnte die Vietnamisierung Deutschlands zur Folge haben. Dem stehen, so hoffen wir, die Vernunft und die Interessen der benachbarten Völker entgegen. Korea und Vietnam sind Beispiele, die nicht nach Wiederholung verlangen.

Vielmehr ist zu erwarten, daß die beiden deutschen Staaten in ihrer Verschiedenheit und Gegensätzlichkeit dem überlieferten Begriff Nation einen neuen Sinn geben, indem sie den althergebrachten Konfliktstoff Nation überwinden. Das neue Verständnis der Nation setzt allerdings voraus, daß es an Aufgaben wächst, die der alten, zerschlagenen und nicht wieder zu restaurierenden Nation unbekannt waren.

Der Bundeskanzler hat in seinem 20-Punkte-Programm gegenwärtig realisierbare Aufgaben niedergelegt, die nur von beiden deutschen Staaten zu lösen sind. Ich will versuchen, weitere Aufgaben zu skizzieren, die in die Zukunft weisen und heute ausgesprochen – so kurz nach Kassel – den Geruch des Utopischen an sich haben mögen.

Als erste Aufgabe der zwei Staaten deutscher Nation nenne ich das gemeinsame Austragen der jüngsten deutschen Geschichte und ihrer Folgen. Die DDR wie die Bundesrepublik sind die Nachfolgestaaten des Dritten Reiches; keiner der beiden Staaten wird sich aus dieser für beide Staaten verbindlichen Konsequenz herausschwindeln können. Wenn Willy Brandt und Willi Stoph bei Erfurt das ehemalige Konzentrationslager Buchenwald und in Kassel ein Denkmal des Antifaschismus besucht haben, dann geschah zweimal mehr als übliche staatspolitische Routine, weil beide Politiker den Spuren deutscher Geschichte nachzugehen gezwungen waren und es fortan auch sein werden. Die neue Nation wird, wenn sie sich in aller Konsequenz begreifen will, die Konkursmasse der alten Nation auf beiden Schultern tragen müssen.

Als zweite Aufgabe der zwei Staaten deutscher Nation nenne ich ihre verantwortliche Zusammenarbeit, sobald es darum gehen wird, Entspannungspolitik in Europa und den bislang leeren Begriff »Friedliche Koexistenz« zu konkretisieren. Der Bundesrepublik und der DDR als Partner des Nordatlantischen Bündnisses und des Warschauer Paktes stehen Aufgaben ins Haus, die im Interesse der neuen Nation zugleich europäische Aufgaben sind. Der oft verkündete Wille nach schrittweiser Abrüstung der beiden Blocksysteme könnte in den beiden deutschen Staaten seine erste Probe ablegen und also dem neugefaßten Begriff Nation Sinn geben.

Als dritte Aufgabe ergibt sich aus dem vorher Gesagten die Zusammenarbeit der beiden deutschen Staaten auf dem Gebiet der Friedens- und Konfliktforschung. Wo, wenn nicht in Deutschland, wäre genügend Anlaß, wo, wenn nicht in Berlin, wäre der geeignete Ort, diese neu anmutende

Wissenschaft an der Realität und ihren ständig nachwachsenden Konflikten zu erproben und zu entwickeln, zumal Frieden, Krieg und Konflikt aus kommunistischer, aus demokratischer Sicht bisher verschieden und sogar gegensätzlich motiviert wurden.

Als vierte Aufgabe bietet sich den zwei deutschen Staaten deutscher Nation die Zusammenarbeit auf dem Gebiet der Entwicklungspolitik für die Staaten der Dritten Welt an. Die Bundesrepublik und die DDR sind Industriestaaten; also fällt ihnen wie allen anderen Industriestaaten die Verpflichtung zu, eine Entwicklungspolitik zu betreiben, die nicht mehr am neokolonialen Machtdenken der Blocksysteme orientiert ist. Wenn die Bundesrepublik und die DDR eines Tages – sei es in Afrika, sei es in Südamerika – gemeinsam erarbeitete Entwicklungsprojekte zu realisieren beginnen werden, wird der Begriff »Zwei Staaten deutscher Nation« den Nationalismus alter Schule überwunden haben und sich als etwas erweisen, das anderen geteilten Nationen bei der Lösung ihrer Konflikte hilfreich sein könnte.

Es mag Ihnen bedenklich vorkommen, wenige Tage nach Kassel und im Zustand allgemeiner Ernüchterung jemanden so ungebrochen die Zukunft anpeilen zu sehen. Dennoch werden wir gezwungen sein, Willy Brandts Hinweis auf eine »konkrete Utopie« ernstzunehmen, und zwar weil uns die gegenwärtige, zumeist formaljuristisch zurechtgeschnittene Heckenlandschaft Übersicht und Weitblick zu nehmen droht: Das Wort »Realpolitik« hat sich, wie zu beweisen ist, allzu oft nur als Synonym für Kurzsichtigkeit ausgewiesen.

Realpolitik sollte perspektivenreich genug sein, um der Zukunft ein Stück utopische Kontur abgewinnen zu können. Realpolitik sollte gleichfalls geduldig genug sein, um unter dem Übereinander widersprüchlicher und irrationaler Wirkungen – wie sie in Kassel zutage traten – die Ursachen freizulegen.

Wer das Stelldichein der extremen politischen Gruppierungen, bei gleichzeitiger Lethargie der Mitte und Mehrheit, beobachtet hat, wem gleichzeitig nicht entging, daß es in der Mehrzahl junge Leute gewesen sind, die, vom bloßen Anblick her austauschbar, den abgestandenen Wortschatz politischer Fehlentwicklungen vor sich herschoben, der sollte begreifen, wie wenig es in der Bundesrepublik während der vergangenen zwanzig Jahre gelungen ist, trotz forschem Antikommunismus und emsiger Schuldemokratie, den Nationalsozialismus um seine Nachwirkungen zu bringen und dem stalinistischen Kommunismus die Weihe der Heilslehre zu nehmen. Solange in der Bundesrepublik Minderheiten das Feld frei finden, um wie Mehrheiten auftreten zu können, werden die Massenmedien, selbst bei bestem Willen, nicht umhin können, verzeichnete Bilder als Wirklichkeit auszustrahlen. So wurde Kassel einerseits zur Spielwiese rechts- und linksradikaler Traditionsgruppen und andererseits ohnmächtiger Ausdruck einer kaum sichtbaren demokratischen Mehrheit. Politik und Zukunft der Bundesrepublik werden gewiß nicht an den Machtansprüchen radikaler Gruppierungen scheitern; es ist die Unbetroffenheit weiter Bevölkerungskreise, die der sozialen Demokratie und ihrem empfindlichen parlamentarischen Instrument auf die Dauer Boden und Kontrolle entziehen könnte.

Einem Alptraum gleich ist die Vorstellung von einer nach dem Krieg geborenen Generation, die in das überlieferte und rüstungsähnliche Kostüm der Nationalstaatlichkeit hineinwachsen könnte, nur weil dem neuen Verständnis zweier Staaten deutscher Nation vorerst die politische Substanz und die aufklärenden Möglichkeiten der Öffentlichkeit fehlen. Allein der Versuch, meinen zwölfjährigen Söhnen zu erklären, welche bis heute wirksamen Folgen der überlieferte Nationalismus hat und wie notwendig es wäre, die deutsche Nation als etwas zu begreifen, das sich konkrete soziale, entwicklungspolitische und den Frieden sichernde Aufgaben zu stellen hat, macht mir deutlich, wie groß das nationale Vakuum ist und wie rasch es, mit Hilfe allzeit abrufbereiter Demagogen, abermals aufzufüllen wäre. Der nationalistische Sud von vorgestern ist zwar angesäuert, aber immer noch findet er Märkte.

Hier beginnen pädagogische Aufgaben vordringlich zu werden, auf die ich besonders in Ihrem Kreis hinweisen möchte.

Weit schwieriger, weil verfestigter, nimmt sich die Lage im anderen Staat deutscher Nation aus. Die DDR hat den raschen, fast nahtlosen Übergang vom Nationalsozialismus zum Stalinismus, ohne die geringste Chance demokratischer Selbstdarstellung, ertragen müssen. Im gleichen Maße wie sich die Bundesrepublik zur Zeit Konrad Adenauers dem Separatismus und der Eigenstaatlichkeit verschrieb, forcierte die SED in der DDR eine nationalstaatliche Restauration, die, zumindest geographisch folgerichtig, am Vorbild Preußens orientiert war. So konnte es nicht verwundern, wenn im benachbarten Polen die DDR als Nachfolgestaat Preußens mißtrauisch erkannt wurde.

Der Alleinvertretungsanspruch der Bundesrepublik und das so untaugliche wie kostspielige Instrument der Hallstein-Doktrin trugen erheblich dazu bei, das Trauma des Nichtanerkanntseins offenzuhalten und zu erweitern. Niemand hat Grund, erstaunt zu sein, wenn heutzutage die

DDR ihren Wunsch nach Anerkennung so harthörig Argumenten gegenüber und gezeichnet von infantilem Trotz vorträgt. Hinzu kommt, daß diese Fixiertheit auf Anerkennung, gestützt auf vergleichsweise ökonomische Macht, die DDR innerhalb des Ostblocks nicht gerade Sympathie gewinnen ließ. Die Beteiligung von Truppeneinheiten der Nationalen Volksarmee bei der Okkupation der Tschechoslowakei hat nicht nur im okkupierten Land, sondern auch bei den anderen Okkupationsmächten des Warschauer Paktes Erinnerungen wachgerufen, die den Deutschen insgesamt zu Buche schlagen.

Wohlgenährt, doch in merkwürdig schlechtsitzenden, teils modisch, teils altväterlich zugeschnittenen Kleidern stehen sich die beiden Staaten deutscher Nation gegenüber und benehmen sich linkisch, weil ihnen unterbewußt ist, wie gespreizt sie sich im Blickfeld ihrer aus guten Gründen mißtrauischen Nachbarn bewegen.

Demokratische Willensbildung hat im vergangenen Jahr, zumindest im Ansatz, der Bundesrepublik zu einem neuen Selbstverständnis ihrer selbst und ihrer politischen Aufgaben in der Mitte Europas verholfen. Seitdem Gustav Heinemann Bundespräsident ist und Willy Brandt als Bundeskanzler die Richtlinien der Politik bestimmt, wird die Bundesrepublik mehr im Ausland denn im Inland ein wachsendes Maß demokratischer Mündigkeit zugesprochen. Das lange tragfähige Wortfeld – westdeutscher Revanchismus, Militarismus, Neonazismus – trägt nicht mehr.

Doch diese nützliche Veränderung im Gesamtbild der Bundesrepublik hat sich bislang nicht verändernd und die bekannten Fixierungen ablösend auf die DDR übertragen lassen. Die Angst vor der sozialdemokratischen Alternative ist dem stalinistischen Kommunismus so immanent, daß besonderts dort, wo Sozialdemokraten und Kommunisten in gleicher Geschichte stehen, mögliche Veränderungen abgeblockt werden; denn jede Veränderung des Bestehenden setzt Dogmen außer Kraft, die einzig im Bestehenden fußen.

Seitdem die sozialliberale Koalitionsregierung mit der neuen Deutschland- und Ostpolitik begonnen hat und seitdem der Begriff »Zwei Staaten deutscher Nation« zwar proklamiert, aber politisch noch nicht faßbar ist, wird, angesichts der Mühsal langwieriger Verhandlungen, warnend oder – nach Rückschlägen – entschuldigend von einem »steinigen Weg«, von einer »Durststrecke«, von einer »langwierigen Aufgabe für das vor uns liegende Jahrzehnt« gesprochen. Die so warnen, übertreiben nicht. Die Geschichte macht keine Sprünge. Und wenn sich die Geschichte im Sprung versucht, sehen wir sie alsbald zurückfallen: Der Fortschritt gehorcht keiner Sprungtechnik.

Ich bemühte mich, Schwierigkeiten und Widersprüche aufzuzeigen. Doch mein Versuch, den Begriff »Zwei Staaten deutscher Nation« aus verschiedener Perspektive zu reflektieren, bliebe verengt und in deutscher Esoterik verhaftet, wenn ich ihn nicht zum Schluß insgesamt in Frage stellen wollte durch einen kurzen, mehr aufreißenden als klärenden Hinweis auf die Weltpolitik und ihren zur Zeit irrational anmutenden Trend.

Die Vereinigten Staaten von Amerika und die Sowjetunion sind innen- wie außenpolitisch, ideologisch wie moralisch nicht mehr in der Lage, in ihren Weltreichen die Rolle der Ordnungsmacht, sprich: Weltpolizisten, zu spielen. Ein Übermaß an weitverzweigtem Interesse und Verantwortlichkeit läßt das sattsam bekannte Selbstbewußtsein der beiden Großmächte als gebrochen erscheinen. Zerfahren und empfindlich, gelegentlich kleinmütig, dann überlaut reagieren sie. Die Rolle der chinesischen Volksrepublik war in ihrem Stück nicht vorgesehen. Wir wissen nicht und können kaum beeinflussen, welchen Anteil die Vernunft an der Weltpolitik zukünftig haben wird. Der Beitrag von unserer Seite, das heißt, die Aufgaben der beiden Staaten deutscher Nation sollten, gerade weil Deutschland immer wieder der Brautgarten des Irrationalismus gewesen ist, fortan ausschließlich auf Vernunft im Sinne der europäischen Aufklärung gründen; es sei denn, wir schwören dieser besten europäischen Tradition ab und folgen vernunftlos den Orakelsprüchen der politischen Wetterfrösche.

Gesamtdeutscher März

Gustav Steffen zum Andenken

Die Krisen sprießen, Knospen knallen,
in Passau will ein Biedermann
den Föhn verhaften, Strauß beteuert,
daß er nicht schuld sei, wenn es taut;
in Bayern wird viel Bier gebraut.

Der Schnee verzehrt sich, Ulbricht dauert.
Gesamtdeutsch blüht der Stacheldraht.
Hier oder drüben, liquidieren
wird man den Winter laut Beschluß:
die Gärtner stehn Gewehr bei Fuß.

In Schilda wird ein Hochhaus, fensterlos,
das Licht verhüten; milde Lüfte
sind nicht gefragt, der alte Mief
soll konservieren Würdenträger
und Prinz Eugen, den Großwildjäger.

Im Friedenslager feiert Preußen
das Osterfest, denn auferstanden
sind Stechschritt und Parademarsch;
die Tage der Kommune sind vorbei,
und Marx verging im Leipz'ger Allerlei.

Bald wärmt die Sonne und der greise,
schon legendäre Fuchs verläßt
zum Kirchgang-Wahlkampf seinen Bau;
der Rhein riecht fromm nach Abendland,
und Globke lächelt aus dem Zeugenstand.

Heut gab es an der Grenze keinen Toten.
Nun langweilt sich das Bild-Archiv.
Seht die Idylle: Vogelscheuchen
sind beiderseits der Elbe aufmarschiert;
jetzt werden Spatzen ideologisiert.

Oh, Deutschland, Hamlet kehrte heim:
»Er ist zu fett und kurz von Atem...«
und will, will nicht, auf kleiner Flamme
verkocht sein Image: Pichelsteiner Topf;
die Bundesliga spielt um Yoricks Kopf.

Bald wird das Frühjahr, dann der Sommer
mit all den Krisen pleite sein, –
glaubt dem Kalender, im September
beginnt der Herbst, das Stimmenzählen;
ich rat Euch, Es-Pe-De zu wählen.

Was Erfurt außerdem bedeutet

Auch für den 1. Mai werden wir uns zu Beginn der siebziger Jahre um einen neuen Inhalt bemühen müssen, wenn er nicht zur feierlich hohlklingenden Leerformel werden soll. Dieser Feiertag darf nicht als Podest für landläufige Lobreden hergeliehen werden.

Der 1. Mai eignet sich nicht für die routinemäßige Beförderung tagespolitischer Gewerkschaftspolitik, so wichtig sie ist und soviel sie bewegt. Heute, am 1. Mai, soll historischen Ursachen nachgegangen werden, deren Wirkungen uns immer noch einholen und oft genug überrascht sehen.

Nach zwanzig Jahren Bundesrepublik und Deutscher Demokratischer Republik, nach zwanzig Jahren DGB und FDGB, nach nunmehr fünfzehn Jahren Bundeswehr und Volksarmee beginnt, nach dem Regierungswechsel in Bonn, lang verdrängte deutsche Geschichte mit ihren Konsequenzen auf uns zuzukommen: Wir können nicht mehr ausweichen. Des Wunschdenkens überdrüssig, tun wir etwas, das lange unter Verbot stand: Wir beginnen, Wirklichkeit anzuerkennen.

Diese Wirklichkeit ist nicht erfreulich. Sie schmerzt, weil sie Teilung bewußt macht; und manch einer mag bedauern, daß die alten und so harmonischen Wunschbilder dank neuer Politik archiviert worden sind. Das Wort »Wiedervereinigung« und der Wunsch nach Wiedervereinigung waren zwanzig Jahre lang stärker als die uns täglich belehrende Realität. Man muß nur fest daran glauben! so hieß es. Und wenn immer wir Anlaß sahen zur Feier – sei es am 17. Juni, sei es am 1. Mai –, begannen wir, uns diesen Ersatzglauben abzuverlangen und einzuschwören.

Doch der Glaube an die Wiedervereinigung hat keinen Berg, geschweige denn die Berliner Mauer versetzen können. Heute wagen wir auszusprechen, was viele wußten, aber nur hinter der hohlen Hand sagten, was viele ahnten, sich aber aus allzu verständlicher Gutgläubigkeit nicht eingestehen wollten. Es wird keine Wiedervereinigung geben: keine unter den Vorzeichen unseres Gesellschaftssystems, keine unter kommunistischen Vorzeichen. Zwei deutsche Staaten deutscher Nation, die gegensätzlicher und einander feindlicher nicht gedacht werden konnten, müssen lernen, nebeneinander zu leben und miteinander die Hypotheken gemeinsamer Geschichte zu tragen.

Wie macht man das? Wir haben so wenig Praxis. Wie lebt man neben- und miteinander? Wir haben die Bilder aus Erfurt gesehen. Willy Brandt und Willi Stoph: zwei Männer, die sich kühl einzuschätzen wußten. Zwei Politiker auf schmalem Grat: Den einen möchte Herr Strauß zum Stolpern bringen; der andere spürt seinen parteiinternen Gegenspieler Honecker im Rücken. Honecker und Strauß: Ideologisch liegen Welten zwischen ihnen, aber das Dogma des Kalten Krieges eint sie und läßt sie auf einen Mißerfolg des Erfurter Beginns hoffen. Oft hat es den Anschein, als gäbe es gesamtdeutsche Gemeinsamkeiten nur noch in der absoluten Verneinung.

Aber wir sahen auch den Platz zwischen Bahnhof und Hotel. Spontane Freude und vorsichtige Hoffnung ließ sich den Fotos ablesen, aber auch die bestellte und verbitterte Gegenagitation.

Was wir nicht sahen, aber mittlerweile wissen, daß einige Bürger der DDR, nur weil sie spontan reagierten, in Schwierigkeiten gerieten, weil der Kommunismus keine Spontaneität duldet und weil die inhumane Konsequenz des kommunistischen Dogmas selbst dort Härte unter Beweis stellen muß, wo das Eingeständnis der Schwäche den verantwortlichen Politikern der DDR Sympathie eintrüge.

Dabei hat sich in Erfurt nur Freundliches zugetragen: Wir erlebten, daß ein Politiker, den man vor kurzer Zeit noch in beiden deutschen Staaten, also zweistimmig diffamiert hat, das Vertrauen unserer benachbarten Landsleute besitzt: Willy Brandt trat ans Fenster, nicht um Ovationen entgegenzunehmen, sondern um zu danken und um Rücksicht für seine schwierige Aufgabe zu bitten.

Man verstand ihn. Aber haben wir jenes Bild verstanden, das den Bundeskanzler der Bundesrepublik im ehemaligen Konzentrationslager Buchenwald zeigte? Eine Kranzniederlegung. Nur die übliche Geste? Oder mehr? Im Konzentrationslager Buchenwald wurden deutsche Kommunisten und Sozialdemokraten von deutschen Nationalsozialisten ermordet. Wo wir auch hintreten, wir stoßen uns an den harten Rückständen der Vergangenheit. Kaum eine Grundlage, die nicht doppelbödig, kaum ein Wort, das nicht doppelsinnig wäre.

Auch Erfurt bedeutet mehr als das Treffen vom 19. März 1970. In der über hundertjährigen Geschichte deutscher Sozialdemokratie und deutscher Gewerkschaftsbewegung beweist die Geschichte der Stadt Erfurt bedrückender Gewicht als sich viele Sozialdemokraten und Gewerkschaftler eingestehen wollen.

Es sollte Ihnen und mir ein nützliches Vergnügen sein, heute, am 1. Mai, zurückzublicken, damit wir uns daran erinnern, was Erfurt außerdem bedeutet.

1891, ein Jahr nach dem Fortfall der Bismarckschen Sozialistengesetze, fand in Erfurt ein Parteitag der Sozialdemokratischen Partei Deutschlands statt. Auf diesem folgen-reichen Parteitag wurde das Erfurter Programm verabschiedet. An diesem Parteiprogramm entzündete sich ein parteiinterner Streit, der lange anhielt, bald die Arbeiterbewegung in ganz Europa erschütterte und unter kaum veränderten Vorzeichen sogar heute noch stattfindet. Ich spreche vom Revisionismusstreit und seinen Folgen, von einem Konflikt also, der die sozialistische Arbeiterschaft jahrelang geschwächt, später endgültig gespalten und am Ende in tödliche Feindschaft geführt hat. Erfurt 1891 – und Erfurt 1970: Die Geschichte wiederholt sich nicht, aber sie hat ein Elefantengedächtnis. Blättern wir zurück.

Bis zum Erfurter Parteitag war die deutsche Sozialdemokratie mehr von den Theorien Lassalles als von Marx und Engels geprägt. Als die Eisenacher Sozialdemokraten unter Bebel und die Lassalleaner 1875 in Gotha die Sozialistische Arbeiterpartei gründeten, blieben Marx und Engels skeptisch. Distanz und Mißtrauen, gegenseitige Bewunderung und zunehmende Mißverständnisse lagen zwischen der praktischen Arbeit der deutschen Sozialdemokraten und den beiden gestrengen Theoretikern im Londoner Exil. Selbst August Bebels Emanzipationsschrift *Die Frau und der Sozialismus* war eher von dem französischen Frühsozialisten Charles Fourier denn von Marx und Engels beeinflußt.

Das bis dahin vorliegende, auf dem Parteitag in Gotha verabschiedete Programm war seinerzeit von Karl Marx heftig kritisiert worden; sein Verfasser, Wilhelm Liebknecht, konnte sich seitdem nicht mehr als erster Programmatiker der Partei behaupten.

Während der zwölfjährigen Verfolgungszeit, der Zeit der Sozialistengesetze, waren alle sozialdemokratischen Zeitungen und Zeitschriften verboten gewesen. Nirgends hatte sich der Ort gefunden, die Theorien des Ferdinand Lassalle weiterzuentwickeln und sie von den Fesseln preußisch-staatssozialistischer Voreingenommenheit zu befreien. Zwar überlebte die SPD die Verfolgungszeit, stark an Mitgliedern und neuen Hoffnungen, aber sie befand sich in einem geistigen und theoretischen Vakuum.

Einzig die beiden sozialdemokratischen Theoretiker Karl Kautsky und Eduard Bernstein hielten während der achtziger Jahre engen Kontakt mit Friedrich Engels: Gestützt auf ihn und auf die Autorität August Bebels verfaßten sie das Erfurter Programm. Wenige Jahre nach Karl Marx' Tod fanden zum erstenmal marxistische Wissenschaftlichkeit und marxistischer Dogmatismus in die programmatischen Grundlagen der deutschen Arbeiterbewegung. Das Erfurter Programm ist in zwei Teilen angelegt: Auf Kautsky läßt sich der theoretische Teil, auf Bernstein der praktische Teil zurückführen. Von dieser Dualität zwischen revolutionärer Forderung und praktischem Reformwillen datiert der Beginn der Parteispaltung in Revolutionäre einerseits und Reformisten andererseits. Kautsky und Bernstein, die Väter des Erfurter Programms, sind auch die Väter des bis heute anhaltenden Konfliktes. Es war gewiß nicht ihre Absicht gewesen, die Partei zu spalten; es sind die schon bei Marx gesetzten Widersprüche im Marxismus gewesen, die eine dialektische Synthese von Theorie und Praxis nicht zulassen wollten.

Fast könnte man meinen, die sozialistische Arbeitswoche sei, laut Erfurter Programm, eingeteilt gewesen in einen revolutionären Sonntag und in sechs praxisüberladene, die Reform betreibende Wochentage. Dabei war der Revolutionsanspruch des Kautsky- und Bebelflügels rein rhetorischer Natur. Die Reformpolitiker Bernstein und Vollmar spotteten über die revolutionären Sonntagsreden einiger Sozialdemokraten, die wochentags nüchtern und praktisch ihrer mühsamen Reformarbeit nachgingen.

Hier nun die Gegensätze im Erfurter Programm.

Kautsky – und mit ihm Bebel – setzt ein Endziel: die Verwandlung des kapitalistischen Privateigentums an Produktionsmitteln in gesellschaftliches Eigentum. Beide bauen auf die marxistische Theorie vom bald zu erwartenden Zusammenbruch und Ableben des Kapitalismus und damit der bürgerlichen Gesellschaft. Ihr Programm, soweit es theoretisch bleibt, bedeutet eine radikale Kampfansage an das bestehende Gesellschaftssystem; es schließt eine Zusammenarbeit im Parlament, selbst in der Rolle der Opposition, von vornherein aus.

Demgegenüber das praktische Arbeitsprogramm: Bernstein und Georg von Vollmar, der in der Programmkommission mitarbeitet, bieten einen handfesten Katalog zur Verbesserung der sozialen Lage der Arbeiter und der Frauen. Durchaus wird an die staatliche Sozialgesetzgebung angeknüpft, wird das Parlament als demokratischer Arbeitsplatz für die geplanten Reformen anerkannt, werden sozialdemokratische Ziele genannt, die damals schon praktische Politik bedeuteten, obgleich sie erst Jahrzehnte später erreicht werden: zum Beispiel das Frauenwahlrecht und die Abschaffung der Todesstrafe.

Die Tendenz des praktischen Programmteils zielt auf den Ausbau einer teils plebiszitären, teils repräsentativen Demokratie, in der die »Selbstverwaltung des Volks in Reich, Staat, Provinz und Gemeinde« sowie die »Wahl der Behörden durch das Volk« Gewicht haben.

Wenn wir heute nach den Ursachen fragen, die die nahezu tragikomischen Gegensätze im Erfurter Programm so verwirrend wirksam sein ließen, dann gibt der Hinweis auf Marx und seine den Untergang des Kapitalismus suggerierende Katastrophentheorie nur eine Teilantwort. Es ist die lange Zeit der Unterdrückung gewesen, die selbst bei den gemäßigten Sozialdemokraten die Hoffnung auf Befreiung durch Revolution hat wachsen lassen. Der Briefwechsel zwischen August Bebel und Friedrich Engels belegt, wie jede Krise im kapitalistischen Wirtschaftssystem die Spekulationen dieser beiden sonst so nüchternen Männer zu fördern imstande gewesen ist. Man hoffte geradezu auf die Verelendung der arbeitenden Massen und war dennoch bereit, durch alltägliche Reformarbeit der Verelendung entgegenzuwirken. Die Revolution galt als heiliger Glaubensartikel, doch die soziale Not war vordringlicher. August Bebel hat zur Zeit der Sozialistengesetze, während zwölfjähriger Verfolgung, diesen Zwiespalt überbrücken können; er selbst, in seinem Glauben an die Revolution und in seiner Praxis als großer Parlamentarier, war Teil und Ausdruck dieses Zwiespalts.

Insgesamt läßt sich sagen, daß der theoretische Teil des Erfurter Programms eine Gesellschaftsform ablehnt, die der praktische Teil des gleichen Programms als gegeben ansieht, zur Demokratie ausbauen und durch soziale Reformen festigen will.

Ein gutes Jahrhundert später wird es wenig Sinn haben, besserwisserisch Schelte anzumelden und einerseits den Verrat der revolutionären Ideen, andererseits die unwissenschaftliche Praxisferne anzuklagen. Wir haben wenig Vorstellung von den Belastungen durch die Sozialistengesetze. Wir ahnen kaum, wie groß August Bebels Leistung gewesen ist, als es darum ging, die mittellose und desorganisierte Arbeiterbewegung über eine zwölfjährige Durststrecke zu erhalten. Damals fand das Erfurter Programm den Beifall der ganzen Partei; es wurde fast einstimmig angenommen. Man war nach der Zeit der Verfolgung froh, wieder Boden unter den Füßen zu haben.

Heute erkennen wir: Unvereinbar, ja, einander ausschließend standen sich Theorie und Praxis gegenüber, geeignet, die Arbeiterbewegung nicht nur in Deutschland, sondern, wie sich zeigen sollte, in ganz Europa zu spalten. Denn die deutsche sozialdemokratische Partei galt in Europa als Beispiel: In ihrer Stärke und Schwäche machte sie Schule.

Schon wenige Jahre später versuchten die Praktiker der Politik, den unheilvollen Gegensatz zwischen der Praxis und der utopischen, teilweise unwissenschaftlichen Theorie zu überbrücken, indem sie auf den folgenden Parteitagen eine Revision des Erfurter Programms betrieben: Man nannte sie »Revisionisten«; ein politisches Schimpfwort, das sich bis in unsere Zeit gehalten hat. Alexander Dubček und Ota Sik, die Theoretiker des tschechoslowakischen Reformkommunismus, wurden nach der Okkupation der CSSR als Revisionisten verketzert.

Wer die Geschichte nach Vergleichbarem befragt, wird in den Ketzerprozessen des Mittelalters ähnlich dogmatische Versteinerung finden: Ob Giordano Bruno oder die Albigenser, ob Hussiten oder Lutheraner, sie alle galten dem katholischen Dogma als Revisionisten und zahlten dafür.

Eduard Bernstein, der bedeutendste Revisionist seiner Zeit, unterlag damals dem verbalrevolutionären Flügel seiner Partei. Erst heute begreifen wir, mit welchem Weitblick und wie wissenschaftlich kühl Bernstein seiner Zeit voraus gewesen ist. Indem er frühzeitig dem Endziel »Diktatur des Proletariats« widersprach, wurde er später, als Lenin diesen Weg beschritt, zu einem der ersten Kritiker des kommunistischen Totalitarismus. Bernstein hat es als erster gewagt, dem marxistischen Aberglauben vom baldigen Zusammenbruch der bürgerlich-kapitalistischen Gesellschaft zu widersprechen. Er warnte davor, den Wunsch und das Wunschdenken zur Theorie zu erheben. Er hat nachgewiesen, daß die kapitalistische Wirtschaft »Anpassungsmöglichkeiten« besitzt, also keinen unumstößlichen, von Marx bis in alle Ewigkeit dauernden Gesetzen folgt. Dennoch: So oft sich Bernsteins Analyse bestätigt hat, innerhalb der sozialistischen Parteien konnten Wunschdenken und dogmatischer Aberglaube überleben.

Um ein Beispiel aus unserer Zeit zu nennen: Wo immer die Neue Linke den Kapitalismus als »Spätkapitalismus« bezeichnet, hängt sie dem überlieferten Wunschdenken an, indem sie beweislos suggeriert, der Kapitalismus befinde sich in einer Spät-, also Endphase.

Dabei könnte uns die Geschichte lehren, daß der Kapitalismus so alt oder so jung wie der Sozialismus ist, daß sie einander bedingen und beeinflussen, ja, daß die Enteignung des Privatkapitals, unter dem Druck der Diktatur des Proletariats, nicht etwa zum Untergang des Kapitalismus, sondern zu einer neuen, durch Lenin etablierten Unterdrückungsform, zum sozialistischen Staatskapitalismus geführt hat. Als Willy Brandt und Willi Stoph, der Sozialdemokrat und der Kommunist, einander in Erfurt begegneten, repräsentierten sie, außer der historischen Spaltung des Sozialismus und der Nation, jeweils die privatkapitalistische und die staatskapitalistische Gesellschaftsordnung: Zu Recht hat Eduard Bernstein vor mehr als siebzig Jahren von den »Anpassungsmöglichkeiten« der kapitalistischen Wirtschaft gesprochen; sie ist auf Privatbesitz nicht festgelegt.

Doch bevor ich abermals über Erfurt 1970 spreche, will

ich noch einmal an Erfurt 1891 erinnern. Es lohnt sich, zurückzublättern und den Ursachen sozialistischer Selbstzerstörung wie den Anfängen moderner sozialdemokratischer Reformpolitik nachzugehen. Denn so folgenreich das Erfurter Programm die europäische Arbeiterbewegung schwächte und schließlich spaltete, so nachhaltig haben die ihm folgenden Auseinandersetzungen das Selbstbewußtsein jener Arbeiter gestärkt, die sich unmittelbar am Arbeitsplatz organisiert hatten. Der Beginn des Revisionismus datiert den Beginn des politischen Machtzuwachses der Gewerkschaftsbewegung. Die Genossenschaftler und Gewerkschaftler, die tagtäglich mit den praktischen Anforderungen der Politik konfrontiert wurden, verstanden als erste, wie notwendig es war, die weltfremden Theorien des Erfurter Programms einer Revision zu unterwerfen.

Bernsteins Konzept einer genossenschaftlichen Durchdringung und Kontrolle der Produktionsmittel kann als erster Entwurf heute diskutierter Modelle der Mitbestimmung gelten. So ist auch das Godesberger Programm als ein später Sieg revisionistischer Reformpolitik zu verstehen. Allein deshalb verlangt es jetzt schon nach Revision, weil alle Reformpolitik der permanenten Revision bedarf.

Die Mitbestimmung, insofern sie sich als wirksames Kontrollinstrument versteht, könnte die demokratische Alternative sein zum überlieferten Privatkapitalismus unserer Gesellschaftsordnung wie zum überlieferten Staatskapitalismus der kommunistischen Gesellschaftsordnung: Nur als eine Gesamtreform in allen Bereichen der Gesellschaft wird sie sich – in den Schulen und Universitäten, am Arbeitsplatz wie im Rechtswesen – verwirklichen lassen. Als einer Reformaufgabe ist ihr der evolutionäre Weg vorgeschrieben.

Es würde wenig Sinn haben, für die Mitbestimmung nach

dem Beispiel des Erfurter Programms eine revolutionäre Theorie als Schrittmacher zu entwerfen. Denn soviel sollte uns der Rückblick in die Geschichte lehren: Ein Parteiprogramm, dessen theoretischer Teil revolutionäre Sprungtechnik übt, während sein praktischer Teil die langsamen Pflichtübungen der Reform vorschreibt, wird allenfalls die Bewußtseinsspaltung fördern: Es gibt keine springenden Schnecken.

Aber – so fragen wir uns – kann es nach der Spaltung der Arbeiterbewegung nicht endlich doch noch zu einer Aussöhnung zwischen Revolutionären und Reformisten, zwischen Kommunisten und Sozialdemokraten kommen? Könnte es sein, daß die Begegnung zwischen Willy Brandt und Willi Stoph auch in diese Richtung einen Anfang setzen kann?

Wer genau hinsieht, der vermag zu erkennen, daß auf dem Verhandlungstisch in Erfurt 1970 auch jene Konflikte als Zündstoff lagen, die vor nunmehr bald achtzig Jahren im Erfurter Programm ihren ersten Ausdruck fanden. Zu lange ist der undogmatische Weg zum Sozialismus als Revisionismus diffamiert worden. Zu hoch sind die Kosten und Opfer gewesen, die dem revolutionären Teil der europäischen Arbeiterbewegung zu Buche schlugen. Zu groß ist der Verlust an demokratischen Grundrechten in den kommunistischen Staaten, als daß ihn die Verwandlung des Privatkapitalismus in Staatskapitalismus, also der Austausch einer älteren Unterdrückungsform gegen eine neuere, aufwiegen könnte.

Sozialdemokratie und Kommunismus können wohl nebeneinander existieren; vermischen lassen sie sich nicht. Wer hier eine Wiedervereinigung träumt, wird sich an Realitäten sehr bald wachstoßen. Wer hier auf Hoffnung baut, dem hat die Geschichte keine Lehre erteilen können. Unversöhnlich sieht der Kommunismus in der Sozialdemokratie immer noch seinen ersten Gegner. Man schlage Ulbrichts Sprachgebrauch nach: Revisionismus, Reformismus, Sozialdemokratismus sind ihm gleichermaßen ketzerisch und der Verfolgung preisgegeben.

Doch auch im Westen ist der Revisionismusstreit bis heute nicht abgeschlossen. Wer die studentischen Diskussionen der letzten drei Jahre aufmerksam verfolgt hat, dem mußte bald auffallen, daß sich die revolutionären Forderungen einer Minderheit nicht mit den Reformzielen einer Mehrheit verbinden ließen. Wie heftig und doch auch wie anachronistisch wurde der Streit um die Rechtmäßigkeit der Gewaltanwendung geführt. Wie rhetorisch war der Gebrauch des Wortes »Revolution«, und wie modisch wechselten die revolutionären Attitüden. Wie verbittert bekämpften sich selbst innerhalb des revolutionären Flügels die einzelnen Gruppen, und wie unbelehrbar durch geschichtliche Erfahrungen bezichtigten sie einander.

Doch was der SDS an Gruppenkämpfen zu bieten hatte, war nur ein Reflex der zunehmend weltweiten Spannungen innerhalb des kommunistischen Sozialismus. Die gleiche Sowjetunion, die zuerst den jugoslawischen Titoismus und dann den tschechoslowakischen demokratischen Sozialismus als Revisionismus bekämpft hat, wird heute von der chinesischen Volksrepublik der gleichen Ketzerei angeklagt.

Es fragt sich wohl niemand mehr, was das Wort »Revisionismus« bedeutet und wie notwendig die permanente Revision des Bestehenden ist. Ungeprüft wurde und wird das mittlerweile klassische Schimpfwort übernommen; dabei besteht Anlaß, angesichts so vieler dogmatischer Verhärtungen die Beschuldigung »Revisionist!« wie einen Ehrentitel zu tragen.

Also benutze ich den 1. Mai 1970 als Anlaß, den vielverketzerten Eduard Bernstein einen bedeutenden und weitblickenden Sozialdemokraten zu nennen.

Solche Gedächtnisstützen sind notwendig. Allzu fahrlässig und vergeßlich sind die SPD und der Deutsche Gewerkschaftsbund mit ihrer eigenen Vergangenheit umgegangen. Allzu oft genieren sich heute junge Sozialdemokraten, den Namen Eduard Bernstein zu nennen, obgleich sie wie Revisionisten die Verhärtungen in der eigenen Partei bekämpfen: Das Gift der Diffamierung wirkt bis in unsere Tage.

Eduard Bernstein wurde 1850 als siebtes Kind eines Lokomotivführers in Berlin geboren. Als Zweiundzwanzigjähriger wurde er Mitglied der damals seit drei Jahren bestehenden Sozialdemokratischen Arbeiterpartei. Von Beruf war Bernstein Bankangestellter. Zur Zeit der Sozialistengesetze mußte er Deutschland verlassen. Sieben Jahre lang war er Redakteur der Zeitschrift *Sozialdemokrat* in Zürich. Danach lebte er in London und hielt engsten Kontakt mit Friedrich Engels, dessen Nachlaßverwalter er ab 1895 wurde. Der lange Englandaufenthalt hat Bernsteins Verhältnis zur Demokratie und besonders zum Parlamentarismus geprägt und für die deutsche Sozialdemokratie wirksam gemacht. Seit dem Erfurter Parteitag begann er, die parteioffizielle Marx-Orthodoxie zu kritisieren und an der allseits praktizierten Reformpolitik zu messen. Sein Hauptwerk *Die Voraussetzungen des Sozialismus und die Aufgaben der Sozialdemokratie* ist die theoretische Zusammenfassung seiner Revision. Da er im Verlauf des Ersten Weltkrieges gegen die Bewilligung der Kriegskredite stimmte, schloß er sich zeitweilig der USPD an. Heftig angegriffen und verleumdet, hat Eduard Bernstein bis zu seinem Tod, 1932, die Grundlagen für eine moderne und undogmatische Sozialdemokratie erarbeitet. Wenn heute zum erstenmal sozialdemokratische Politik in der Bundesrepublik regierungsverantwortlich zeichnet, dann kommt der Vorarbeit Eduard Bernsteins ein Großteil Verdienst an diesem Erfolg zu.

Wer Erfurt 1970, die Begegnung zwischen dem Sozialdemokraten Willy Brandt und dem Kommunisten Willi Stoph, voll begreifen will, der wird Erfurt 1891, also das Erfurter Programm und dessen Auswirkungen, zur Kenntnis nehmen müssen. Geschichtliche Ereignisse sind nicht isoliert zu verstehen. Die Spaltung der deutschen Arbeiterbewegung und die Spaltung der deutschen Nation sind Wirklichkeiten von heute, deren Ursachen allzu lange verdrängt worden sind.

Die Geschichte bietet uns keinen Trost. Harte Lektionen teilt sie aus. Zumeist liest sie sich absurd. Zwar schreitet sie fort, aber Fortschritt ist nicht ihr Ergebnis. Die Geschichte schließt nicht ab: Wir befinden uns in und nicht außerhalb der Geschichte.

Ich sprach vom jüngsten geschichtlichen Anlaß: Erfurt 1970. Kein besserer Tag als der 1. Mai, uns alle daran zu erinnern, was Erfurt außerdem bedeutet.

Gleisdreieck

Die Putzfraun ziehen von Ost nach West.
Nein Mann, bleib hier, was willst du drüben;
komm rüber Mann, was willst du hier.

Gleisdreieck, wo mit heißer Drüse
die Spinne, die die Gleise legt,
sich Wohnung nahm und Gleise legt.

In Brücken geht sie nahtlos über
und schlägt sich selber Nieten nach,
wenn, was ins Netz geht, Nieten lockert.

Wir fahren oft und zeigen Freunden,
hier liegt Gleisdreieck, steigen aus
und zählen mit den Fingern Gleise.

Die Weichen locken, Putzfraun ziehn,
das Schlußlicht meint mich, doch die Spinne
fängt Fliegen und läßt Putzfraun ziehn.

Wir starren gläubig in die Drüse
und lesen, was die Drüse schreibt:
Gleisdreieck, Sie verlassen sogleich

Gleisdreieck und den Westsektor.

Die kommunizierende Mehrzahl

Vor mehr als einem Monat wurde mit wohlorganisierten pompes funèbres hierzulande Geschichte beschworen: Konrad Adenauers Abschied von seinen Anhängern und Gegnern bot Gelegenheit, einen Markstein zu setzen, von dem die augenzwinkernde Arglosigkeit annimmt, er lasse sich nicht mehr verrücken. Wie schrieb *Die Welt:* »Der Kanzler ist tot. Ein Mythos ist geboren.«

Wir kennen diese Geburtsanzeigen. Das Volk ist dankbar, wenn ihm Geschichte als kolossales Fatum auf Breitwand oder aus Springers Weltsicht geboten wird: Von der Schlacht im Teutoburger Wald über den Bußgang nach Canossa bis zur bewußten Verfälschung des 17. Juni 1953 sind wir reich an bombastischen Fatalitäten. Das schlägt sich nieder in Schulbüchern; das klammert sich an Jahreszahlen. Wenn wir nur wissen, von wann bis wann der Dreißigjährige Krieg gedauert hat, ist es schon recht. Über Wallenstein belehrt uns Friedrich Schiller; und damit die Bezüge auch stimmen, sendet das Deutsche Fernsehen einen Tag nach Konrad Adenauers Tod eine Wallenstein-Inszenierung: Geschichte kinderleicht gemacht. Die Raben vom Dienst überm Kyffhäuser. Der Alte im Sachsenwald. Hindenburglichter werden uns aufgesteckt, die als Wiedervereinigungskerzen Argumente ersetzen und die Stimmung beleben sollen.

Solcher Theatralik gegenüber darf der Bürger die Geschichte als breiten und mächtig schwellenden Strom sehen, gegen den anzuschwimmen es mir heute ein Vergnügen sein wird. Meine Rede heißt: *Die kommunizierende Mehrheit.*

Ich werde versuchen, einer Unzahl etablierter Antworten

gegenüber, die nationale Frage zu stellen. Nicht, daß ich vorhabe, revolutionäre Thesen an diese oder jene ehrbare Tür zu schlagen; Selbstverständliches soll zur Sprache kommen, wenn sich auch nicht verhindern läßt, daß das Selbstverständliche dem einen oder anderen Ohr revolutionär klingt.

Vor sechs Wochen etwa führte der Grundstock dieser Rede den Arbeitstitel *Der Milchpfennig und die nationale Frage*. Mit Siegfried Lenz und dem Historiker Eberhard Jäckel bereiste ich Schleswig-Holstein. Aber der Tod eines Politikers oder vielmehr: die byzantinische Darstellung seines Todes beeinflußte die Wählerentscheidung gewichtiger, als es das Wirtschaftsprogramm der SPD vermochte.

Nur um die Voraussetzungen dieser Rede darzulegen, sei gesagt: Ich versuchte in Kiel, Eutin und anderswo zu klären, inwieweit der berühmt-berüchtigte Pfennig und die berüchtigt-berühmte Frage nach der Nation zusammenhängen.

Der Milchpfennig war ein Jahrzehnt lang unsere nationale Nebenwährung. Denn wie die Kirche im Mittelalter gegen Geld Sünden abließ, blieb es christlichen Politikern des 20. Jahrhunderts vorbehalten, den Milchpfennig, also den säkularisierten Ablaß, in die Welt zu setzen. Doch der Glaube an den Milchpfennig vermochte genausowenig unsere ranzig werdenden Butterberge zu versetzen, wie unser naiver Glaube an die Wiedervereinigung ein Steinchen aus der besagten Mauer zu rücken vermochte.

Zwei Worte: Milchpfennig und Wiedervereinigung. Zwei Statussymbole und jahrelang Tabus. Zwar wird jetzt der Milchpfennig langsam abgebaut; zwar dämmert es langsam selbst unseren Sonntagsrednern, daß das Wörtchen »Wiedervereinigung« den Applauszähler nicht mehr ausschlagen läßt; weil aber die Deutschen wenig eint und die Milchpfennigwährung wie die Wiedervereinigungsstimulanz einigen Ersatz für fehlende nationale Einheit zu bieten vermochten, trennen wir uns nur langsam vom Milchpfennig – zum Beispiel, vom Glauben an die Wiedervereinigung: beispiellos.

Da Schleswig-Holstein mit seinen Wahlergebnissen hinter uns liegt, erlaube ich mir, die Milchpfennigwährung auf ein Sperrkonto zu überweisen. Wir konzentrieren uns auf die nationale Frage.

Bilden die Deutschen eine Nation? Sollen die Deutschen eine Nation bilden?

Zwar verfügen wir über viele mutige bis halbherzige Vorschläge zur Deutschland-Politik und, dank Hans Magnus Enzensberger, über einen *Katechismus zur deutschen Frage,* zwar gibt es von Rüdiger Altmanns Utopie *Der Deutsche Bund heute am 1. November* 1976 über Wilhelm Wolfgang Schütz' Versuch, das Sackgassendenken des Kuratoriums umzuleiten, bis zum Gaus/Wehner-Gespräch eine Menge Ansätze, die einseitig westlich-orientierte Außenpolitik der Bundesrepublik zu revidieren, aber die Grundlage für diese Versuche, nämlich die Vermittlung des nationalen Selbstverständnisses, fehlt noch. Selbst Enzensbergers schroffer Katechismus verzichtet auf diese Basis. Der neue Begriff »Konföderation« produziert, gleichgültig, ob Walter Ulbricht oder Herbert Wehner ihn verwenden, nichts als Mißverständnisse. Welcher Briefsteller berät uns, wenn es gilt, dem Ministerpräsidenten Stoph zu antworten? Es ist wie überall: Wir haben Schwierigkeiten mit der Terminologie.

Zum Beispiel: Was verstehen wir unter Wiedervereinigung? Wer soll mit wem unter welchen politischen Bedingungen wiedervereinigt werden? Heißt Wiedervereinigung

Wiederherstellung des Deutschen Reiches in den Grenzen von 1937?

Es gibt immer noch Roßtäuscher, die als Politiker solcher Hybris das Wort reden. Wir haben es erleben müssen, wie über ein Jahrzehnt lang und eigentlich bis heutzutage jedem Deutschen, dessen Wählerstimme begehrenswert schien, die Wiedervereinigung in Frieden und Freiheit versprochen wurde. Wohlgemerkt: in den Grenzen von 1937 und das in Frieden und Freiheit.

So absurd es klingt: Diese Blüten politischer Falschmünzerei wurden vom Wähler als Bargeld gewertet. Es regierte uns ohne Unterlaß eine Partei, die bis heutzutage nicht in der Lage ist, genau und unumwunden zu sagen, was Wiedervereinigung bedeutet, wer mit wem und unter welchen politischen Bedingungen vereinigt werden soll und wie man den Ursachen Rechnung tragen will, die zur Zerschlagung des Reiches, zur Minderung des Reichsgebietes und zur Teilung des restlichen Landes führten. Als Surrogat wurde uns ein vulgärer Antikommunismus geboten, dessen Schlagzeilenfertigkeit Konrad Adenauers Spracharmut auf das Niveau des Franzosenhasses im 19. Jahrhundert drückte: »Der Russe ist an allem schuld.« Im übrigen hatte die Beschwörungsformel »Wiedervereinigung« als Lückenbüßer zu dienen.

Dabei ließe sich dieses Wort auch ganz anders verstehen: Zur Zeit des Heiligen Römischen Reiches Deutscher Nation konnten die Deutschen immerhin auf eine wenn auch mystische und politisch nicht faßbare Reichseinheit hinweisen; doch seit Beginn des Konfessionsstreites im 16. Jahrhundert und spätestens seit Abschluß des Westfälischen Friedens war das Römische Reich Deutscher Nation konfessionell und also politisch in zwei Hälften geteilt. Zwar

war der Protestantismus anfangs eine Sache aller Deutschen, doch niemals konnte der Protestantismus Sache eines Kaisers werden, der zugleich König von Spanien war. Die Gegenreformation siegte im Süden und Westen des Reiches; der Norden und Osten blieben, bis auf regionale Einsprengsel, protestantisch. Noch heute tut die Main-Linie ihre politische Wirkung: Die dreihundert Jahre alten Gegensätze zwischen Bayern und Schleswig-Holstein wurzeln tiefer als der noch junge ideologische Gegensatz zwischen Mecklenburg und Niedersachsen. Dennoch sollten wir nicht vergessen, daß die Teilung, wie wir sie heute vorfinden, schon lange vor 1945 vorbereitet worden ist. Vom Rheinland her gesehen, hat es immer ein Ostelbien gegeben. Östlich der Elbe, so sagte und sagt man, ging und geht es preußisch, protestantisch, also heidnisch, kurzum kommunistisch zu. Der von uns verursachte Krieg und der ihm folgende Kalte Krieg, den beide Deutschland weit unter dem Gefrierpunkt zu führen verstanden, hat die ostelbische gedachte Grenzlinie in eine befestigte Staatsgrenze verwandelt. Es mußte grotesk anmuten, wenn Konrad Adenauer, ein dezidierter Westelbier, endlich am Ziel seiner Wünsche, also als Schmied der separaten Bundesrepublik, dennoch von »Wiedervereinigung in Frieden und Freiheit« sprach. Sein Tod macht den Bankrott offenbar: Die Wiedervereinigung ist ein sinnentleerter Begriff, den wir, wollen wir glaubwürdig werden, streichen müssen.

Und was setzen wir anstelle?

Neue Wählerfallen und Surrogate?

Soll das Haus Springer abermals aus kritischer Quadratur, Mars und Uranus, aus günstigem Doppel-Sextil, Jupiter-Sonne, Venus-Merkur, seine gesamtdeutschen Heilslehren keltern dürfen?

Wir kennen diesen Warenhauskatalog mit seinen immer wieder und jeweils in verbesserter Ausführung angebotenen Ladenhütern. Da wird uns Hoffnung gemacht auf den wenn nicht morgen, dann übermorgen zu erwartenden Zusammenbruch des kommunistischen Systems. Selbst China muß herhalten als Garant der Wiedervereinigung. Und alle paar Jahre wird unsere gesamtdeutsche Verstopfung mit dem Europa-Klistier behandelt.

Denn sobald wir in nationale Sackgassen geraten, bieten sich europäische Lösungen als utopische Zuflucht an. Unser abendländisches Deckmäntelchen nennt sich einerseits christlich und soll andererseits bis zum Ural reichen. Altfränkisch ist sein Zuschnitt. Es wurde schon oft getragen. Es hat schon vieles bemäntelt: Zur Zeit der Heiligen Allianz gediehen im Schatten einer verblasenen Europa-Vision handfeste Reaktionen und feingesponnenes Polizeiwesen. Wenige Jahre nach dem Wiener Kongreß, und nachdem ein wirrköpfiger Student einen emsigen Lustspielschreiber umgebracht hatte, fand diese Reaktion unter Metternichs Führung Gelegenheit, in Karlsbad Beschlüsse zu fassen; Furcht vor der Revolution und das Unvermögen, mit Hilfe von Reformen die notwendige Evolution einzuleiten, zeichneten eine Epoche, die wir der schönen Möbel wegen schätzen und Biedermeier nennen.

Es lohnte die Untersuchung, wie tief wir *heute* im Biedermeier stecken. Vor wenigen Wochen hat Walter Ulbricht der Reaktion abermals *seine* Reverenz erwiesen. Der Tatort hieß, zufällig, Karlsbad. Fürst Metternich gab, wie zufällig, den Segen. Aber auch *unsere* Karlsbader Beschlüsse, die politische Strafjustiz und das KPD-Verbot, stehen in zufällig biedermeierlichem Verhältnis zur Bundesgartenschau und zur gediegenen Schönheit der neuesten Mercedes-Modelle. »Das Bestehende erhalten«, wollte Metternich; unser Credo setzte den Imperativ: »Keine Experimente!« Und in der DDR wurde der wiederbelebte Stechschritt der paradierenden Volksarmee zum augenfälligen Beweis fortschrittlicher Restauration.

»Deutschland ist ein Land der halben und niemals beendeten Revolutionen, der geglückten Konterrevolutionen und der versäumten Evolutionen«, sagte Hans Werner Richter. Eine traurige Bilanz, der wir mit einem Ausspruch des ehemaligen Wirtschaftsministers Kurt Schmücker zur biedermeierlichen Ausgewogenheit verhelfen können: »Wir sind die zweitgrößte Handelsnation der Welt. Uns kann überhaupt nichts passieren.«

Zwei unvereinbare Positionen, die abermals Teilung – ich gehe weiter –, das Schisma belegen, wobei es dem christlichen Politiker vorbehalten bleibt, dem vulgärsten Materialismus das Wort zu reden, während dem linken Schriftsteller die Hoffnung von gestern zur Definition der Niederlage gerinnt. Ein Vergleich des Deutschen Bundes von 1815 bis 1866 mit der ausklingenden Ära Ulbricht/Adenauer gibt Hans Werner Richter erschreckend recht. Doch immerhin gelang es damals dem Schwaben Friedrich List, trotz Verfolgung, Diffamierung und zeitweiliger Emigration, den Deutschen Zollverein zu gründen. Ein Mann der Aufklärung setzte zwischen den wabernden Nebeln urburschenschaftlicher Deutschtümelei und die verstiegenen Weltreformpläne des Wilhelm Weitling Maßstäbe für den evolutionären Fortschritt. Friedrich Lists Freitod, noch vor der 1848er Revolution, nahm deren Ende voraus. Dieser bedeutende Politiker und Ökonom, dessen Liberalismus mit dem frühen Marx zu korrespondieren verstand, dieser vorausschauende Praktiker der Vernunft fehlt uns heute; es sei denn, Willy Brandt und Karl Schiller sehen sich in der Lage, uns in politisch-ökonomischer Personalunion den fehlenden Friedrich List zu ersetzen und unseren Mangel am notwendigen Selbstverständnis zu beheben.

Ohne dieses Selbstverständnis wird sich das vernünftigste Deutschland-Konzept nicht realisieren lassen; ohne dieses Selbstverständnis werden wir immer wieder dem nächstbesten nationalistischen Ohrenbläser ausgeliefert sein. Ohne dieses Selbstverständnis werden wir weiterhin zwischen Extremen schlingern und die Besorgnis unserer Nachbarn nähren. Deshalb sollen hier in aller Gelassenheit die nationalen Möglichkeiten und Unmöglichkeiten der Deutschen formuliert werden; denn zwischen dem permanenten Hang zum kleinstaatlichen Separatismus und dem permanenten Gefälle in nationalistische Hybris ist ein Vakuum entstanden. Es ist an der Zeit, *klare* Sätze zu machen.

Zuallererst: Wer heute von Deutschland spricht, muß wissen, daß zwei verschiedene Deutschland, zuerst das kaiserliche, dann das nationalsozialistische, in diesem Jahrhundert je einen Weltkrieg angefangen und verloren haben. (Bewußt verzichte ich auf Gesprächspartner, die meinen, mit dem Stammtischthema der Kriegsschuldfrage ein Nationalgefühl erhitzen zu können, das allzu gerne mit Nationalbewußtsein verwechselt werden möchte.)

Zudem: Die mangelnde Begabung, aus einem verlorenen Krieg zu lernen, ja, überhaupt zu begreifen, daß wir den einen und auch den nächsten Krieg aus Gründen verloren hatten, zeichnete und zeichnet das Unvermögen der jeweiligen Nachkriegspolitik, die sich bis ins Irrationale verstieg und versteigt; die Summe dieser Ignoranz liegt in einem Satz, der Umgangsdeutsch geworden ist: Wir wollen nicht anerkennen.

Mittlerweile hat sich der Wert dieser Anerkennung bis zur Unerheblichkeit überfälliger Formalitäten reduziert. Wir haben den Überblick verloren. Wir doktern an den Symptomen einer von Anbeginn falschen Politik herum. Dabei hat uns Gustav Heinemann zum frühesten Zeitpunkt, lange vor Abschluß der Pariser Verträge, gewarnt; dabei hätte uns die Große Anfrage der SPD vom 15. Dezember 1954 eine letzte Warnung sein müssen. Es ging um die Wiederbewaffnung. Die Sozialdemokraten plädierten für den Vorrang von Verhandlungen zur Wiedervereinigung Deutschlands. Was antwortete damals Kurt Georg Kiesinger den Sozialdemokraten? Ich zitiere aus dem Bundestagsprotokoll: »›Nun sagen *Sie* uns: Wenn wir ratifiziert haben, ist alles dahin, ist die letzte Chance verspielt, mit den Russen über eine Wiedervereinigung erfolgreich zu verhandeln. Herr Ollenhauer, glauben Sie *das* wirklich? *Ich* kann es nicht glauben, daß *Sie* es glauben!‹ (Heiterkeit und Beifall bei den Regierungsparteien.)«

Zwölf Jahre später waren wir vergeßlich genug, den Bock zum Gärtner einer neuen Deutschland-Politik zu machen. Was muß in diesem Land passieren, damit politische Schlüsse aus politischen Gegebenheiten gezogen werden?

Fehlte und fehlt es an profunden Ratschlägen?

Alles ist wiederholt genau und dennoch vergeblich gesagt worden; zum Beispiel von Golo Mann in seiner *Deutschen Geschichte des 19. und 20. Jahrhunderts*. Aus dem letzten Kapitel dieses Buches, das den vielsagenden Titel *Les Allemagnes* führt, also bewußt den Plural, mehrere Deutschland voraussetzt, erlaube ich mir, einen längeren Absatz zu zitieren, der beide Deutschland in Beziehung zueinander setzt:

»Als ein neuer Staat wird die DDR von ihrer Offizialität

verstanden. Sie macht wohl Versuche, an gewisse Episoden der deutschen und preußischen Geschichte Anschluß zu finden. Aber sie betrachtet das Deutschen Reich als aufgelöst und muß es, da sonst ihr Staat keine rechtliche Basis hätte. Darum ist sie gern bereit, die Bundesrepublik anzuerkennen; sie verficht die Theorie von ›zwei deutschen Staaten‹. Die Bundesrepublik tut das nicht. Sie ist nicht bereit, die DDR anzuerkennen; sie betrachtet sich als den Statthalter des Deutschen Reiches, das rechtens noch existiert und faktisch wieder hergestellt werden soll.

Die Wirklichkeit hat seit 1949 sich diesem theoretischen Standpunkt nicht angenähert, sie hat sich weiter und weiter von ihm entfernt; die Bundesrepublik hat eine Identität gewonnen, welche nicht die des ›Reiches‹ ist. Ihre Außenpolitik ist rheinisch und süddeutsch gewesen, nicht gesamtdeutsch. Gesamtdeutsche Außenpolitik hätte auch Ostpolitik sein müssen, und die Bundesrepublik hat keine Ostpolitik gehabt.«

Wir dürfen im Jahre 1967 feststellen: Die Politik der Stärke hat die Festigung der Sowjetzone zum Staat DDR bewirkt. Der Alleinvertretungsanspruch oder die Fiktion, es sei die Bundesrepublik legitime Nachfolgerin des »Reiches« in den Grenzen von 1937, sind nur Beweise, wie schizoid die Ergebnisse dieser rhetorisch gesamtdeutschen, in Wirklichkeit separaten Politik kaschiert worden sind. Die Politik des »Alles oder nichts« hat uns erlaubt, das Nichts als Ernte einzufahren.

Dabei ist die Ausgangsposition für das geteilte Deutschland nach der Kapitulation nicht ungünstig gewesen. Nach der Streichung des Morgenthau-Planes, nach dem Abflauen des Stalinismus bot sich in beiden Teilen Deutschlands mehrmals die Möglichkeit, im Nebeneinander und Miteinander die Konsequenzen des verlorenen Krieges zu tragen und das Vertrauen der gestern noch feindlichen Nachbarvölker wiederzugewinnen. Diesen von den Siegermächten in beide Teile Deutschlands investierten Kredit haben das eine und das andere Deutschland verspielt, indem das eine Deutschland den Stalinismus wieder aufleben ließ und sich innerhalb seines Bündnissystems isolierte, indem die Bundesrepublik bei noch günstigeren Startbedingungen noch weniger ihre Chance begreifen wollte: Alle Marksteine der Ära Adenauer – von der Wiederbewaffnung bis zur Hallstein-Doktrin – widersprachen der Grundgesetz-Präambel. Sie trugen dazu bei, das eine wie das andere Staatsprovisorium zu festigen; heute haben wir zwei Deutschland. Die Gewöhnung an diesen Zustand einerseits und hysterisches Reagieren andererseits bezeugen die zu begründende Tatsache, daß die Deutschen nicht in der Lage sind, eine Nation zu bilden.

Denn die Struktur der beiden deutschen Staaten ist von der Anlage her föderalistisch. In beiden Staaten wird diese föderalistische Struktur vom Gesetz bestätigt. Der Artikel I der DDR-Verfassung sagt immer noch: »Deutschland ist eine unteilbare demokratische Republik; sie baut sich auf den Ländern auf...« Doch nur in der Bundesrepublik hat sich der Föderalismus auswirken und bewähren können. Der andere Staat, also die DDR, gibt sich preußisch-einheitlich und versucht, über die gegebenen Unterschiede, zwischen Mecklenburg und Sachsen zum Beispiel, hinwegzutäuschen. Dabei ist der Föderalismus, das heißt das rechtmäßige Miteinander, Nebeneinander und, im staatsbürgerlichen Sinn, Füreinander der einzelnen Länder die einzig zu vertretende Grundlage der beiden deutschen Staaten. Diese beiden deutschen Staaten haben bisher nur vom Gegeneinander gelebt. So wurde die Tradition des Dualismus konsequent bis zur Spaltung fortgesetzt.

Deutschland ist selten und immer nur zwangsweise ein nationaleinheitlicher Block gewesen, dem die Kontrolle der Länder, der Föderalismus gefehlt hat. Andererseits lehrt die deutsche Geschichte, daß die föderalistische Struktur unseres Landes uns immer wieder und bis heutzutage in den Separatismus getrieben hat. Eintausendsiebenhundertneunundachtzig territoriale Herrschaften trieben zur Zeit der Französischen Revolution, während in Frankreich der Nationalstaat geboren wurde, ihren absolutistischen Kleinhandel; und selbst Napoleons Werk, die Vereinfachung der deutschen Landkarte, hat sich nach dem Wiener Kongreß, innerhalb des Deutschen Bundes, sechsunddreißigmal separat betragen. Erst die preußisch-nationale Roßkur führte zu den bekannten und gleichfalls extremen Ergebnissen. Wir haben das Maß nicht finden können. Zwischen Nationalismus und Separatismus liegt jedoch unsere einzige und selten genutzte Möglichkeit: die Konföderation oder der wirtschaftlich feste, politisch und kulturell lockere Bund der Länder. Er könnte uns Patria sein; doch schon und abermals verwirren sich die Begriffe.

Es wäre jetzt an der Zeit, das altmodische, oft mißbrauchte und gleichwohl treffende Wort »Vaterland« zu definieren, zumal sich das »Vaterland« zwanglos den konföderierten Ländern überordnen ließe. Aber der nationalistische Verschleiß dieses Begriffes, von der »vaterländischen Gesinnung« bis zum »Europa der Vaterländer«, bereitet uns Sprachschwierigkeiten; wie überhaupt verworrene Terminologie geschwätzige Sprachlosigkeit belegt, sobald die Frage nach der Nation gestellt wird. Da verwirren sich Nationalbewußtsein und Nationalgefühl. Nationalhymne steht gegen Nationalhymne. *Unsere* hebt sich akustisch auf, indem wir gleichzeitig die erste und dritte Strophe des Deutschlandliedes singen: eine Katzenmusik, die sich zur Ouvertüre einer nationalen Farce eignen könnte. Selbstverständlich leistet sich die Bundesrepublik eine Fußballnationalmannschaft, während auf der anderen Seite, je nach Gusto des Fernsehsprechers, die mitteldeutsche bzw. Zonenmannschaft gewinnt, verliert oder ein Unentschieden erkämpft. Zwar vermag uns keiner der nationalen Schönredner den Begriff »Nation« zu definieren, doch sollte zumindest Rainer Barzel in der Lage sein, uns gelegentlich zu verraten, was er unter »nationaler Würdelosigkeit« versteht. Um nicht Bruno Hecks Aufschwünge beim Namen nennen zu müssen – denn unser Minister für Familie und Jugend überbietet erfolgreich die Verstiegenheiten der NPD – erlaube ich mir, aus Eugen Gerstenmaiers Versuch, das nationale Soll zu erfüllen, kurz aber vielsagend zu zitieren: »Ein Volk in unserer Lage, mit unserer Geschichte und Veranlagung braucht einfach den Geist der Hingabe, des Opfermuts, der Ehrerbietung und auch des Gehorsams.«

Diese Töne klingen in unseren Breiten nicht neu. Wenn wir bedenken, wie mysteriös-phantastisch der Reichs-Begriff sich aus dem Mittelalter bis in unser Jahrhundert konservieren konnte; wenn wir, um ein Beispiel zu nennen, die widersprechende Reichsschau der Landesfürsten – ich nenne Moritz von Sachsen und Maximilian I. von Bayern –, also den realpolitischen Separatismus mit der Reichsutopie des genialen Scharlatans Wallenstein vergleichen, und wenn wir bemerken, wie einerseits Moritz von Sachsen und andererseits Wallenstein immer mehr oder weniger begabte Nachfolger gefunden haben, dann wird uns deutlich, wie sehr es den Deutschen an Selbstverständnis mangelt, wie blindlings sie mangelndes Selbstverständnis durch komplexes Selbstbewußtsein zu ersetzen versuchen, wie leicht verführbar sie sein müssen, welche Chance einerseits Konrad Adenauer, andererseits Walter Ulbricht hatten und wahrnahmen, indem sie die erweiterte Maximilian-von-Bayern-Position und die erweiterte Moritz-von-Sachsen-Position verwirklichten und gleichzeitig Wallenstein-Töne improvisierten.

Seitdem dieser neudeutsche Separatismus in Gestalt zweier Staaten durchaus separate Geschichte macht, ist eine Generation aufgewachsen, die sich einerseits als Bürger der Bundesrepublik und andererseits als Bürger der Deutschen Demokratischen Republik versteht. Diese Generation weiß wenig voneinander. Bewußt haben zwei gegensätzliche Schulsysteme diese Generation voneinander weg erzogen und verzogen. Die Entfremdung der beiden deutschsprachigen Staaten hatte sich im Verlauf der fünfziger Jahre derart verhärtet und ideologisiert, daß man in der Bundesrepublik ohne Skrupel bereit war, die selbstgestellte Frage »Ist Walter Ulbricht ein Deutscher?« mit »Nein« zu beantworten. Zu Recht befindet man im westlichen wie östlichen Ausland: Warum soll es nicht bei zwei Staaten bleiben, wenn die Deutschen es so zielstrebig zu zwei Staaten gebracht haben?

Ich möchte in diesem Zusammenhang auf den im August 1962 im *Monat* veröffentlichten und immer noch aktuellen Aufsatz *Patriotische Fragezeichen* von Arnulf Baring hinweisen. Dieser Aufsatz schließt bewußt provokativ und nur scheinbar paradox: »Jede Wiederannäherung in Deutschland setzt die Anerkennung der Spaltung voraus!«

Ergänzend hierzu sei gesagt: Nur von den Gegebenheiten, also vom verlorenen Krieg her, den wir bezahlen müssen, von den Konsequenzen des verlorenen Krieges her und basierend auf der föderalistischen Struktur beider deutschen Staaten, läßt sich ein konföderiertes Deutschland denken und bei Geduld und politischer Einsicht verwirklichen, wobei der selbstverständlichste Teil dieser Einsicht die endliche Anerkennung der Oder-Neiße-Grenze bedeuten muß. Doch sollte diese Anerkennung mit dem rechtmäßigen Anspruch auf die Konföderation der beiden deutschen Staaten verbunden und als Vorleistung für einen Friedensvertrag deklariert werden.

Um dieses Ziel erreichen zu können, fehlen in beiden deutschen Staaten vorerst die Voraussetzungen. Denn weder die preußisch-stalinistische Staatsvorstellung der DDR noch die halbeingestandene Rheinbündelei der Bundesrepublik bieten ausreichend Ansätze für die Konföderation zweier deutscher Staaten. Schon zeichnet sich ein Alptraum ab, der, wie viele deutsche Alpträume, Chancen birgt, Realität zu werden: Nur wenig spricht dagegen, daß sich in den siebziger Jahren der starke preußisch-stalinistische Flügel in der DDR einig wird mit dem immer stärker werdenden national-konservativen Flügel in der Bundesrepublik, einig auf Kosten des liberalen Föderalismus, einig auf Kosten der sozialen Demokratie. Deutschnationale Rechte plus stalinistische Rechte könnten die Spottgeburt einer Nation in die Welt setzen, deren furchterregende Existenz durch das wachsende Selbstverständnis der Deutschen verhindert werden möge.

Wir sollten begreifen lernen, daß der Begriff Nation an sich keinen Wert darstellt.

Wir sollten erkennen, daß die französische Nation auf historische Voraussetzungen gründet, die uns nicht gegeben sind. Wir sollten andererseits am Beispiel der Schweiz lernen, daß die Konföderation ein Nationalbewußtsein nicht aufhebt.

Wir sollten trotz aller ideologischen Versteinerung, hier wie drüben, und ohne das übliche Schielen nach Vorbildern, deren Zentralismus uns eher ein warnendes Beispiel sein müßte, eine Politik betreiben, die den Rückfall in die Nationalstaatlichkeit ausschließt, die den sinnentleerten Begriff »Wiedervereinigung« vermeidet und dafür eine schrittweise Annäherung versucht, die sich die Konföderation zweier deutscher Länderbünde als Ziel setzt.

Am 6. Mai 1947 begann in München, unter dem Vorsitz des damaligen bayerischen Ministerpräsidenten Ehard, die erste und letzte Nachkriegskonferenz aller deutschen Ministerpräsidenten. Schon am gleichen Tag kam es, der Tagesordnung wegen, zum Bruch: Die fünf Länderchefs der Sowjetzone reisten ab. Wenn eine Politik der Annäherung zwanzig Jahre später neu ansetzen will, wird sie sich der mißglückten Konferenz vom Mai 1947 und der Gründe des Scheiterns erinnern müssen. Gleichzeitig sollten sich Volkskammer- wie Bundestagsabgeordnete bewußt sein, daß einerseits die geplante und endgültige DDR-Verfassung, andererseits unsere Notstandsgesetze neue Zeugnisse des Separatismus sein werden.

Meine These heißt: Da wir, gemessen an unserer Veranlagung, keine Nation bilden können, da wir, belehrt durch geschichtliche Erkenntnis – und unserer kulturellen Vielgestalt bewußt – keine Nation bilden sollten, müssen wir endlich den Föderalismus als einzige Chance begreifen. Nicht als geballte Nation, nicht als zwei wider einander gesetzte Nationen, nur als friedlich wettstreitende Länderbünde können wir unseren Nachbarn in Ost und West

Sicherheit bieten. Denn auch Polen und der Tschechoslowakei wäre eine föderalistische Deutsche Demokratische Republik ein weniger unheimlicher Nachbar als es die zum preußischen Nachfolgestaat zentralisierte DDR ist.

Konkret gesprochen müßte, bei gleichzeitiger Anerkennung des zweiten Staates und bei Aufgabe des Alleinvertretungsanspruches, der Deutschen Demokratischen Republik nahegelegt werden, die Länderhoheit innerhalb ihres Staatsbereiches verfassungsmäßig zu verwirklichen, damit die Voraussetzungen für die föderative Zusammenarbeit der zehn Länder innerhalb der Bundesrepublik mit dem Land Berlin und den fünf Ländern innerhalb der DDR im Sinne einer Konföderation beider Staaten gegeben sind. Es werden christdemokratisch regierte, sozialdemokratisch regierte und kommunistisch regierte Bundesländer in dieser Konföderation zusammenarbeiten müssen. Was für Italien und Frankreich als selbstverständlich gilt, das oft disharmonische Konzert gegensätzlicher Parteien, sollte auch uns selbstverständlich werden. Politische Gegner, die einander bis heute bedingungslos ausschlossen, werden sich morgen zur Diskussion bequemen müssen. Es wird dem Gremium dieser Konföderation, das seinen Sitz alternierend in Leipzig und Frankfurt am Main haben möge, nicht an Aufgaben fehlen: Es gilt, zwei stehende Armeen Zug um Zug abzurüsten; es gilt, mit den freiwerdenden Mitteln gemeinsame Forschungsprojekte und Entwicklungshilfe zu finanzieren; es gilt, in beiden konföderierten Staaten die politische Strafjustiz aufzuheben; es gilt, gemeinsam Verhandlungen einzuleiten, deren Ziel der Friedensvertrag sein sollte; es gilt, einen Anfang zu wagen, denn die Zeit arbeitet nicht für uns. Nichts spricht dagegen, unsere westlichen wie östlichen Nachbarn vom Sinn und Nutzen dieser Konföderation zweier förderalistischer deutscher Staaten zu überzeugen, zumal diese Annäherung keine Wiedervereinigung bedeuten soll, sondern Sicherheit garantieren will, zumal diese Annäherung die Entspannung zwischen Ost und West beispielhaft fördern könnte und einer zukünftigen europäischen Lösung, die gewiß eine föderalistische Lösung sein wird, entgegenkäme.

Einigkeit, europäische wie deutsche, setzt nicht Einheit voraus. Deutschland ist nur zwangsweise, also immer zu seinem Schaden, eine Einheit gewesen. Denn die Einheit ist eine Idee, die wider den Menschen gesetzt ist; sie schmälert die Freiheit. Einigkeit verlangt den freien Entschluß der Vielzahl. Deutschland sollte endlich das Mit-, Neben- und Füreinander der Bayern und Sachsen, der Schwaben und Thüringer, der Westfalen und Mecklenburger werden. Das singuläre Deutschland ist eine Rechnung, die nie mehr aufgehen möge; denn genau gerechnet ist Deutschland eine kommunizierende Mehrzahl.

Ich war vermessen genug, vor deutschen Journalisten zu sprechen, die mit den Fiktionen wie mit den realen Möglichkeiten der Deutschlandpolitik seit Jahren vertraut sind. Es kann sein, daß während der nun beginnenden Diskussion ein Sack voller Fakten ausgeschüttet wird, woraufhin der eine oder andere jeweils seine Lieblingsfakten ausrufen könnte; denn wir haben uns daran gewöhnt, uns in einer Art Faktensicherheit zu wiegen, die, weil ein allgemeines Selbstverständnis fehlt, der einzelnen Position Genüge verschafft. Wenn ich es auch gewohnt bin, dem Mißverständnis, ja, der bewußten Fehlinterpretation als, mittlerweile, vertrautem Weggenossen zu begegnen, möchte ich Sie dennoch bitten, Ihre eigene Position, sooft Sie als Journalist faktisch recht haben mögen, nun im größeren Zusammenhang, dem mangelnden Selbstverständnis der Deutschen gegenüber, zu prüfen.

Wer der Autor gewesen sein mag, Goethe oder Schiller; für Mannheim und Jena, für Weimar wie für Frankfurt sei zum Schluß aus den Xenien zitiert:

»Deutscher Nationalcharakter

Zur Nation euch zu bilden, ihr hoffet es, Deutsche, vergebens;

Bildet, ihr könnt es, dafür freier zu Menschen euch aus.«

Was ist des Deutschen Vaterland?

So heißt meine Rede, und mit dieser Frage beginnt ein Gedicht, das ich Ihnen nicht vorenthalten möchte.

Was ist des Deutschen Vaterland?
Ist's Preußenland, ist's Schwabenland?
Ist's, wo am Rhein die Rebe blüht?
Ist's, wo am Belt die Möwe zieht?
O nein! nein! nein!
Sein Vaterland muß größer sein.

Was ist des Deutschen Vaterland?
Ist's Bayerland, ist's Steierland?
Ist's, wo des Marsen Rind sich streckt?
Ist's, wo der Märker Eisen reckt?
O nein! nein! nein!
Sein Vaterland muß größer sein.

Was ist des Deutschen Vaterland?
Ist's Pommerland, Westfalenland?
Ist's, wo der Sand der Dünen weht?
Ist's, wo die Donau brausend geht?
O nein! nein! nein!
Sein Vaterland muß größer sein.

Was ist des Deutschen Vaterland?
So nenne mir das große Land!
Ist's Land der Schweizer, ist's Tirol?
Das Land und Volk gefiel mir wohl;
Doch nein! nein! nein!
Sein Vaterland muß größer sein.

Was ist des Deutschen Vaterland?
So nenne mir das große Land!
Gewiß es ist das Österreich,
An Ehren und an Siegen reich?
O nein! nein! nein!
Sein Vaterland muß größer sein.

Was ist des Deutschen Vaterland?
So nenne mir das große Land!
So weit die deutsche Zunge klingt
Und Gott im Himmel Lieder singt:
Das soll es sein!
Das, wackrer Deutscher, nenne dein!

Das ist des Deutschen Vaterland?
Wo Eide schwört der Druck der Hand,
Wo Treue hell vom Auge blitzt
Und Liebe warm im Herzen sitzt –
Das soll es sein!
Das, wackrer Deutscher, nenne dein!

Das ist des Deutschen Vaterland,
Wo Zorn vertilgt den welschen Tand,
Wo jeder Franzmann heißet Feind,
Und jeder Deutsche heißet Freund –
Das soll es sein!
Das ganze Deutschland soll es sein!

Das ganze Deutschland soll es sein!
O Gott vom Himmel, sieh darein
Und gib uns rechten deutschen Mut,
Daß wir es lieben treu und gut.

Das soll es sein!
Das ganze Deutschland soll es sein!

Trotz einiger Anklänge: Diese Hymne wurde nicht im Ministerium für Gesamtdeutsche Fragen ausgeheckt; der Verfasser dieses Gedichtes heißt Ernst Moritz Arndt. Sein Denkmal steht in Bonn. Und ich habe dieses Unikum in der Schule noch auswendig lernen müssen. Heute wage ich zu hoffen, daß die Gedächtnisse, etwa der Neuwähler, nicht mit dererlei Strophenreichtum belastet worden sind. Allenfalls zeitgenössische und immer noch eifrige Karl-May-Leser werden im Schlußkapitel des Bandes *Der blaurote Methusalem* eine feucht-fröhliche Männerrunde versammelt finden, die sich mehrstimmig beteuert, was alles des Deutschen Vaterland ist. Dennoch können wir uns mit Hilfe dieses Liedes und der erwähnten Karl-May-Sangesrunde ausdenken, welch ein sättigendes und die nationale Hybris nährendes Fressen dieses Poem, von Wilhelms bis zu Adolfs Zeiten, für fröhliche Liedertafeln, Abiturientenfeiern und sonstige große Tage gewesen ist. Aber man täte Ernst Moritz Arndt Unrecht, wollte man ihm den späteren Mißbrauch seiner noch aus den Befreiungskriegen nachwehenden Begeisterung aufbürden. Ich bin dem Kollegen, der so vielen deutschen Gymnasien seinen Namen geliehen hat, seiner interessanten Fragestellung wegen dankbar. Was ist des Deutschen Vaterland?

Arndt zählt mit Fleiß die Provinzen auf und ist dabei mehr dem Reimzwang als dem genauen Grenzverlauf verpflichtet. – »Sein Vaterland muß größer sein.« Wenn die Aufgabe, lyrisch-geographisch Bestand aufzunehmen, heute gestellt würde, wie gingen Lyriker unserer Tage das heiße Eisen an oder um den Brei herum? Etwa Peter Rühmkorf sänge vom Westen aus, Freund Bobrowski erhöbe die Stimme in Ostberlin. Ich als Berliner müßte, wie vor Monaten, gleich Korber und Wendt lavieren, um nicht als Sänger der Dreistaaten-Theorie einerseits oder als Imperialist, der den Bonner Ultras hörig sei, andererseits beschimpft zu werden. Gar nicht auszudenken ist Arndts heikle Frage, wenn sich die Österreicherin Ingeborg Bachmann ihrer annähme. Was also ist des Deutschen Vaterland?

Wenn nun jemand glauben sollte, ich sei entschlossen, nach solchem Anlauf schnurstracks Vorschläge zur Wiedervereinigung zu unterbreiten, oder ich wisse, wie man Konrad Adenauers Wahlversprechen an die Flüchtlinge: »Ihr alle kommt in Eure alte Heimat zurück!« endlich einlösen könne, den muß ich enttäuschen. Der Bundesregierung ist es spätestens ab 1955, als der Deutschlandvertrag unterzeichnet wurde, und bis in unsere Mauerbau-Zeiten hinein gelungen, die Teilung des restlichen Deutschland, zum kurzfristigen Nutzen der Bundesrepublik, zum andauernden Schaden der Landsleute in der DDR, zu zementieren; und was jene Provinzen angeht, die im Lied des Ernst Moritz Arndt, mehr oder weniger umschrieben, noch vorkommen – Schlesien, Hinterpommern, Ostpreußen –, kann ich, also jemand, der von da unten kommt, nur zähneknirschend und gegen die eigene Brust schlagend die Wahrheit aussprechen: Wir haben diese Provinzen vertan, verspielt, eine Welt herausfordernd verloren. Ernst Moritz Arndts Lied *Was ist des Deutschen Vaterland?* ist kürzer geworden. Wenn auch nicht so kurz, wie wir zu fürchten Anlaß haben. Vielleicht finden sich in der nächsten Bundesregierung realistische Politiker, die auf der Basis eines Friedensvertrages zu verhandeln verstehen, denn über den Verbleib von Stettin und über den Lausitzzipfel waren sich die Siegermächte in Jalta und Potsdam nicht einig.

Herr Seebohm röhrt gelegentlich sonntags seine Ansprüche aufs Sudetenland der entsetzten Welt in die Ohren. Meine Landsleute aus Danzig unterhalten in Lübeck sogar einen Schattensenat, der seit Jahr und Tag den alten Leutchen aus der Stadt und dem Werder verspricht, eines Tages gäbe es sie wieder, die Freie Stadt Danzig. Lügen und Zynismus alten Menschen gegenüber, die im Westen nicht heimisch werden konnten, die sich ihre breite und langsam die Butter aufs Brot schmierende Sprache erhalten haben, verbale Seifenblasen müssen seit Jahren eine konstruktive Außenpolitik ersetzen. Noch einmal: Wenn es uns an Stettin und der Lausitz wirklich gelegen ist, sollten wir den Mut aufbringen, Königsberg und Breslau, Kolberg und Schneidemühl aus unserem Lied *Was ist des Deutschen Vaterland?* als geographische Begriffe zu streichen; aber nicht notwendig ist es deshalb, die Heimatverbände aufzulösen und jene Provinzen, die einmal des Deutschen Vaterland gewesen sind, zu vergessen. Gewiß, Schluß mit den kostspieligen und Funktionäre mästenden Flüchtlingstreffen. Aber an ihrer Stelle forderte ich die ernsthafte Erforschung aussterbender Dialekte und – ich fürchte nicht das Lächeln der Oberschlauen – die Gründung von gutgeplanten, durchaus lebensfähigen und nicht nur musealen Städten, die Neu-Königsberg, Neu-Allenstein, Neu-Breslau, Neu-Görlitz, Neu-Kolberg und Neu-Danzig heißen mögen.

Laßt uns Stadtgründer sein! Wir haben Platz in der Eifel, im Hunsrück, im Emsland und im Bayrischen Wald. Es mangelt nicht an unterentwickelten Gebieten, die auf solch realistische Art erschlossen werden können. Gerne bin ich bereit, bei der Grundsteinlegung der Stadt Neu-Danzig, sie muß nicht an der Ostsee liegen, meinen Teil beizutragen. Wer sagt da Utopie? Nichts davon. Hier wird die Frage: »Was ist des Deutschen Vaterland?« realistisch beantwortet. Es bedarf der Vernunft und einer Portion Pioniergeist, wie ihn die deutschen Auswanderer in Amerika bewiesen haben, als sie Hamburg, Frankfurt und Berlin im Mittleren Westen gründeten, um uns wenn nicht verlorene Provinzen, so doch die Essenz dessen wiederzugewinnen, was einst des Deutschen Vaterland gewesen ist.

Nach dem Krieg haben die Glasbläser und Glasschmuckfabrikanten des sudetendeutschen Städtchens Gablonz ein Beispiel dieses Pioniergeistes gegeben, als sie in Süddeutschland die Stadt Neu-Gablonz gründeten. Unser Land ist reich genug, diese Neugründungen zu wagen. Moderne, kühn geplante Städte sehe ich entstehen, die, da es ohnehin an Universitäten und Hochschulen mangelt, wissenschaftliche Zentren sein können. Architekten könnten Wagnisse eingehen, die uns aus unseren städtebaulichen Sackgassen herausführen. Traditionelle Industrien, wie früher in Breslau, Danzig, Königsberg, sehe ich Fuß fassen. Und vielleicht werden auch die aussterbenden Dialekte, Gerhart Hauptmanns Schlesisch und mein geliebtes Danziger Platt, grotesk gemischt mit friesischer und bayrischer Mundart, eine Renaissance erleben.

Jetzt werden tausend Soziologen den Kopf schütteln. Rufe wie: Zu spät! Das hätte man vor zehn Jahren! Der spinnt! lassen sich erahnen. Das Wörtchen »Verzichtpolitiker« klettert aus der Mottenkiste. Ergraute Ostlandreiter sehe ich den eingefetteten SA-Dolch ziehen. Sie wollen sich aus mir den üblichen vaterlandslosen Gesellen, den Kommunisten von der Stange schnitzen. Und womöglich werden sich die von mir so geschätzten Sozialdemokraten für dererlei Schützenhilfe bedanken; mir jedoch kommt es darauf an, die alte Frage des Ernst Moritz Arndt zu beantworten: »Was ist des Deutschen Vaterland?« Was wir aus ihm machen. Welche Güter wir obenan stellen: die Aussprüche des Panzergenerals Guderian oder die mutige Rede des sozialdemokratischen Reichstagsabgeordneten Otto Wels. Nach soviel verlorenen Kriegen, nach Blitzsiegen und Kesselschlachten, nach all dem Horror, dessen wir fähig sind, sollten wir endlich die Vernunft, das Maß und die eigentliche Stärke unseres Vaterlandes siegen lassen: den einst blühenden, nun immer mehr verdrängten Hang zu den Wissenschaften. Die Wahl liegt bei uns.

In New York, um den 8. Mai herum, habe ich im amerikanischen Fernsehen Ausschnitte aus der Ostberliner Siegesparade gesehen. Der Telstar Early Bird machte es möglich. Dort marschierte sie, die Volksarmee, zackig am Schnürchen. Ein nachgemachtes Preußen. Schamlos wurde in Ulbrichts Machtbereich eine korrumpierte Tradition übernommen. Furchterregend, auch komisch, wie jede aufgeblähte Macht, zog es vorbei. Insgesamt ein Bild, das vergessen machte, daß dieser Möchtegern-Staat sich »Friedenslager« nennt. O bärtiger großer Marx! Was haben sie dir dort angetan? In welchem Gefängnis würdest du heute dort sitzen?

Zwanzig Jahre nach der bedingungslosen Kapitulation eines Landes, das sich Groß-Deutschland genannt hatte, saß ich in einem New Yorker Hotel vor der Mattscheibe und sah dieselbe beineschmeißende Unnatur, Parademarsch genannt, die meiner Jugend den Rhythmus diktiert hat. Auch das ist des Deutschen Vaterland. Aber ist es nur das? Wer in Berlin lebt, weiß, daß die Mehrzahl unserer Landsleute in der DDR abseits von dieser preußisch-stalinistischen Spielart des Stechschrittes lebt. Im Herbst vergangenen Jahres war ich für wenige Tage in Weimar. Sprechen wir nicht von dem lächerlichen Kongreß, der dort stattfand und sich bemühte, den althergebrachten Vulgär-Marxismus am Leben zu halten. Aber in den Pausen, sobald es nicht mehr darauf ankam, Kafka, Joyce oder unsere, wie Herr Erhard kürzlich zu sagen beliebte, »entartete Kunst« gegen kleinkarierte Funktionäre und also das gesamtdeutsche Banausentum zu verteidigen, nahm ich Gelegenheiten wahr und schaute mich um.

Wer Ohren hat, höre: Es ist fünf Minuten vor zwölf. Unsere Landsleute, die fleißige Sonntagsredner zu Brüdern und Schwestern stilisiert haben, sind bereit, uns abzuschreiben. Sie wissen alles. Sie hören Westsender. Unser Sprachgebrauch, vom »Gesamtdeutschen Anliegen« bis zu den feierlichen Allgemeinplätzen des 17. Juni und dem Kuratorium-Zitat aus unserem Arndt-Gedicht: »Das ganze Deutschland soll es sein!«, hat ihre Ohren zermürbt. Ohne Umschweif und ohne den leicht verächtlichen Unterton zu kaschieren, werden dort vierzehn Jahre westdeutsche Wiedervereinigungspolitik drastisch realistisch zusammengefaßt. Ich hörte sagen: »Euer Adenauer, der hat schon gewußt, was er tat. Wiedervereinigung kam nicht in die Tüte. Das hätte ja eine gesamtdeutsche SPD-Regierung bedeutet. Außerdem sind wir nicht katholisch.« Man kann gerne und mit Fleiß diesen Satz verfeinern und verästeln, das Wenn und Aber berücksichtigen, auch läßt sich die Schuld, je nach Belieben, auf dem Konto der Alliierten oder der bösen Russen abbuchen, wer aber den Selbstbetrug satt hat, wer, mit Vernunft und untrüglichem Gedächtnis ausgerüstet, bereit ist zur nationalen Inventaraufnahme und sich, getreu unserem Motto, die Frage stellt: »Was ist des Deutschen Vater-

land?«, der wird recht bald erkennen, daß dieselben Schrei-
hälse und Kreuzzügler, die das Sudetenland und Gleiwitz
heim ins Reich holen wollen, den wahren Ausverkauf unseres Vaterlandes, den verschleierten Verzicht auf Dresden
und Magdeburg, auf Weimar und Rostock, nicht ohne Ge-
schick betrieben haben.

Schauen wir zurück: Am 16. und 17. Juni 1953 fand in
Ostberlin und in der sowjetisch besetzten Zone ein deutscher Arbeiteraufstand statt, der in seinen stärksten Mo-
menten, im Beginn auf der Stalinallee wie im Scheitern,
deutlich sozialdemokratische Züge trug und Walter Ulbrichts Diktatur, wenn auch nur für Stunden, ins Wanken
brachte. Dieser Arbeiteraufstand ist von der DDR-Regie-
rung zum faschistischen Putschversuch und von verant-
wortlicher westdeutscher Seite zu einer Volkserhebung verfälscht worden, obgleich sich ohne Mühe beweisen läßt,
daß das Bürgertum und die Bauern, Beamte und Intellektuelle bis auf löbliche Ausnahmen zu Hause geblieben sind.
Deutsche Arbeiter gaben den Anstoß, Arbeiter aus Hen-
ningsdorf, Buna, Leuna, Halle und Merseburg nahmen das
Risiko auf sich, und uns blieb es überlassen, ihre verzwei-
felte, bewegende, wie, am Ende, hilflose Tat als Feiertag
einzuebnen. Auch das ist des Deutschen Vaterland: dieser
zwei Tage lang während Moment der Wahrheit und die
zwölf Jahre lang immer mehr Speck ansetzende Lüge. Wo
ist die Jugend, und wo ist meine gebrannte Generation, die
es besser wissen müßte, wo sind sie, die sich dieses Eintopf-
gericht widerspruchslos haben einlöffeln lassen? Sagt nicht,
das ist uns neu. Davon wußten wir nichts. Ihr *Spiegel*- und
Pardon-Leser, Ihr *konkret*- und *Civis*-Abonnenten, Ihr kor-
porierten und nichtkorporierten Studenten, zuckt nicht mit
den Achseln: »Das ist doch gleich, ob Arbeiter- oder Volks-

aufstand, genützt hat es doch nix.« So leicht sprechen Euch unsere Landsleute, die zur Anklage bereit sind, nicht frei, zumal hören konnte, wer seine Ohren nicht mit Totozahlen, Ferienplänen und »Keine Experimente« verstopft hatte.

Ein im Juni 1953 noch relativ unbekannter Berliner Bundestagsabgeordneter, Willy Brandt, hat am 1. Juli 1953, als der 17. Juni zum »Tag der deutschen Einheit« erklärt wurde, eine scharfe Rede gehalten. Willy Brandt hat als erster vor der Verfälschung des Arbeiteraufstandes gewarnt. Erlauben Sie mir, eine längere Passage dieser großen und immer noch gültigen Rede zu zitieren. Brandt sagte: »Wer heute noch glaubt, die demokratische und nationale Zuverlässigkeit der deutschen Arbeiterbewegung und der deutschen Sozialdemokratie in Frage stellen zu können, der nimmt dadurch die Verantwortung für eine nochmalige, eine zusätzliche Spaltung unseres Volkes auf sich.

Die Illusionen auf außenpolitischem Gebiet in den hinter uns liegenden Jahren und der Mangel an Realismus lagen bei denen, die Verhandlungen zwischen West und Ost nicht mit einkalkuliert haben. Wir sehen übrigens die größere Gefahr noch immer darin, daß die Mächte bis auf weiteres über eine Lösung der deutschen Frage überhaupt nicht verhandeln. Die deutsche Politik darf nichts tun, was diese Gefahr vergrößern könnte.

Es gibt keine andere Lösung als die friedliche Lösung der deutschen Frage. Es gibt keine andere Möglichkeit als die von Verhandlungen über die deutsche Frage. Wir fordern mehr Aktivität, mehr Zielklarheit, mehr Entschlossenheit im Kampf um die deutsche Einheit in Frieden und Freiheit.«

So sprach damals der unbekannte Abgeordnete, so

spricht heute noch der Regierende Bürgermeister Willy Brandt. Damals in den Wind gesprochen. Wird er heute Gehör finden? Damals ließen parteipolitisches Taktieren und Kommunistenfurcht die Scheuklappen wachsen. Sind wir heute bereit, aus der Stärke unserer demokratischen Verfassung heraus, selbstbewußt und endlich mündig dem politischen Gegner in langwährenden und Schritt für Schritt geführten Verhandlungen zu begegnen, oder sollen sich weitere Jahrzehnte lang Bundeswehr und Volksarmee als der Weisheit letzter Schluß gegenüberstehen? Die Bundestagswahlen am 19. September werden Antwort geben, was heute und morgen des Deutschen Vaterland ist und sein wird. Unsere Landsleute, denen Ulbricht das freie Wahlrecht heute noch vorzuenthalten vermag, werden uns zuschauen bei unserer Stimmabgabe. Ich meine, wen immer noch Skrupel bewegen, von seinem Stimmrecht Gebrauch zu machen, der möge bedenken, wie viele der Arbeiter, die im Juni 1953 gegen Unrecht und Diktatur aufstanden, bereit wären, an seiner Stelle zu wählen. Gebt es nicht leichtfertig auf, unser teuer erkauftes Wahlrecht!

Ich habe diese Rede Anfang Juni in Amerika konzipiert. Dort, auf diesem und jenem amerikanischen Universitätsgelände, auf den üblichen Empfängen, bei Gesprächen in der Hotelhalle, wo immer ich deutschen Emigranten begegnete, drängte sich jenes groteske Schulgedicht auf, das wir Ernst Moritz Arndt verdanken. Auch sie, die Beleidigten und Verbitterten, die Stillen, denen es dreiunddreißig die Sprache verschlagen hat, die Schüchternen, denen im Verlauf der Jahre Worte abhanden gekommen sind, die alten, nach Heidelberg und Göttingen fragenden Professoren, Kaufleute, denen Leipzig und Frankfurt immer noch anhängen, sie alle, die uns heute fehlen, bewohnen eine grenzenlose, weil weltweite Provinz, die schmerzhaft und oft wider Willen des Deutschen Vaterland ist.

In den letzten Jahren ist die deutsche Emigration oft genug, und sei es, um Willy Brandt zu diffamieren, mit Dreck beworfen worden, den die Arbeitsgemeinschaft Kapfinger-Strauß allen Interessenten, so auch unserem Altbundeskanzler, kostenlos zur Verfügung gestellt hat. Wenn diese geistige Provinz deutscher Emigration nicht auch noch unserem Vaterland verlorengehen soll, werden die Bürger der Bundesrepublik und besonders die Jugend jene immer noch fortlebende Sprachschleuder des Joseph Goebbels abstellen müssen. Heute noch von »Entarteter Kunst« zu sprechen, Herr Ludwig Erhard, heißt, den verfolgten und verfemten, den toten wie überlebenden Malern, Schriftstellern und Komponisten im Lande und in der Emigration abermals ins Gesicht zu schlagen. Paul Klee und Max Beckmann, Alban Berg und Kurt Weill, Alfred Döblin und Else Lasker-Schüler sind, Herr Erhard, mit Ihrer nachgeplapperten und deshalb doppelt unverantwortlichen Formulierung aus unserm Land getrieben worden. Wenn schon nicht Einsicht und Kunstverstand Ihnen gegeben sind, so sollte Sie doch Schamgefühl hindern, die Sprache der Nationalsozialisten zu benutzen, denn sie, das sollte gewiß sein, die mit dem »Durchführen« und »Ausmerzen«, mit den Sprachungeheuern »volklich« und »entartet« eine uns heute noch bedrückende Bilanz hinterließ, sollte nicht oder nie wieder des Deutschen Vaterland sein.

Lassen Sie mich einen letzten Versuch unternehmen, die Frage des Ernst Moritz Arndt zu beantworten. In New York und jene Provinz deutscher Emigration erahnend, die ich dem Deutschen Vaterland gerne zurechnen möchte, habe ich die *Transatlantische Elegie* geschrieben:

Zum Lächeln aufgelegt, und Erfolg, das Hündchen, immer
bei Fuß.
So unterwegs im Lande Walt Whitmans, mit leichtem Ge-
päck.
Frei schwimmend zwischen den Konferenzen, getragen vom
Redefluß.
Doch während Pausen, solang sich gewürfeltes Eis
klirrend mit Gläsern ausspricht,
rührt es dich an und nennt seinen Namen.
In New Haven und Cincinnati von Emigranten befragt,
die damals, als uns der Geist emigrierte,
nichts mitnehmen durften, als Sprache,
und immer noch schwäbisch, sächsisch und hessisch
die gutgelaunte und jedes Wort streichelnde
Vielfalt der Zunge belegen,
in Washington und New York fragten sie mich,
mit Händen den Whisky erwärmend:
Wie sieht es aus drüben?
Sagt man noch immer?
Und eure Jugend?
Weiß sie? Will sie? Man hört so wenig.
      Es dehnte Schüchternheit diese Fragen,
      und sie erinnerten sich mit Vorsicht,
      als wollten sie jemanden schonen:
Sollte man wieder zurück?
Ist da noch Platz für unsereins?
Und wird mein Deutsch – es ist altmodisch, ich weiß –
nicht jedermann verraten, daß ich solange …?
      Und ich antwortete, den Whisky erwärmend:
Es ist besser geworden.
Wir haben eine gute Verfassung.
Jetzt, endlich, rührt sich auch meine Generation.

Bald, im September, sind Wahlen.
     Und als ich Mangel an Worten litt,
     halfen sie mir
     mit ihrer emigrierten und schöngebliebenen
     Sprache.
Hört die Legende von drüben:
     Es war ein tausendfältiger Bibliothekar,
     der die Nachlässe jener verwahrte,
     deren Bücher gebrannt hatten, damals.
Er lächelte konservativ und wünschte mir Glück für den
September.

Offener Brief an Anna Seghers

Berlin, am 14. August 1961

An die Vorsitzende des Deutschen
Schriftstellerverbandes in der DDR

Verehrte Frau Anna Seghers,

als mich gestern eine der uns Deutschen so vertrauten und geläufigen plötzlichen Aktionen mit Panzernebengeräuschen, Rundfunkkommentaren und obligater Beethovensymphonie wach werden ließ, als ich nicht glauben wollte, was ein Radiogerät mir zum Frühstück servierte, fuhr ich zum Bahnhof Friedrichstraße, ging zum Brandenburger Tor und sah mich den unverkennbaren Attributen der nackten und dennoch nach Schweinsleder stinkenden Gewalt gegenüber. Ich habe, sobald ich mich in Gefahr befinde – oftmals überängstlich, wie alle gebrannten Kinder –, die Neigung, um Hilfe zu schreien. Ich kramte im Kopf und im Herzen nach Namen, nach hilfeverheißenden Namen; und Ihr Name, verehrte Frau Anna Seghers, wurde mir zum Strohhalm, den zu fassen ich nicht ablassen will.

Sie waren es, die meine Generation oder jeden, der ein Ohr hatte, nach jenem nicht zu vergessenden Krieg unterrichtete, Recht und Unrecht zu unterscheiden; Ihr Buch, *Das siebte Kreuz,* hat mich geformt, hat meinen Blick geschärft und läßt mich heute die Globke und Schröder in jeder Verkleidung erkennen, sie mögen Humanisten, Christen oder Aktivisten heißen. Die Angst Ihres Georg Heisler hat sich mir unverkäuflich mitgeteilt; nur heißt der Kommandant des Konzentrationslagers heute nicht mehr Fahrenberg, er heißt Walter Ulbricht und steht Ihrem Staat vor. Ich bin nicht Klaus Mann, und Ihr Geist ist dem Geist des Faschisten Gottfried Benn gegengesetzt, trotzdem berufe ich mich mit der Anmaßung meiner Generation auf jenen Brief, den Klaus Mann am 9. Mai 1933 an Gottfried Benn richtete. Für Sie und für mich mache ich aus dem 9. Mai der beiden toten Männer einen lebendigen 14. August 1961: Es darf nicht sein, daß Sie, die Sie bis heute vielen Menschen der Begriff aller Auflehnung gegen die Gewalt sind, dem Irrationalismus eines Gottfried Benn verfallen und die Gewalttätigkeit einer Diktatur verkennen, die sich mit Ihrem Traum vom Sozialismus und Kommunismus, den ich nicht träume, aber wie jeden Traum respektiere, notdürftig und dennoch geschickt verkleidet hat.

Vertrösten Sie mich nicht auf die Zukunft, die, wie Sie als Schriftstellerin wissen, in der Vergangenheit stündlich Auferstehung feiert; bleiben wir beim Heute, beim 14. August 1961. Heute stehen Alpträume als Panzer an der Leipziger Straße, bedrücken jeden Schlaf und bedrohen Bürger, indem sie Bürger schützen wollen. Heute ist es gefährlich, in Ihrem Staat zu leben, ist es unmöglich, Ihren Staat zu verlassen. Heute – und Sie deuten mit Recht auf ihn – bastelt ein Innenminister Schröder an seinem Lieblingsspielzeug: am Notstandsgesetz. Heute – *Der Spiegel* unterrichtete uns – trifft man in Deggendorf, Niederbayern, Vorbereitungen zu katholisch-antisemitischen Feiertagen. Dieses Heute will ich zu unserem Tag machen: Sie mögen als schwache und starke Frau Ihre Stimme beladen und gegen die Panzer, gegen den gleichen, immer wieder in Deutschland hergestellten Stacheldraht anreden, der einst den Konzentrationslagern Stacheldrahtsicherheit gab; ich aber will nicht müde werden, in Richtung Westen zu sprechen: Nach Deggendorf in Niederbayern will ich ziehen und in eine Kirche spucken, die den gemalten Antisemitismus zum Altar erhoben hat.

Dieser Brief, verehrte Frau Anna Seghers, muß ein »offener Brief« sein. Das Brieforiginal schicke ich Ihnen über den Schriftstellerverband in Ostberlin. Mit der Bitte um Veröffentlichung schicke ich einen Durchschlag an die Tageszeitung *Neues Deutschland,* einen zweiten Durchschlag an die Wochenzeitung *Die Zeit.*

Hilfesuchend grüßt Sie
Günter Grass

Es war einmal ein Land

Es war einmal ein Land, das hieß Deutsch.
Schön war es, gehügelt und flach
und wußte nicht, wohin mit sich.
Da machte es einen Krieg, weil es überall
auf der Welt sein wollte und wurde klein davon.
Nun gab es sich eine Idee, die Stiefel trug,
gestiefelt als Krieg ausging, um die Welt zu sehen,
als Krieg heimkam, harmlos tat und schwieg,
als habe sie Filzpantoffeln getragen,
als habe es auswärts nichts Böses zu sehen gegeben.
Doch rückläufig gelesen, konnte die gestiefelte Idee
als Verbrechen erkannt werden: so viele Tote.
Da wurde das Land, das Deutsch hieß, geteilt.
Nun hieß es zweimal und wußte,
so schön gehügelt und flach es war,
immer noch nicht, wohin mit sich.
Nach kurzem Bedenken bot es für einen dritten Krieg
sich beiderseits an.
Seitdem kein Sterbenswort mehr, Friede auf Erden.

Quellennachweis

»Lastenausgleich«, Rede auf dem Parteitag der SPD in Berlin, 18. Dezember 1989, zuerst in: Frankfurter Rundschau, Frankfurt, 19. Dezember 1989.

»Viel Gefühl, wenig Bewußtsein«, Ein Spiegel-Gespräch, geführt von Willi Winkler, in: Der Spiegel Nr. 47, Hamburg, 20. November 1989.

»Die Zwiemacht aus Zwietracht«, in: Die Rättin, Darmstadt und Neuwied 1986.

»Scham und Schande«, Rede zum 50. Jahrestag des Kriegsausbruchs, zuerst in: Süddeutsche Zeitung, München, 2. September 1989.

»Nachdenken über Deutschland«, Stefan Heym und Günter Grass diskutieren am 21. November 1984 in Brüssel (anläßlich des 25jährigen Bestehens des Goethe-Instituts Brüssel), vollständig zuerst in: Berlin Brüssel 1984.

»Nationalstiftung«, in: Kopfgeburten oder Die Deutschen sterben aus, Darmstadt und Neuwied 1980.

»Sieben Thesen zum demokratischen Sozialismus«, Rede in Bièvres bei Paris am 24. Februar 1974 auf einem internationalen Kolloquium über das »tschechoslowakische Experiment«, zuerst in: Werkausgabe in zehn Bänden, hg. von Volker Neuhaus, Band IX, Darmstadt und Neuwied 1987. Anmerkungen in Band IX ab S. 943.

»Deutschland – zwei Staaten – eine Nation?«, Rede auf einem Seminar der Friedrich-Ebert-Stiftung in Bergneustadt am 23. Mai 1970, zuerst in: Die Neue Gesellschaft, Bonn, Juli/Aug. 1970, auch in: Werkausgabe in zehn Bänden, a. a. O.

»Gesamtdeutscher März«, zuerst in: Plädoyer für eine neue Regierung oder Keine Alternative, hg. von Hans Werner Richter, Hamburg 1965, auch in: Ausgefragt, Gedichte und Zeichnungen, Neuwied und Berlin 1967.

»Was Erfurt außerdem bedeutet«, Rede zum 1. Mai 1970 in Baden-Baden, zuerst in: Vorwärts, Bonn, 11. Mai 1970, auch in: Werkausgabe in zehn Bänden, a. a. O.

»Gleisdreieck«, zuerst in: Forum academicum. Zeitschrift für die Heidelberger Studenten, 11. Jg., Heft 3, 1960, auch in: Gleisdreieck, Darmstadt und Neuwied 1960.

»Die kommunizierende Mehrzahl«, Rede vor dem Presseclub Bonn am 29. Mai 1967, unter dem Titel »Sollen die Deutschen eine Nation bilden?«, zuerst in: Süddeutsche Zeitung, München, 29. Mai 1967, auch in: Werkausgabe in zehn Bänden, a. a. O.

»Was ist des Deutschen Vaterland?«, Rede im Bundestagswahlkampf 1965, zuerst als Einzelveröffentlichung: Neuwied und Berlin 1965, auch in: Werkausgabe in zehn Bänden, a. a. O.

»Offener Brief an Anna Seghers«, Brief vom 14. August 1961 an die Vorsitzende des Deutschen Schriftstellerverbandes in der DDR, unter dem Titel »Und was können die Schriftsteller tun?«, zuerst in: Die Zeit, Hamburg, 18. August 1961, auch in: Werkausgabe in zehn Bänden, a. a. O.

»Es war einmal ein Land«, in: Die Rättin, Darmstadt und Neuwied 1986.

Die Werkausgabe von Günter Grass

im Luchterhand Literaturverlag

Werkausgabe in zehn Bänden
Hg. von Volker Neuhaus
6476 Seiten
Broschierte Ausgabe im Schuber
Leinenausgabe im Schuber

Band I
Gedichte und Kurzprosa

Band II
Die Blechtrommel

Band III
Katz und Maus / Hundejahre

Band IV
örtlich betäubt
Aus dem Tagebuch einer Schnecke

Band V
Der Butt

Band VI
Das Treffen in Telgte / Kopfgeburten
oder Die Deutschen sterben aus

Band VII
Die Rättin

Band VIII
Theaterspiele

Band IX
Essays Reden Briefe Kommentare

Band X
Gespräche mit Günter Grass

»Insgesamt ist diese Werkausgabe nicht nur ein Editions-Ereignis, sondern bietet auch – und gerade – wegen ihrer zahlreichen Kommentierungen und Sacherklärungen zu Personen, Ereignissen und kulturellen Vorgängen ein historisch höchst aufschlußreiches literarisch-politisches Bild aus 40 Jahren Bundesrepublik.« *Stuttgarter Nachrichten*

Günter Grass

im Luchterhand Literaturverlag

Zunge zeigen
240 Seiten mit 80 Abb. Gebunden

»Noch war das Buch kaum erschienen, da wurde es schon von einigen tonangebenden Meinungsbildnern so drastisch abqualifiziert oder doch in Frage gestellt, daß einem die Lust verging, sich auf dieses *Zunge zeigen* einzulassen. . . . Ich erwähne das, weil es schon jetzt zur Geschichte des Buches gehört, daß es sich – wenn überhaupt – gegen einen seit dem Roman *Die Rättin* umgehenden, geschickt erzeugten . . . zähen öffentlichen Widerwillen behaupten muß, in dem die Intention und der Ertrag der Grass'schen Reise nach Kalkutta sich ins Kleinliche und Fragwürdige entstellen. Es lohnt sich, das so wirkungsvoll lancierte Vorurteil zu überprüfen – es stimmt hinten und vorn nicht. *Zunge zeigen* kommt der Wahrheit dessen, worum es hier geht, der Wahrheit des menschlichen Elends in der außerhalb der Wohlstandsinseln galoppierend verkommenden sogenannten Dritten Welt literarisch und künstlerisch so nahe wie kein anderes mir bekanntes Werk. . . . Was Grass als ›letztmögliche Schönheit‹ bezeichnet, das ist Zeichen der Menschlichkeit, der Würde noch der Elendesten. Dies zu erkennen und auszusprechen und für sich selbst sprechen zu lassen, ist etwas ganz anderes als Ästhetisierung. Auch hieraus, vor allem hieraus begründet Grass seine ›ungerufene Liebe zu dieser Stadt, die verflucht ist, jedem menschlichen Elend Quartier zu bieten‹.«
Heinrich Vormweg

DE...
for...
rec...
Qu...
Co...
inc... and Ted
Hugh... He was awarded the Nobel Prize for
Literature.

Walcott was educated at St Mary's College in St Lucia, and
at the University of the West Indies. After graduating he
taught in Jamaica and then worked as a journalist on the
Trinidad Guardian. He is also known for his work in the
theatre, as a director. He now divides his time between
Trinidad and the United States, where he teaches at Boston
University.

Other works by Derek Walcott

POETRY

In a Green Night (1962)

The Castaway (1965)

The Gulf (1970)

Another Life (1973)

Sea Grapes (1976)

The Star-Apple Kingdom (1979)

The Fortunate Traveller (1982)

Midsummer (1983)

Collected Poems 1948–1984 (1986)

Arkansas Testament (1988)

Omeros (1990)

Odyssey (1992)

PLAYS

Henri Christophe (1950)

Henri Dernier (1951)

Ione (1954)

Drums and Colours (1961)

Dream on Monkey Island and Other Plays (1970)

The Joker of Seville and *O Babylon* (1978)

Remembrance and *Pantomime* (1980)

Three Plays: The Last Carnival; Beef, No Chicken;
   A Branch of the Blue Nile (1988)

DEREK WALCOTT

SELECTED POETRY

Selected, annotated and introduced
by Wayne Brown

HEINEMANN

Heinemann is an imprint of Pearson Education Limited, a
company incorporated in England and Wales, having its registered
office at Edinburgh Gate, Harlow, Essex, CM20 2JE.
Registered company number: 872828

www.heinemann.co.uk

Heinemann is a registered trademark of Pearson Education Limited

In a Green Night first published 1962, © Derek Walcott 1962
The Castaway first published 1965, © Derek Walcott 1963, 1964, 1965
The Gulf first published 1969, © Derek Walcott 1969
Another Life first published in Great Britain 1973, © Derek Walcott 1972, 1973
Sea Grapes first published in Great Britain 1976, © Derek Walcott 1976
The Star-Apple Kingdom first published in Great Britain 1980, © Derek Walcott
1977, 1978, 1979

This collection first published in the Caribbean Writers series in 1981
Reprinted in this edition in 1993

The right of Derek Walcott to be identified as the author
of this work has been asserted by him in accordance with the
Copyright, Designs and Patents Act 1988.

British Library Cataloguing in Publication Data
A catalogue record for this book is available from the British Library.

ISBN 9780435911973

Printed and bound in Great Britain by
Cox & Wyman Ltd, Reading, Berkshire

08   15   14

Contents

Introduction

One often hears the complaint that Derek Walcott's poetry is 'difficult'. Though the note of resentment is seldom justified (it usually masks laziness or a kind of defiant philistinism on the plaintiff's part), still, it adheres to the truth: many of Walcott's poems *are* difficult. Their difficulty, however, is almost never due to any impulse towards obscurantism in a poet who, from the very beginning, has sought to write 'verse ... clear as sunlight', and only infrequently to some incoherence of thought or expression. Rather, it is the ineluctable product of a mind predisposed to obliquity and thrown back on its own resources by the absence of a West Indian literary tradition or any consensus of culture – an educated and embattled mind, engaged in true thinking (which is always difficult), aware of the revelatory power of metaphor, the solace of allusion, the economy and philosophical mischief of a pun – and prepared, in the face of a climate of often stultifying parochialism, to riffle the vast vocabulary and supple syntax of Unabridged English for help in tracking down and expressing some nuance of thought or feeling. A characteristic Walcott poem thus exhibits a sophistication of language and a density of meaning which can make the exploration of it as delightful an exercise for the adventurous reader as it must be repellent to the mentally staid.

There are writers – the Trinidadian novelist V. S. Naipaul is one – whose books, like a surveyor's measurements, constitute successive examinations, from different angles, of the same terrain. Derek Walcott's poems comprise the opposite: a study of different vistas from the same viewpoint – or rather (since over the years the poet's angle of vision has altered, in exact relationship to the evolution of his style) from the slowly evolving perspective of someone taking a stroll. The reader of the 200-plus poems (apart from juvenilia) which Walcott has so far published thus comes away from them with a sense of their author as an identifiable, consistent and maturing character using poetry to explore the manifold aspects of life in and around him.

Nonetheless, in Walcott's verse certain subjects recur oftener than others. Chief among these are West Indian history, politics and the West Indian landscape; the nature of memory, and of the creative imagination, and the relationship between them; the poet's own marriages and loves; his precocious and enduring awareness of Time, and of his eventual death. If in the poems these concerns often seem to yield their particulars and blur towards allegory (so that one is tempted to describe Walcott's main themes simply as the unwavering themes of all literature: love, war, exile and death) this is because Walcott writes as someone simultaneously aware of himself as individual and as archetype – as a man belonging to a certain race, region and age, and as a witness for mankind.

Ultimately, a poet's claim to stature depends upon his mastery of, and influence upon, the language in which he writes. Much has been written (see also the note to 'The Schooner *Flight*: Chapter 11') about Walcott's search for his 'true' voice – i.e. for a language forged from the different tongues which together make up the babble of West Indian history – and it is worth reflecting upon the ebullience and creative possibilities of a linguistically heterogeneous region like the Caribbean. Yet Robert Graves's early comment, that Walcott 'handles English with a closer understanding of its inner magic than most (if not any) of his English-born contemporaries', remains, after twenty years, probably the most pertinent single remark about his work. In that time Walcott has moved from a consuming predilection for the iambic pentameter (the main line of English verse, and a line in which this West Indian poet has always seemed wholly at ease) to a mastery of other metres and, most recently, to an unusually supple *vers libre* exhibiting many of the virtues (if occasionally the odd vice) of prose, so that today, employing a variety of metres and forms, he writes, in the words of one commentator, like someone who knows exactly what he is doing. This process he initiated by means of a conscious, indeed wilful, rebellion against the iambic pentameter (see note to 'The Cast-away'); yet one has the impression that the pentameter remains the natural vehicle for his sensibility. A Walcott poem which accepts its lineaments is almost never derailed.

Though it is a flexible line which easily accommodates the extremes of contemplative observation ('Deciduous beauty prospered and is gone') and ejaculatory slang ('Man, all the men in that damned country mad!') the pentameter has tended in recent times to reflect the irony and epigrammatic mischief of its eighteenth-century adherents rather than the measured, meditative minds of its major architects since Shakespeare: Milton, Wordsworth, Tennyson, Yeats. The bulk of Walcott's verse composed to this metre stands in opposition to this trend. In his hands the line is deliberately slowed, heightened and left open, the paragraph displacing the couplet or end-stopped line as the unit of thought. Detailing all the ways in which Walcott achieves these effects lies beyond the scope of this note, but one of them should be mentioned here, since it is also a defining characteristic of his style, and that is his instinctive subversion of those parts of speech which Auden has called the bane of English pentametrical verse: the definite and indefinite articles. In a Walcott poem, often as not, the definite article is displaced by the demonstrative 'that', particularizing its object and slowing speech; and the sense of the indefinite is heightened (and dramatized) by its replacement by the throwaway 'some', which likewise slows the line. It is not difficult to understand why in a generalizing, impatient age the sensibility behind such mannerisms should be defined – or should define itself – as conservative; or to deduce in what ways such a relationship between the poet and his audience is likely to influence, in its turn, the former's language, perspective and themes.

In itself, however, a catalogue of a poet's themes and metres is not a reliable indication of his true concerns and sensibility – there may be individual poems which are more or less emotionally ingenuous or structurally uneasy or internally discordant. In choosing these poems, therefore, I have tried to resist the temptation to produce a 'representative' anthology, preferring simply to select from those poems which struck me as best equipped to repay rereading. Because the real biography of a writer is to be found in the evolution of his style, I have left the poems in roughly the order of their original publication, rather than attempting to categorize them by theme or metre – though of course there exists a sound scholarly justification of the latter method. With the exception of those pertaining to the extracts of *Another Life** the notes which follow the poems are extensive but by no means exhaustive. Though aware that an approach which emphasizes either form or content at the other's expense greatly impoverishes the experience of poetry, I have come down rather heavily on the side of 'comprehension' – an unavoidable bias, I think, in a book of this kind. Even so, many of the notes will need the intercession of the teacher (I have assumed, for example, a knowledge of prosody which many students will not have had imparted to them, but without which, it seems to me, it is impossible to treat a poem as much more than an exercise in

---

* The extracts of the 150 page autobiographical poem, *Another Life* (Cape, 1973) presented the annotator with certain problems. A long poem moves at a comparatively leisurely or ponderous pace; thus, in order to maintain the fiction of their (structural) autonomy, it was necessary that the extracts themselves be lengthy. Furthermore, in attempting to annotate them on the same scale as the rest of the poems the annotator would have been forced constantly to refer beyond them to the unreproduced, and major, portion of the poem. All this prefigured a veritable cascade of notes, occupying perhaps as many pages as the extracts themselves, and beyond the scope of this book. For various reasons, the alternative (i.e. halving the number of extracts) seemed undesirable. I have therefore limited myself to the barest synopsis of each extract, along with the odd explanatory note. The teacher who is disinclined to treat these extracts merely as Material for Further Reading or as exercises in research ('who was Michelangelo?') may prefer to compare the language of different passages – the taut trimeters of 'E', for example, with the transparent prose of 'F' – or to select a few extracts for closer attention over a number of sessions. The interested student should be referred to the text in its entirety, and then, for help, to Edward Baugh's engaging explication of it, entitled *Derek Walcott: Memory as Vision: Another Life* (Longman, 1978). No serious analysis of the poem's form(s) has to my knowledge yet been published.

comprehension, and a botched and trivial 'comprehension' at that).

Finally, it is worth recalling Frost's dictum that a poem should 'begin in delight and end in wisdom'. Inherent in an annotator's task is the danger that in concentrating upon a poem's wisdom he may give short shrift to its delights. This is a trap which I have not always avoided.

I believe that the teacher who consciously counters this tendency of the notes, even going at times to the other extreme, will find his or her efforts rewarded; and that the student who submits to being led like a tourist among a poem's delights (its metaphors, its wit, some elegant turn of phrase or appropriate rhythm or rhyme) will ineluctably stumble upon its wisdom.

Selections from

In a Green Night

The Harbour

The fishermen rowing homeward in the dusk,
Do not consider the stillness through which they move,
So I, since feelings drown should no more ask
For the safe twilight which your calm hands gave.
And the night, urger of old lies
Winked at by stars that sentry the humped hills,
Should hear no secret faring-forth; time knows
That bitter and sly sea, and love raises walls.
Yet others who now watch my progress outward
On a sea which is crueller than any word
Of love, may see in me the calm my passage makes,
Braving new water in an antique hoax;
And the secure from thinking may climb safe to liners
Hearing small rumours of paddlers drowned near stars.

To a Painter in England

(for Harold Simmons)

Where you rot under the strict, grey industry
Of cities of fog and winter fevers, I
Send this to remind you of personal islands
For which Gauguins sicken, and to explain
How I have grown to learn your passionate
Talent with its wild love of landscape.

2

It is April and already no doubt for you,
As the journals report, the prologues of spring
Appear behind the rails of city parks,
Or the late springtime must be publishing
Pink apologies along the wet, black branch
To men in overcoats, who will conceal
The lines of songs leaping behind their pipes.

And you may find it difficult to imagine
This April as a season where the tide burns
Black, leaves crack into ashes from the drought,
A dull red burning, like heart's desolation.
The roads are white with dust and the leaves
Of the trees have a nervous, spinsterish quiet.
And walking under the trees today I saw
The canoes that are marked with comic names;
Daylight, St Mary Magdalen, Gay Girl.

They made me think of your chief scenes for painting,
Of days of instruction at the soft villa,
When we watched your serious experience, learning.
So you will understand how I feel lost
To see our gift wasting before the season,
You who defined with an imperious palette
The several postures of this virginal island,
You understand how I am lost to have
Your brush's zeal and not to be explicit.

But the grace we avoid, that gives us vision,
Discloses around corners an architecture whose
Sabbath logic we can take or refuse;
And leaves to the single soul its own decision
After landscapes, palms, cathedrals or the hermit-thrush,
And wins my love now and gives it a silence
That would inform the blind world of its flesh.

Ruins of a Great House

though our longest sun sets at right
declensions and makes but winter
arches, it cannot be long before we
lie down in darkness, and have our
light in ashes ...
BROWNE: Urn Burial

Stones only, the *disjecta membra* of this Great House,
Whose moth-like girls are mixed with candledust,
Remain to file the lizard's dragonish claws;
The mouths of those gate cherubs streaked with stain.
Axle and coachwheel silted under the muck
Of cattle droppings.

                Three crows flap for the trees,
And settle, creaking the eucalyptus boughs.
A smell of dead limes quickens in the nose
The leprosy of Empire.

             'Farewell, green fields'
             'Farewell, ye happy groves!'

Marble as Greece, like Faulkner's south in stone,
Deciduous beauty prospered and is gone;
But where the lawn breaks in a rash of trees
A spade below dead leaves will ring the bone
Of some dead animal or human thing
Fallen from evil days, from evil times.

It seems that the original crops were limes
Grown in the silt that clogs the river's skirt;
The imperious rakes are gone, their bright girls gone,
The river flows, obliterating hurt.

I climbed a wall with the grill ironwork
Of exiled craftsmen, protecting that great house
From guilt, perhaps, but not from the worm's rent,
Nor from the padded cavalry of the mouse.
And when a wind shook in the limes I heard
What Kipling heard; the death of a great empire, the abuse
Of ignorance by Bible and by sword.

A green lawn, broken by low walls of stone
Dipped to the rivulet, and pacing, I thought next
Of men like Hawkins, Walter Raleigh, Drake,
Ancestral murderers and poets, more perplexed
In memory now by every ulcerous crime.
The world's green age then was a rotting lime
Whose stench became the charnel galleon's text.
The rot remains with us, the men are gone.
But, as dead ash is lifted in a wind,
That fans the blackening ember of the mind,
My eyes burned from the ashen prose of Donne.

Ablaze with rage, I thought
Some slave is rotting in this manorial lake,
And still the coal of my compassion fought:
That Albion too, was once
A colony like ours, 'Part of the continent, piece of the main'
Nook-shotten, rook o'er blown, deranged
By foaming channels, and the vain expense
Of bitter faction.

                         All in compassion ends
So differently from what the heart arranged:
'as well as if a manor of thy friend's ...'

Tales of the Islands

CHAPTER III

la belle qui fut ...

Miss Rossignol lived in the lazaretto
For Roman Catholic crones; she had white skin,
And underneath it, fine, old-fashioned bones;
She flew like bats to vespers every twilight,
The living Magdalen of Donatello;
And tipsy as a bottle when she stalked
On stilted legs to fetch the morning milk,
In a black shawl harnessed by rusty brooches.
My mother warned us how that flesh knew silk
Coursing a green estate in gilded coaches.
While Miss Rossignol, in the cathedral loft
Sang to her one dead child, a tattered saint
Whose pride had paupered beauty to this witch
Who was so fine once, whose hands were so soft.

CHAPTER X

'adieu foulard ...'

I watched the island narrowing the fine
Writing of foam around the precipices then
The roads as small and casual as twine
Thrown on its mountains; I watched till the plane
Turned to the final north and turned above
The open channel with the grey sea between
The fishermen's islets until all that I love
Folded in cloud; I watched the shallow green
That broke in places where there would be reef,
The silver glinting on the fuselage, each mile

6

Dividing us and all fidelity strained
Till space would snap it. Then, after a while
I thought of nothing, nothing, I prayed, would change;
When we set down at Seawell it had rained.

A Careful Passion

Hosanna, I build me house, Lawd,
De rain come wash it 'way.
                    JAMAICAN SONG

The Cruise Inn, at the city's edge,
Extends a breezy prospect of the sea
From tables fixed like islands near a hedge
Of foam-white flowers, and to deaden thought,
Marimba medleys from a local band,
To whose gay pace my love now drummed a hand.
I watched an old Greek freighter quitting port.

You hardly smell the salt breeze in this country
Except you come down to the harbour's edge.
Not like the smaller islands to the south.
There the green wave spreads on the printless beach.
I think of wet hair and a grape red mouth.
The hand which wears her husband's ring, lies
On the table idly, a brown leaf on the sand.
The other brushes off two coupling flies.
'Sometimes I wonder if you've lost your speech.'
Above our heads, the rusty cries
Of gulls revolving in the wind.
Wave after wave of memory silts the mind.

7

The gulls seem happy in their element.
We are lapped gently in the sentiment
Of a small table by the harbour's edge.
Hearts learn to die well that have died before.
My sun-puffed carcass, its eyes full of sand,
Rolls, spun by breakers on a southern shore.
'This way is best, before we both get hurt.'
Look how I turn there, featureless, inert.
That weary phrase moves me to stroke her hand
While winds play with the corners of her skirt.

Better to lie, to swear some decent pledge,
To resurrect the buried heart again;
To twirl a glass and smile, as in pain,
At a small table by the water's edge.
'Yes, this is best, things might have grown much worse ...'

And that is all the truth, it could be worse;
All is exhilaration on the eve,
Especially, when the self-seeking heart
So desperate for some mirror to believe
Finds in strange eyes the old original curse.
So cha cha cha, begin the long goodbyes,
Leave the half-tasted sorrows of each pledge,
As the salt wind brings brightness to her eyes,
At a small table by the water's edge.

I walk with her into the brightening street;
Stores rattling shut, as brief dusk fills the city.
Only the gulls, hunting the water's edge
Wheel like our lives, seeking something worth pity.

Castiliane

I

The GOLONDRINA is a sour hotel,
Redeemed, like Creole architecture,
By its ornate, wrought-iron balcony;
A floral asterisk to grace a lecture
On 'Spanish Art In The Last Century'.
And though its rusting quaintness is no cure
Against the encroaching odours of the port,
Its failing apertures inhale the sea;
Besides, a wraith haunts there whom I know well,
Having created her in noon's despair.

Frail Donna of another century,
A grace of muslin, vineleaf and guitars,
She comes at noon, guarded by black duennas
To flute and bandol music from the bars,
Above the flies, molasses, donkey carts,
Above the clash of voices from the pier
Of stevedores gambling over tepid beer,
And stands as mute as old embroidery
On an old fashioned cushion of the heart.

II

Why should she hide against the dirty lace
Which stirs so still, its drift is scarcely seen
From the hot street? Why is that haunted face,
Dim as an antique faun's, fin de siècle style,
Imprisoned in the grillwork's leafless green
Who can evoke Alhambras with a smile?

9

Assailed by memory, desire stirs;
Yet that white hand against a rose cheek sleeping
That to the idler makes a subtle sign
Becomes a pigeon from a dark coign sweeping
As the coarse odour from the street defers
Anticipation of dark cellared wine.

Albums of lost Alhambras, swaying cypresses,
Brooding, daggered Moors and fanfares from da Falla,
A sable papa munching his moustache,
The scented note, the fearful assignation:
'I must, I must go now . . .', sighing, she sweeps
Her jewelled laces up as bells
Shatter the crystal park. The dark
Duennas weep,
They know the true necessity of that sleep
That withers centuries or the virgin rose.
Jesu Maria, what nonsense . . . I suppose . . .

III

I stir to smell the male, malodorous sea.
Another trance of mine is moving water.
How would it end? A merchant claims the daughter,
A man who hawks and profits in this heat,
Jeering at poets with a goldtoothed curse.
Girl, you were wise, whoever lived by verse?
The future is in cheap enamel wares.

Yet, Doña Maria, like a worn-out song
That keeps a phrase of wisdom in our ears,
Like the sad gaiety of a drunk guitar,
Like the bright gardens which blind vendors sell,
I watch your ancient, simple spirit where
Its letters flake across the balcony
From the façade of a third-rate hotel.

A Lesson for this Sunday

The growing idleness of summer grass
With its frail kites of furious butterflies
Requests the lemonade of simple praise
In scansion gentler than my hammock swings
And rituals no more upsetting than a
Black maid shaking linen as she sings
The plain notes of some protestant hosanna
Since I lie idling from the thought in things,

Or so they should. Until I hear the cries
Of two small children hunting yellow wings,
Who break my sabbath with the thought of sin.
Brother and sister, with a common pin,
Frowning like serious lepidopterists.
The little surgeon pierces the thin eyes.
Crouched on plump haunches, as a mantis prays
She shrieks to eviscerate its abdomen.
The lesson is the same. The maid removes
Both prodigies from their interest in science.
The girl, in lemon frock, begins to scream
As the maimed, teetering thing attempts its flight.
She is herself a thing of summery light,
Frail as a flower in this blue August air,
Not marked for some late grief that cannot speak.

The mind swings inward on itself in fear
Swayed towards nausea from each normal sign.
Heredity of cruelty everywhere,
And everywhere the frocks of summer torn,
The long look back to see where choice is born,
As summer grass sways to the scythe's design.

11

Allegre

Some mornings are as full of elation
As these pigeons crossing the hill slopes,
Silver as they veer in sunlight and white
On the warm blue shadows of the range.

And the sunward sides of the shacks
Gilded, as though this was Italy.

The bird's claws fasten round the lignum-vitae,
The roots of delight growing downward,
As the singer in his prime.

And the slopes of the forest this sunrise
Are thick with blue haze, as the colour
Of the woodsmoke from the first workman's fire.
A morning for wild bees and briersmoke,
For hands cupped to boys' mouths, the holloa
Of their cries in the cup of the valley.

The stream keeps its edges, wind-honed,
As the intellect is clear in affections,
Calm, with the rivulet's diligence.

Men are sawing with the wind on those ridges,
Trees arching, campeche, gommiers, canoe-wood,
The sawn trunks trundled down hillsides
To crash to the edge of the sea.
No temples, yet the fruits of intelligence,
No roots, yet the flowers of identity,
No cities, but white seas in sunlight,
Laughter and doves, like young Italy.

12

Yet to find the true self is still arduous,
And for us, especially, the elation can be useless and empty
As this pale, blue ewer of the sky,
Loveliest in drought.

Conqueror

'March of Triumph'

This bronze, praised flayer of horses, who bred
Direction not valour in armies, has halted
On the crest of a ridge, in drizzling light;
His scaled gloves at rest
On the pommels, the wet-metal blaze
Of the sun in his sunken eye,
At the still, directionless hour
Of a changing, dragonish sky.

Iron deliverer whom the furies choose!
Half-human and half-deity in repose,
Envying each victim as its ravening grows,
Aye, the invincible! but whose
Armour cages a sigh no slaughter can depose.

Below him a thin harvest rusts in rain,
Lean flocks come limping to the herder's fife.
In that brown light, a mounted traveller
Splashes a silver river scarcely flowing
Through banks of ageing poplars;
On those unconquered peaks, it may be snowing.
On amber landscapes, hardly true to life

13

Is laid sometimes the quiet of unknowing
That elsewhere murderous teeth champ and devour,
As if such art placated nature's laws.
The small furred beast, spent beyond trembling
Contains such peace between its torturer's claws.

Take these small sparrows, witless if you will
That in the frightful glory of this hour
Flirt with that armed mass quiet on the hill,
Who dip, twitter, alight
On windless pennons, on these iron sheaves;

What are they? Fables of innocence trusting in power,
Or natural thoughts that haunt their source still?
If one cried out pity might shake the mind
Like a limp pennon in a sudden wind,
And joy remembered make rage the more.
And at that cry, the god must raise his hand
However wearily, and all respite end
In noise and neighing thunder, in a wealth
Of sounding brass and the conqueror, sighing descend
Down to the desolation of self.

Selections from

The Castaway

The Castaway

The starved eye devours the seascape for the morsel
Of a sail.

The horizon threads it infinitely.

Action breeds frenzy. I lie,
Sailing the ribbed shadow of a palm,
Afraid lest my own footprints multiply.

Blowing sand, thin as smoke,
Bored, shifts its dunes.
The surf tires of its castles like a child.

The salt green vine with yellow trumpet-flower,
A net, inches across nothing.
Nothing: the rage with which the sandfly's head is filled.

Pleasures of an old man:
Morning: contemplative evacuation, considering
The dried leaf, nature's plan.

In the sun, the dog's faeces
Crusts, whitens like coral.
We end in earth, from earth began.
In our own entrails, genesis.

If I listen I can hear the polyp build,
The silence thwanged by two waves of the sea.
Cracking a sea-louse, I make thunder split.

Godlike, annihilating godhead, art
And self, I abandon
Dead metaphors: the almond's leaf-like heart,

The ripe brain rotting like a yellow nut
Hatching
Its babel of sea-lice, sandfly and maggot,

That green wine bottle's gospel choked with sand,
Labelled, a wrecked ship,
Clenched seaward nailed and white as a man's hand.

The Swamp

Gnawing the highway's edges, its black mouth
Hums quietly: 'Home, come home . . .'

Behind its viscous breath the very word 'growth'
Grows fungi, rot;
White mottling its root.

More dreaded
Than canebreak, quarry, or sun-shocked gully-bed
Its horrors held Hemingway's hero rooted
To sure, clear shallows.

It begins nothing. Limbo of cracker convicts, Negroes.
Its black mood
Each sunset takes a smear of your life's blood.

Fearful, original sinuosities! Each mangrove sapling
Serpentlike, its roots obscene
As a six-fingered hand,

17

Conceals within its clutch the mossbacked toad,
Toadstools, the potent ginger-lily,
Petals of blood,

The speckled vulva of the tiger-orchid;
Outlandish phalloi
Haunting the travellers of its one road.

Deep, deeper than sleep
Like death,
Too rich in its decrescence, too close of breath,

In the fast-filling night, note
How the last bird drinks darkness with its throat,
How the wild saplings slip

Backward to darkness, go black
With widening amnesia, take the edge
Of nothing to them slowly, merge

Limb, tongue and sinew into a knot
Like chaos, like the road
Ahead.

The Flock

The grip of winter tightening, its thinned
volleys of blue-wing teal and mallard fly
from the longbows of reeds bent by the wind,
arrows of yearning for our different sky.
A season's revolution hones their sense,
whose target is our tropic light, while I
awoke this sunrise to a violence

of images migrating from the mind.
Skeletal forest, a sepulchral knight
riding in silence at a black tarn's edge
hooves cannonading snow
in the white funeral of the year,
antlike across the forehead of an alp
in iron contradiction crouched
against those gusts that urge the mallards south.
Vizor'd with blind defiance of his quest,
its yearly divination of the spring.
I travel through such silence, making dark
symbols with this pen's print across snow,
measuring winter's augury by words
settling the branched mind like migrating birds,
and never question when they come or go.

The style, tension of motion and the dark,
inflexible direction of the world
as it revolves upon its centuries
with change of language, climate, customs, light,
with our own prepossession day by day
year after year with images of flight,
survive our condemnation and the sun's
exultant larks.
       The dark, impartial Arctic
whose glaciers encased the mastodon,
froze giant minds in marble attitudes
revolves with tireless, determined grace
upon an iron axle, though the seals
howl with inhuman cries across its ice
and pages of torn birds are blown across
whitening tundras like engulfing snow.

Till its annihilation may the mind
reflect its fixity through winter, tropic,
until that equinox when the clear eye

19

clouds, like a mirror, without contradiction,
greet the black wings that cross it as a blessing
like the high, whirring flock that flew across
the cold sky of this page when I began
this journey by the wintry flare of dawn,
flying by instinct to their secret places
both for their need and for my sense of season.

The Whale, His Bulwark

To praise the blue whale's crystal jet,
To write, 'O fountain!' honouring a spout
Provokes this curse:
      'The high are humbled yet'
From those who humble Godhead, beasthood, verse.

Once, the Lord raised this bulwark to our eyes,
Once, in our seas, whales threshed,
The harpooner was common. Once, I heard
Of a baleine beached up the Grenadines, fleshed
By derisive, antlike villagers: a prize
Reduced from majesty to pygmy-size.
Salt-crusted, mythological,
And dead.

The boy who told me couldn't believe his eyes,
And I believed him. When I was small
God and a foundered whale were possible.
Whales are rarer, God as invisible.
Yet, through His gift, I praise the unfathomable,
Though the boy may be dead, the praise unfashionable,
The tale apocryphal.

20

Missing the Sea

Something removed roars in the ears of this house,
Hangs its drapes windless, stuns mirrors
Till reflections lack substance.

Some sound like the gnashing of windmills ground
To a dead halt;
A deafening absence, a blow.

It hoops this valley, weighs this mountain,
Estranges gesture, pushes this pencil
Through a thick nothing now,

Freights cupboards with silence, folds sour laundry
Like the clothes of the dead left exactly
As the dead behaved by the beloved,

Incredulous, expecting occupancy.

The Almond Trees

There's nothing here
this early;
cold sand
cold churning ocean, the Atlantic,
no visible history,

except this stand
of twisted, coppery, sea-almond trees
their shining postures surely
bent as metal, and one

foam-haired, salt-grizzled fisherman,
his mongrel growling, whirling on the stick
he pitches him; its spinning rays
'no visible history'
until their lengthened shapes amaze the sun.

By noon,
this further shore of Africa is strewn
with the forked limbs of girls toasting their flesh
in scarves, sunglasses, Pompeian bikinis,

brown daphnes, laurels, they'll all have
like their originals, their sacred grove,
this frieze
of twisted, coppery, sea-almond trees.

The fierce acetylene air
has singed
their writhing trunks with rust, the same
hues as a foundered, peeling barge.
It'll sear a pale skin copper with its flame.

The sand's white-hot ash underheel,
but their aged limbs have got their brazen sheen
from fire. Their bodies fiercely shine!
They're cured,
they endure their furnace.

Aged trees and oiled limbs share a common colour!

Welded in one flame,
huddling naked, stripped of their name,
for Greek or Roman tags, they were lashed
raw by wind, washed
out with salt and fire-dried,
bitterly nourished where their branches died,

their leaves' broad dialect a coarse,
enduring sound
they shared together.

Not as some running hamadryad's cries
rooted, broke slowly into leaf
her nipples peaking to smooth, wooden boles

Their grief
howls seaward through charred, ravaged holes.

One sunburnt body now acknowledges
that past and its own metamorphosis
as, moving from the sun, she kneels to spread
her wrap within the bent arms of this grove
that grieves in silence, like parental love.

Veranda

(for Ronald Bryden)

Grey apparitions at veranda ends
like smoke, divisible, but one
your age is ashes, its coherence gone,

23

Planters whose tears were marketable gum, whose voices
scratch the twilight like dried fronds
edged with reflection,

Colonels, hard as the commonwealth's greenheart,
middlemen, usurers whose art
kept an empire in the red,

Upholders of Victoria's china seas
lapping embossed around a drinking mug,
bully-boy roarers of the Empire club,

To the tarantara of the bugler, the sunset furled
round the last post,
the 'flamingo colours' of a fading world,

A ghost steps from you, my grandfather's ghost!
Uprooted from some rainy English shire,
you sought your Roman

End in suicide by fire.
Your mixed son gathered your charred, blackened bones,
in a child's coffin.

And buried them himself on a strange coast.
Sire,
why do I raise you up? Because

Your house has voices, your burnt house,
shrills with unguessed, lovely inheritors,
your genealogical roof tree, fallen, survives,
like seasoned timber through green, little lives.

I ripen towards your twilight, sir, that dream
where I am singed in that sea-crossing, steam
towards that vaporous world, whose souls,

like pressured trees brought diamonds out of coals.
The sparks pitched from your burning house are stars.
I am the man my father loved and was.

Whatever love you suffered makes amends
within them, father.
I climb the stair

And stretch a darkening hand to greet those friends
who share with you the last inheritance
of earth, our shrine and pardoner,

grey, ghostly loungers at veranda ends.

Lampfall

Closest at lampfall
Like children, like the moth-flame metaphor,
The Coleman's humming jet at the sea's edge
A tuning fork for our still family choir
Like Joseph Wright of Derby's astrological lecture
Casts rings of benediction round the aged.
I never tire of ocean's quarrelling,
Its silence, its raw voice,
Nor of these half-lit, windy leaves, gesticulating higher
'Rejoice, rejoice ...'

But there's an old fish, a monster
Of primal fiction that drives barrelling
Undersea, too old to make a splash,
To which I'm hooked!

Through daydream, through nightmare trolling
Me so deep that no lights flash
There but the plankton's drifting, phosphorescent stars.

I see with its aged eyes,
Its dead green, glaucous gaze,
And I'm elsewhere, far as
I shall ever be from you whom I behold now
Dear family, dear friends, by this still glow,
The lantern's ring that the sea's
Never extinguished.
Your voices curl in the shell of my ear.

All day you've watched
The sea-rock like a loom
Shuttling its white wool, sheer Penelope!
The coals lit, the sky glows, an oven.
Heart into heart carefully laid
Like bread.
This is the fire that draws us by our dread
Of loss, the furnace door of heaven.

At night we have heard
The forest, an ocean of leaves, drowning her children,
Still, we belong here. There's Venus. We are not yet lost.

Like you, I preferred
The firefly's starlike little
Lamp, mining, a question,
to the highway's brightly multiplying beetles.

Selections from

The Gulf

Ebb

Year round, year round, we'll ride
this treadmill whose frayed tide
fretted with mud

leaves our suburban shoreline littered
with rainbow muck, the afterbirth
of industry, past scurf-

streaked bungalows
and pioneer factory;
but, blessedly, it narrows

through a dark aisle
of fountaining, gold coconuts, an oasis
marked for the yellow Caterpillar tractor.

We'll watch this shovelled too, but as we file
through its swift-wickered shade there always is
some island schooner netted in its weave

like a lamed heron
an oil-crippled gull;
a few more yards upshore

and it heaves free,
it races the horizon
with us, railed to one law,

ruled, like the washed-up moon
to circle her lost zone,
her radiance thinned.

28

The palm fronds signal wildly in the wind,
but we are bound elsewhere,
from the last sacred wood.

The schooner's out too far,
too far that boyhood.
Sometimes I turn to see

the schooner, crippled, try to tread the air,
the moon break in sere sail,
but without envy.

For safety, each sunfall,
the wildest of us all
mortgages life to fear.

And why not? From this car
there's terror enough in the habitual,
miracle enough in the familiar. Sure ...

Hawk

(for Oliver Jackman)

Leaves shudder the drizzle's shine
like a treng-ka-treng from the cuatros,
beads fly from the tension line.
Gabilan, ay, gabilan,
high shadow, pitiless!
The old men without teeth,
rum-guzzlers, country fiddlers,

29

their rum-heads golden lakes
of a fabulous Yucatan,
Gabilan, ay, gabilan!

Caribs, like toothless tigers;
talons raking, a flash,
arrows like twanging wires,
catgut and ocelot,
merciless, that is man,
Gabilan, eh, gabilan?
Arima to Sangre Grande,
your wings like extended hands,
a grandee waltzing alone,
alone, to the old parang.

Gabilan, ay, gabilan,
the negroes, bastards, mestizos,
proud of their Spanish blood,
of the flesh, dripping like wires,
praising your hook, gabilan.
Above their slack mouths the hawk
floats tautly out of the cedars,
leaves the limbs shaking.

Slaves yearn for their master's talons,
the spur and the cold, gold eyes,
for the whips, whistling like wires,
time for our turn, gabilan!
But this hawk above Rampanalgas
rasps the sea with raw cries.
Hawks have no music.

30

Mass Man

Through a great lion's head clouded by mange
a black clerk growls.
Next, a gold-wired peacock withholds a man,
a fan, flaunting its oval, jewelled eyes;
What metaphors!
What coruscating, mincing fantasies!

Hector Mannix, water-works clerk, San Juan, has entered a
lion,
Boysie, two golden mangoes bobbing for breastplates, barges
like Cleopatra down her river, making style.
'Join us,' they shout, 'O God, child, you can't dance?'
But somewhere in that whirlwind's radiance
a child, rigged like a bat, collapses, sobbing.

But I am dancing, look, from an old gibbet
my bull-whipped body swings, a metronome!
Like a fruit-bat dropped in the silk-cotton's shade,
my mania, my mania is a terrible calm.

Upon your penitential morning,
some skull must rub its memory with ashes,
some mind must squat down howling in your dust,
some hand must crawl and recollect your rubbish,
someone must write your poems.

Landfall, Grenada

(for Robert Head, Mariner)

Where you are rigidly anchored,
the groundswell of blue foothills, the blown canes
surging to cumuli cannot be heard;
like the slow, seamless ocean,
one motion folds the grass where you were lowered,
and the tiered sea
whose grandeurs you detested
climbs out of sound.

Its moods held no mythology
for you, it was a working-place
of tonnage and ruled stars;
you chose your landfall with a mariner's
casual certainty,
calm as that race
into whose heart you harboured;
your death was a log's entry,
your suffering held the strenuous
reticence of those
whose rites are never public,
hating to impose, to offend.
Deep friend, teach me to learn
such ease, such landfall going,
such mocking tolerance of those
neat, gravestone elegies
that rhyme our end.

Homecoming: Anse La Raye

(for Garth St Omer)

Whatever else we learned
at school, like solemn Afro-Greeks eager for grades,
of Helen and the shades
of borrowed ancestors,
there are no rites
for those who have returned,
only, when her looms fade,
drilled in our skulls, the doom-
surge-haunted nights,
only this well-known passage
under the coconuts' salt-rusted
swords, these rotted
leathery sea-grapes leaves,
the seacrabs' brittle helmets, and
this barbecue of branches, like the ribs
of sacrificial oxen on scorched sand;
only this fish-gut reeking beach
whose spindly, sugar-headed children race
whose starved, pot-bellied children race
pelting up from the shallows
because your clothes,
your posture
seem a tourist's.
They swarm like flies
round your heart's sore.

Suffer them to come,
entering your needle's eye,
knowing whether they live or die,

33

what others make of life will pass them by
like that far silvery freighter
threading the horizon like a toy;
for once, like them,
you wanted no career
but this sheer light, this clear,
infinite, boring, paradisal sea,
but hoped it would mean something to declare
today, I am your poet, yours,
all this you knew,
but never guessed you'd come
to know there are homecomings without home.

You give them nothing.
Their curses melt in air.
The black cliffs scowl,
the ocean sucks its teeth,
like that dugout canoe
a drifting petal fallen in a cup,
with nothing but its image,
you sway, reflecting nothing.
The freighter's silvery ghost
is gone, the children gone.
Dazed by the sun
you trudge back to the village
past the white, salty esplanade
under whose palms, dead
fishermen move their draughts in shade,
crossing, eating their islands,
and one, with a politician's
ignorant, sweet smile, nods,
as if all fate
swayed in his lifted hand.

Cold Spring Harbour

From feather-stuffed bolsters of cloud
falling on casual linen
the small shrieks soundlessly float.
The woods are lint-wreathed. Dawn
crackles like foil to the rake
of a field mouse nibbling, nibbling
its icing. The world is unwrapped
in cotton and you would tread wool
if you opened, quietly, whitely,
this door, like an old Christmas card
turned by a child's dark hand, did
he know it was dark then,
the magical brittle branches, the white house
collared in fur, the white world of men,
its bleeding gules and its berry drops?

Two prancing, immobile white ponies
no bigger than mice pulled a carriage
across soundless hillocks of cotton;
bells hasped to their necks didn't tinkle
though you begged God to touch them to life,
some white-haired old God who'd forgotten
or no longer trusted his miracles.
What urges you now towards this white,
snow-whipped wood is not memory
of that dark child's toys, not the card
of a season, forever foreign, that went
over its ridges like a silent
sleigh. That was a child's sorrow, this is
child's play, through which you cannot go,
dumbstruck at an open door,

stunned, fearing the strange violation
(because you are missing your children)
of perfect snow.

Love in the Valley

The sun goes slowly blind.
It is this mountain, shrouding
the valley of the shadow,

widening like amnesia
evening dims the mind.
I shake my head in darkness,

it is a tree branched with cries,
a trash-can full of print.
Now, through the reddening squint

of leaves leaden as eyes,
a skein of drifting hair
like a twig, fallen on snow,

branches the blank pages.
I bring it close, and stare
in slow vertiginous darkness,

and now I drift elsewhere,
through hostile images
of white and black, and look,

like a thaw-sniffing stallion, the head
of Pasternak emerges with its forelock,
his sinewy wrist a fetlock

pawing the frozen spring,
till his own hand has frozen
on the white page, heavy.

I ride through a white childhood
whose pines glittered with bracelets,
when I heard wolves, feared the black wood,

every wrist-aching brook
and the ice maiden
in Hawthorne's fairy book.

The hair melts into dark,
a question mark that led
where the untethered mind

strayed from its first track;
now Hardy's sombre head
upon which hailstorms broke

looms, like a weeping rock,
like wind, the tresses drift
and their familiar trace

tingles across the face
with light lashes.
I knew the depth of whiteness,

I feared the numbing kiss
of those women of winter,
Bathsheba, Lara, Tess,

whose tragedy made less
of life, whose love was more
than love of literature.

Nearing Forty

(for John Figueroa)

The irregular combination of fanciful invention may
delight awhile by that novelty of which the common
satiety of life sends us all in quest. But the pleasures of
sudden wonder are soon exhausted and the mind can
only repose on the stability of truth ...

SAMUEL JOHNSON

Insomniac since four, hearing this narrow,
rigidly-metred, early-rising rain
recounting, as its coolness numbs the marrow,
that I am nearing forty, nearer the weak
vision thickening to a frosted pane,
nearer the day when I may judge my work
by the bleak modesty of middle-age
as a false dawn, fireless and average,
which would be just, because your life bled for
the household truth, the style past metaphor
that finds its parallel however wretched
in simple, shining lines, in pages stretched
plain as a bleaching bedsheet under a gutter-
ing rainspout, glad for the sputter
of occasional insight; you who foresaw
ambition as a searing meteor
will fumble a damp match, and smiling, settle

for the dry wheezing of a dented kettle,
for vision narrower than a louvre's gap,
then watching your leaves thin, recall how deep
prodigious cynicism plants its seed,
gauges our seasons by this year's end rain
which, as greenhorns at school, we'd
call conventional for convectional;
or you will rise and set your lines to work
with sadder joy but steadier elation,
until the night when you can really sleep,
measuring how imagination
ebbs, conventional as any water-clerk
who weighs the force of lightly-falling rain,
which, as the new moon moves it, does its work,
even when it seems to weep.

The Walk

After hard rain the eaves repeat their beads,
those trees exhale your doubt like mantled tapers,
drop after drop, like a child's abacus
beads of cold sweat file from high tension wires,

pray for us, pray for this house, borrow your neighbour's
faith, pray for this brain that tires,
and loses faith in the great books it reads;
after a day spent prone, haemorrhaging poems,

each phrase peeled from the flesh in bandages,
arise, stroll on under a sky
sodden as kitchen laundry,

39

while the cats yawn behind their window frames,
lions in cages of their choice,
no further though, than your last neighbour's gates
figured with pearl. How terrible is your own

fidelity, O heart, O rose of iron!
When was your work more like a housemaid's novel,
some drenched soap-opera which gets
closer than yours to life? Only the pain,

the pain is real. Here's your life's end,
a clump of bamboos whose clenched
fist loosens its flowers, a track
that hisses through the rain-drenched

grove: abandon all, the work,
the pain of a short life. Startled, you move;
your house, a lion rising, paws you back.

Selections from

Another Life

Extract A:

CHAPTER 1

i

Verandahs, where the pages of the sea
are a book left open by an absent master
in the middle of another life—
I begin here again,
begin until this ocean's
a shut book, and, like a bulb
the white moon's filaments wane.

Begin with twilight, when a glare
which held a cry of bugles lowered
the coconut lances of the inlet,
as a sun, tired of empire, declined.
It mesmerized like fire without wind,
and as its amber climbed
the beer-stein ovals of the British fort
above the promontory, the sky
grew drunk with light.
                              There
was your heaven! The clear
glaze of another life,
a landscape locked in amber, the rare
gleam. The dream
of reason had produced its monster:
a prodigy of the wrong age and colour.

All afternoon the student
with the dry fever of some draughtsman's clerk
had magnified the harbour, now twilight

eager to complete itself,
drew a girl's figure to the open door
of a stone boathouse with a single stroke, then fell
to a reflecting silence. This silence waited
for the verification of detail:
the gables of the Saint Antoine Hotel
aspiring from jungle, the flag
at Government House melting its pole,
and for the tidal amber glare to glaze
the last shacks of the Morne till they became
transfigured sheerly by the student's will,
a cinquecento fragment in gilt frame.

The vision died,
the black hills simplified
to hunks of coal,
but if the light was dying through the stone
of that converted boathouse on the pier,
a girl, blowing its embers in her kitchen,
could feel its epoch entering her hair.

Darkness, soft as amnesia, furred the slope.
He rose and climbed towards the studio.
The last hill burned,
the sea crinkled like foil,
a moon ballooned up from the Wireless Station. O
mirror, where a generation yearned
for whiteness, for candour, unreturned.

The moon maintained her station,
her fingers stroked a chiton-fluted sea,
her disc whitewashed the shells
of gutted offices barnacling the wharves
of the burnt town, her lamp
baring the ovals of toothless façades,
along the Roman arches, as he passed

43

her alternating ivories lay untuned,
her age was dead, her sheet
shrouded the antique furniture, the mantel
with its plaster-of-Paris Venus, which
his yearning had made marble, half-cracked
unsilvering mirror of black servants,
like the painter's kerchiefed, ear-ringed portrait: Albertina.

Within the door, a bulb
haloed the tonsure of a reader crouched
in its pale tissue like an embryo,
the leisured gaze
turned towards him, the short arms
yawned briefly, welcome. Let us see.
Brown, balding, a lacertilian
jut to its underlip,
with spectacles thick as a glass paperweight
over eyes the hue of the sea-smoothed bottle glass,
the man wafted the drawing to his face
as if dusk were myopic, not his gaze.
Then, with slow strokes the master changed the sketch.

Extract B:

CHAPTER 1

iii

They sang, against the rasp and cough of shovels,
against the fists of mud pounding the coffin,
the diggers' wrists rounding off every phrase,
their iron hymn, 'The Pilgrims of the Night'.

In the sea-dusk, the live child waited
for the other to escape, a flute
of frail, seraphic mist,
but their black, Bible-paper voices fluttered shut, silence
re-entered every mould, it wrapped the edges
of sea-eaten stone, mantled the blind
eternally gesturing angels, strengthened the flowers
with a different patience, and left
or lost its hoarse voice in the shells
that trumpeted from the graves. The world
stopped swaying and settled in its place.
A black lace glove swallowed his hand.
The engine of the sea began again.

A night-black hearse, tasselled and heavy, lugged
an evening of blue smoke across the field,
like an old wreath the mourners broke apart
and drooped like flowers over the streaked stones
deciphering dates. The gravekeeper with his lantern-jaw
(years later every lantern-swinging porter
guarding infinite rails repeated this), opened
the yellow doorway to his lodge. Wayfarer's station.
The child's journey was signed.
The ledger drank its entry.
Outside the cemetery gates life stretched from sleep.
Gone to her harvest of flax-headed angels,
of seraphs blowing pink-palated conchs,
gone, so they sang, into another light:
But was it her?
Or Thomas Alva Lawrence's dead child,
another Pinkie, in her rose gown floating?
Both held the same dark eyes,
slow, haunting coals, the same curved
ivory hand touching the breast,
as if, answering death, each whispered 'Me?'

Extract C:

CHAPTER 7

i

Provincialism loves the pseudo-epic,
so if these heroes have been given a stature
disproportionate to their cramped lives,
remember I beheld them at knee-height,
and that their thunderous exchanges
rumbled like gods about another life,
as now, I hope, some child
ascribes their grandeur to Gregorias.
Remember years must pass before he saw an orchestra,
a train, a theatre, the spark-coloured leaves
of autumn whirling from a rail-line,
that, as for the seasons,
the works he read described their passage with
processional arrogance; then pardon, life,
if he saw autumn in a rusted leaf.
What else was he but a divided child?

I saw, as through the glass of some provincial gallery
the hieratic objects which my father loved:
the stuffed dark nightingale of Keats,
bead-eyed, snow-headed eagles,
all that romantic taxidermy,
and each one was a fragment of the True Cross,
each one upheld, as if it were The Host;
those venerated, venerable objects
borne by the black hands (reflecting like mahogany)
of reverential teachers, shone the more
they were repolished by our use.

The Church upheld the Word, but this new Word
was here, attainable
to my own hand,
in the deep country it found the natural man,
generous, rooted.
And I now yearned to suffer for that life,
I looked for some ancestral, tribal country,
I heard its clear tongue over the clean stones
of the river, I looked from the bus-window
and multiplied the bush with savages,
speckled the leaves with jaguar and deer,
I changed those crusted boulders
to grey, stone-lidded crocodiles,
my head shrieked with metallic, raucous parrots,
I held my breath as savages grinned,
stalking, through the bush.

ii

About the August of my fourteenth year
I lost my self somewhere above a valley
owned by a spinster-farmer, my dead father's friend.
At the hill's edge there was a scarp
with bushes and boulders stuck in its side.
Afternoon light ripened the valley,
rifling smoke climbed from small labourers' houses,
and I dissolved into a trance.

I was seized by a pity more profound
than my young body could bear, I climbed
with the labouring smoke,
I drowned in labouring breakers of bright cloud,
then uncontrollably I began to weep,
inwardly, without tears, with a serene extinction

47

of all sense; I felt compelled to kneel,
I wept for nothing and for everything,
I wept for the earth of the hill under my knees,
for the grass, the pebbles, for the cooking smoke
above the labourers' houses like a cry,
for unheard avalanches of white cloud,
but 'darker grows the valley, more and more forgetting'.
For their lights still shine through the hovels like litmus,
the smoking lamp still slowly says its prayer,
the poor still move behind their tinted scrim,
the táste of water is still shared everywhere,
but in that ship of night, locked in together,
through which, like chains, a little light might leak,
something still fastens us forever to the poor.

But which was the true light?
Blare noon or twilight,
'the lonely light that Samuel Palmer engraved',
or the cold
iron entering the soul, as the soul sank
out of belief.
                    That bugle-coloured twilight
blew the withdrawal not of legions and proconsuls,
but of pale, prebendary clerks, with the gait and gall
of camels. And yet I envied them,
bent, silent decipherers of sacred texts,
their Roman arches, Vergilian terraces,
their tiered, ordered colonial world
where evening, like the talons of a bird
bent the blue jacaranda softly, and smoke rose with
the leisure and frailty of recollection,
I learnt their strict necrology of dead kings,
bones freckling the rushes of damp tombs,
the light-furred luminous world of Claude,
their ruined temples, and in drizzling twilights, Turner.

48

iii

Our father,
　　　　who floated in the vaults of Michelangelo,
Saint Raphael,
　　　　of sienna and gold leaf,
it was then
　　　　that he fell in love, having no care
for truth,
　　　　that he could enter the doorway of a triptych,
that he believed
　　　　those three stiff horsemen cantering past a rock,
　　　　towards jewelled cities on a cracked horizon,
　　　　that the lances of Uccello shivered him,
　　　　like Saul, unhorsed,
that he fell in love with art,
　　　　and life began.

iv

Noon,
　　　　and its sacred water sprinkles.
A schoolgirl in blue and white uniform,
her golden plaits a simple coronet
out of Angelico, a fine sweat on her forehead,
hair where the twilight singed and signed its epoch.
And a young man going home.
They move away from each other.
They are moving towards each other.
His head roars with hunger and poems.
His hand is trembling to recite her name.
She clutches her books, she is laughing,
her uniformed companions laughing.
She laughs till she is near tears.

Who could tell, in 'the crossing of that pair'
        that later it would mean
that rigid iron lines were drawn between
        him and that garden chair
from which she rose to greet him, as for a train,
        that watching her rise
from the bright boathouse door was like some station
        where either stood, transfixed
by the rattling telegraph of carriage windows
        flashing goodbyes,
that every dusk rehearsed a separation
        already in their eyes,
that later, when they sat in silence, seaward,
        and looking upward, heard
its engines as some moonlit liner chirred
        from the black harbour outward,
those lights spelt out their sentence, word by word?

Extract D:

from CHAPTER 8

i

Around that golden year which I described
Gregorias and that finished soldier quartered
in a brown, broken-down bungalow
whose yard was indistinguishable from bush,
between the broad-leaved jungle and the town.
Shaky, half-rotted treaders, sighing, climbed
towards a sun-warped verandah, one half of which
Gregorias had screened into a studio,

shading a varnished, three-legged table
crawling with exhausted paint-tubes, a lowering quart
of *Pirate* rum, and grey, dog-eared, turpentine-stained editions
of the Old Masters. One day the floor collapsed.
The old soldier sank suddenly to his waist
wearing the verandah like a belt.
Gregorias buckled with laughter telling this,
but shame broke the old warrior.
The dusk lowered his lances through the leaves.
In another year the soldier shrank and died.
Embittered, Gregorias wanted carved on his stone:
PRAISE YOUR GOD, DRINK YOUR RUM, MIND YOUR OWN BUSINESS.

We were both fatherless now, and often drunk.

Drunk,
        on a half-pint of joiner's turpentine,
drunk,
        while the black, black-sweatered, horn-soled fisher-
            men drank
        their *l'absinthe* in sand back yards standing up,
        on the clear beer of sunrise,
        on cheap, tannic Canaries muscatel,
        on glue, on linseed oil, on kerosene,
        as Van Gogh's shadow rippling on a cornfield,
        on Cézanne's boots grinding the stones of Aix
        to shales of slate, ochre and Vigie blue,
        on Gauguin's hand shaking the gin-coloured dew
        from the umbrella yams,
        garrulous, all day, sun-struck,
till dusk glazed vision with its darkening varnish.
Days welded by the sun's torch into days!
Gregorias plunging whole-suit in the shallows,
painting under water, roaring, and spewing spray,
Gregorias gesturing, under the coconuts
wickerwork shade-tin glare-wickerwork shade.

days woven into days, a stinging haze
of thorn trees bent like green flames by the Trades,
under a sky tacked to the horizon, drumskin tight,
as shaggy combers leisurely beard the rocks,
while the asphalt sweats its mirages and the beaks
of fledgling ginger lilies
gasped for rain.
Gregorias, the easel rifled on his shoulder, marching
towards an Atlantic flashing tinfoil,
singing 'O Paradiso',
till the western breakers laboured to that music,
his canvas crucified against a tree.

ii

But drunkenly, or secretly, we swore,
disciples of that astigmatic saint,
that we would never leave the island
until we had put down, in paint, in words,
as palmists learn the network of a hand,
all of its sunken, leaf-choked ravines,
every neglected, self-pitying inlet
muttering in brackish dialect, the ropes of mangroves
from which old soldier crabs slipped
surrendering to slush,
each ochre track seeking some hilltop and
losing itself in an unfinished phrase,
under sand shipyards where the burnt-out palms
inverted the design of unrigged schooners,
entering forests, boiling with life,
goyave, corrosol, bois-canot, sapotille.

Days!
The sun drumming, drumming,
past the defeated pennons of the palms,
roads limp from sunstroke,

52

past green flutes of grass
the ocean cannonading, come!
Wonder that opened like the fan
of the dividing fronds
on some noon-struck Sahara,
where my heart from its rib-cage yelped like a pup
after clouds of sanderlings rustily wheeling
the world on its ancient,
invisible axis,
the breakers slow-dolphining over more breakers,
to swivel our easels down, as firm
as conquerors who had discovered home.

Extract E:

CHAPTER 12

iv

And how could we know then,
damned poet and damned painter,
that we too would resemble
those nervous, inflamed men,.
fisherman and joiner,
with their quivering addiction
to alcohol and failure,
who hover in a fiction
of flaming palely at doors
for the rumshop lamp to glare,
with watered eyes, loose collars
and the badge of a bone stud,
their vision branched with blood,

their bodies trees which fed
a fire beyond control,
drinkers who lost their pride
when pride in drink was lost.
We saw, within their eyes,
we thought, an artist's ghost,
but dignified, dignified
through days eaten with shame;
we were burned out that year
with the old sacred flame,
we swore to make drink
and art our finishing school,
join brush and pen and name
to the joiner's strenuous tool.

And then, one night, somewhere,
a single outcry rocketed in air,
the thick tongue of a fallen, drunken lamp
licked at its alcohol ringing the floor,
and with the fierce rush of a furnace door
suddenly opened, history was here.

Extract F:

CHAPTER 14

—Anna awaking

When the oil green water glows but doesn't catch,
only its burnish, something wakes me early,
draws me out breezily to the pebbly shelf
of shallows where the water chuckles
and the ribbed boats sleep like children,

buoyed on their creases. I have nothing to do,
the burnished kettle is already polished,
to see my own blush burn,
and the last thing the breeze needs is my exhilaration.

I lie to my body with useless chores.
The ducks, if they ever slept, waddle knowingly.
The pleats of the shallows are neatly creased
and decorous and processional,
they arrive at our own harbour from the old Hospital
across the harbour. When the first canoe,
silent, will not wave at me,
I understand, we are acknowledging
our separate silences, as the one silence,
I know that they know my peace as I know theirs.
I am amazed that the wind is tirelessly fresh.
The wind is older than the world.

It is always one thing at a time.
Now, it is always girlish.
I am happy enough to see it as a kind
of dimpled, impish smiling.
When the sleep-smelling house stirs
to that hoarse first cough, that child's first cry,
that rumbled, cavernous questioning of my mother,
I come out of the cave
like the wind emerging,
like a bride, to her first morning.

I shall make coffee.
The light, like a fiercer dawn,
will singe the downy edges of my hair,
and the heat will plate my forehead till it shines.
Its sweat will share the excitement of my cunning.
Mother, I am in love.
Harbour, I am waking.

I know the pain in your budding, nippled limes,
I know why your limbs shake, windless, pliant trees.
I shall grow grey as this light.
The first flush will pass.
But there will always be morning,
and I shall have this fever waken me,
whoever I lie to, lying close to, sleeping
like a ribbed boat in the last shallows of night.

But even if I love not him but the world,
and the wonder of the world in him, of him in the world,
and the wonder that he makes the world waken to me,
I shall never grow old in him,
I shall always be morning to him,
and I must walk and be gentle as morning.
Without knowing it, like the wind,
that cannot see her face,
the serene humility of her exultation,
that having straightened the silk sea smooth, having noticed
that the comical ducks ignore her, that
the childish pleats of the shallows are set straight,
that everyone, even the old, sleeps in innocence,
goes in nothing, naked, as I would be,
if I had her nakedness, her transparent body.
The bells garland my head. I could be happy,
just because today is Sunday. No, for more.

ii

Then Sundays, smiling, carried in both hands
a towelled dish bubbling with the good life
whose fervour steaming, beaded her clear brow,
from which damp skeins were brushed,
and ladled out her fullness to the brim.
And all those faded prints that pressed their scent

56

on her soft, house-warm body,
glowed from her flesh with work,
her hands that held the burnish of dry hillsides
freckled with fire-light,
hours that ripened till the fullest hour
could burst with peace.

'Let's go for a little walk,' she said, one afternoon,
'I'm in a walking mood.' Near the lagoon,
dark water's lens had made the trees one wood
arranged to frame this pair whose pace
unknowingly measured loss,
each face was set towards its character.
Where they now stood, others before had stood,
the same lens held them, the repeated wood,
then there grew on each one
the self-delighting, self-transfiguring stone
stare of the demi-god.
Stunned by their images they strolled on, content
that the black film of water kept the print
of their locked images when they passed on.

iii

And which of them in time would be betrayed
was never questioned by that poetry
which breathed within the evening naturally,
but by the noble treachery of art
that looks for fear when it is least afraid,
that coldly takes the pulse-beat of the heart
in happiness; that praised its need to die
to the bright candour of the evening sky,
that preferred love to immortality;
so every step increased that subtlety
which hoped that their two bodies could be made

one body of immortal metaphor.
The hand she held already had betrayed
them by its longing for describing her.

Extract G:

CHAPTER 15

i

Still dreamt of, still missed,
especially on raw, rainy mornings, your face shifts
into anonymous schoolgirl faces, a punishment,
since sometimes, you condescend to smile,
since at the corners of the smile there is forgiveness.

Besieged by sisters, you were a prize
of which they were too proud, circled
by the thorn thicket of their accusation,
what grave deep wrong, what wound have you brought Anna?

The rain season comes with its load.
The half-year has travelled far. Its back hurts.
It drizzles wearily.

It is twenty years since,
after another war, the shell-cases are where?
But in our brassy season, our imitation autumn,
your hair puts out its fire,
your gaze haunts innumerable photographs,

now clear, now indistinct,
all that pursuing generality,
that vengeful conspiracy with nature,

all that sly informing of objects,
and behind every line, your laugh
frozen into a lifeless photograph.

In that hair I could walk through the wheatfields of Russia,
your arms were downed and ripening pears,
for you became, in fact, another country,

you are Anna of the wheatfield and the weir,
you are Anna of the solid winter rain,
Anna of the smoky platform and the cold train,
in that war of absence, Anna of the steaming stations,

gone from the marsh-edge,
from the drizzled shallows
puckering with gooseflesh,
Anna of the first green poems that startlingly hardened,

of the mellowing breasts now,
Anna of the lurching, long flamingos
of the harsh salt lingering in the thimble
of the bather's smile,

Anna of the darkened house, among the reeking shell-cases
lifting my hand and swearing us to her breast,
unbearably clear-eyed.

You are all Annas, enduring all goodbyes,
within the cynical station of your body,
Christie, Karenina, big-boned and passive,

that I found life within some novel's leaves
more real than you, already chosen
as his doomed heroine. You knew, you knew.

ii

Who were you, then?
The golden partisan of my young Revolution,
my braided, practical, seasoned commissar,

your back, bent at its tasks, in the blue kitchen,
or hanging flags of laundry, feeding the farm's chickens,
against a fantasy of birches,

poplars or whatever.
As if a pen's eye could catch that virginal litheness,
as if shade and sunlight leoparding the blank page
could be so literal,

foreign as snow,
far away as first love,
my Akhmatoval!

Twenty years later, in the odour of burnt shells,
you can remind me of 'A Visit to the Pasternaks',
so that you are suddenly the word 'wheat',

falling on the ear, against the frozen silence of a weir,
again you are bending
over a cabbage garden, tending
a snowdrift of rabbits,
or pulling down the clouds from the thrumming clotheslines.

If dreams are signs,
then something died this minute,
its breath blown from a different life,

from a dream of snow, from paper
to white paper flying, gulls and herons
following this plough. And now,

you are suddenly old, white-haired,
like the herons, the turned page. Anna, I wake
to the knowledge that things sunder
from themselves, like peeling bark,

to the emptiness
of a bright silence shining after thunder.

iii

'Any island would drive you crazy',
I knew you'd grow tired
of all that iconography of the sea

like the young wind, a bride
riffling daylong the ocean's catalogue
of shells and algae,

everything, this flock
of white, novitiate herons
I saw in the grass of a grey parish church,

like nurses, or young nuns after communion,
their sharp eyes sought me out
as yours once, only.

61

And you were heron-like,
a water-haunter,
you grew bored with your island,

till, finally, you took off,
without a cry,
a novice in your nurse's uniform,

years later I imagined you
walking through trees to some grey hospital,
serene communicant,
but never 'lonely',

like the wind, never to be married,
your faith like folded linen, a nun's, a nurse's,
why should you read this now?

No woman should read verses
twenty years late. You go about your calling, candle-like
carrying yourself down a dark aisle

of wounded, married to the sick,
knowing one husband, pain,
only with the heron-flock, the rain,

the stone church, I remembered . . .
Besides, the slender, virginal New Year's
just married, like a birch
to a few crystal tears,

and like a birch bent at the register
who cannot, for a light's flash, change her name,
she still writes '65 for '66;

so, watching the tacit
ministering herons, each at its
work among the dead, the stone church, the stones,

I made this in your honour, when
vows and affections failing
your soul leapt like a heron sailing
from the salt, island grass

into another heaven.

Extract H:

CHAPTER 20

iv

Well, there you have your seasons, prodigy!
For instance, the autumnal fall of bodies,
deaths, like a comic, brutal repetition,
and in the Book of Hours, that seemed so far,
the light and amber of another life,
there is a Reaper busy about his wheat,
one who stalks nearer, and will not look up
from the scythe's swish in the orange evening grass,

and the fly at the font of your ear
sings, Hurry, hurry!
Never to set eyes on this page,
ah Harry, never to read our names,
like a stone blurred with tears I could not read
among the pilgrims, and the mooning child
staring from the window of the high studio.

Brown, balding, with a lacertilian
jut to his underlip,
with spectacles thick as a glass paperweight
and squat, blunt fingers,
waspish, austere, swift with asperities,

with a dimpled pot for a belly from the red clay of Piaille.
Eyes like the glint of sea-smoothed bottle glass,
his knee-high khaki stockings,
brown shoes lacquered even in desolation.

People entered his understanding
like a wayside country church,
they had built him themselves.
It was they who had smoothed the wall
of his clay-coloured forehead,
who made of his rotundity an earthy
useful object
holding the clear water of their simple troubles,
he who returned their tribal names
to the adze, mattock, midden and cookingpot.

A tang of white rum on the tongue of the mandolin,
a young bay, parting its mouth,
a heron silently named or a night-moth,
or the names of villages plaited into one map,
in the evocation of scrubbed back-yard smoke,
and he is a man no more
but the fervour and intelligence
of a whole country.

Leonce, Placide, Alcindor,
Dominic, from whose plane vowels were shorn
odorous as forest,
ask the charcoal-burner to look up
with his singed eyes,
ask the lip-cracked fisherman three miles at sea
with nothing between him and Dahomey's coast
to dip rain-water over his parched boards
for Monsieur Simmons, *pour* Msieu Harry Simmons,
let the husker on his pyramid of coconuts
rest on his tree.

Blow out the eyes in the unfinished portraits.

And the old woman who danced
with a spine like the 'glory cedar',
so lissom that her veins bulged evenly
upon the tightened drumskin of the earth,
her feet nimbler than the drummer's fingers,
let her sit in her corner and become evening
for a man the colour of her earth,
for a cracked claypot full of idle brushes,
and the tubes curl and harden,
except the red,
except the virulent red!

His island forest, open and enclose him
like a rare butterfly between its leaves.

Extract I:

from CHAPTER 22

That child who sets his half-shell afloat
in the brown creek that is Rampanalgas River—
my son first, then two daughters—
towards the roar of waters,
towards the Atlantic with a dead almond leaf for a sail,
with a twig for a mast,
was, like his father, this child,
a child without history, without knowledge of its pre-world,

only the knowledge of water runnelling rocks,
and the desperate whelk that grips the rock's outcrop
like a man whom the waves can never wash overboard;
that child who puts the shell's howl to his ear,
hears nothing, hears everything
that the historian cannot hear, the howls
of all the races that crossed the water,
the howls of grandfathers drowned
in that intricately swivelled Babel,
hears the fellaheen, the Madrasi, the Mandingo, the Ashanti,
yes, and hears also the echoing green fissures of Canton,
and thousands without longing for this other shore
by the mud tablets of the Indian Provinces,
robed ghostly white and brown, the twigs of uplifted hands,
of manacles, mantras, of a thousand kaddishes,
whorled, drilling into the shell,
see, in the evening light by the saffron, sacred Benares,
how they are lifting like herons,
robed ghostly white and brown,
and the crossing of water has erased their memories.
And the sea, which is always the same,
accepts them.
And the shore, which is always the same,
accepts them.

In the shallop of the shell,
in the round prayer,
in the palate of the conch,
in the dead sail of the almond leaf
are all of the voyages.

CHAPTER 23

iii

I looked from old verandas at
verandas, sails, the eternal summer sea
like a book left open by an absent master.
And what if it's all gone,
the hill's cut away for more tarmac,
the groves all sawn,
and bungalows proliferate on the scarred, hacked hillside,
the magical lagoon drained
for the Higher Purchase plan,
and they've bulldozed and bowdlerized our Vigie,
our *ocelle insularum*, our Sirmio
for a pink and pastel New Town where the shacks and huts
  stood
teetering and tough in unabashed unhope,
as twilight like amnesia blues the slope,
when over the untroubled ocean, the moon
will always swing its lantern
and evening fold the pages of the sea,
and peer like my lost reader silently
between the turning leaves
for the lost names
of Caribs, slaves and fishermen?

Forgive me, you folk,
who exercise a patience
subtler, stronger than the muscles
in the wave's wrist,
and you, sea, with the mouth
of that old gravekeeper

white-headed, lantern-jawed,
forgive our desertions, you islands
whose names dissolve like sugar
in a child's mouth. And you, Gregorias.
And you, Anna. Rest.

iv

But, ah Gregorias,
I christened you with that Greek name because
it echoes the blest thunders of the surf,
because you painted our first, primitive frescoes,
because it sounds explosive,
a black Greek's! A sun that stands back
from the fire of itself, not shamed, prizing
its shadow, watching it blaze!
You sometimes dance with that destructive frenzy
that made our years one fire.
Gregorias listen, lit,
we were the light of the world!
We were blest with a virginal, unpainted world
with Adam's task of giving things their names,
with the smooth white walls of clouds and villages
where you devised your inexhaustible,
impossible Renaissance,
brown cherubs of Giotto and Masaccio,
with the salt wind coming through the window,
smelling of turpentine, with nothing so old
that it could not be invented,
and set above it your crude wooden star,
its light compounded in that mortal glow:
Gregorias, Apilo!

April 1965–April 1972

Selections from

Sea Grapes

The Virgins

Down the dead streets of sun-stoned Frederiksted,
the first freeport to die for tourism,
strolling at funeral pace, I am reminded
of life not lost to the American dream;
but my small-islander's simplicities
can't better our new empire's civilized
exchange of cameras, watches, perfumes, brandies
for the good life, so cheaply underpriced
that only the crime rate is on the rise
in streets blighted with sun, stone arches
and plazas blown dry by the hysteria
of rumour. A condominium drowns
in vacancy; its bargains are dusted,
but only a jewelled housefly drones
over the bargains. The roulettes spin
rustily to the wind; the vigorous trade
that every morning would begin afresh
by revving up green water round the pierhead
heading for where the banks of silver thresh.

Adam's Song

The adulteress stoned to death,
is killed in our own time
by whispers, by the breath
that films her flesh with slime.

The first was Eve,
who horned God for the serpent,
for Adam's sake; which makes
everyone guilty or Eve innocent.

Nothing has changed
for men still sing the song that Adam sang
against the world he lost to vipers,

the song to Eve
against his own damnation;
he sang it in the evening of the world

with the lights coming on in the eyes
of panthers in the peaceable kingdom
and his death coming out of the trees,

he sings it, frightened
of the jealousy of God and at the price
of his own death.

The song ascends to God, who wipes his eyes:

'Heart, you are in my heart as the bird rises,
heart, you are in my heart while the sun sleeps,
heart, you lie still in me as the dew is,
you weep within me, as the rain weeps.'

Parades, Parades

There's the wide desert, but no one marches
except in the pads of old caravans,
there is the ocean, but the keels incise
the precise, old parallels,
there's the blue sea above the mountains
but they scratch the same lines
in the jet trails –
so the politicians plod
without imagination, circling
the same sombre garden
with its fountain dry in the forecourt,
the gri-gri palms desiccating
dung pods like goats,
the same lines rule the White Papers,
the same steps ascend Whitehall,
and only the name of the fool changes
under the plumed white cork-hat
for the Independence Parades,
revolving around, in calypso,
to the brazen joy of the tubas.

Why are the eyes of the beautiful
and unmarked children
in the uniforms of the country
bewildered and shy,
why do they widen in terror
of the pride drummed into their minds?
Were they truer, the old songs,
when the law lived far away,
when the veiled queen, her girth
as comfortable as cushions,
upheld the orb with its stern admonitions?

We wait for the changing of statues,
for the change of parades.

Here he comes now, here he comes!
Papa! Papa! With his crowd,
the sleek, waddling seals of his Cabinet,
trundling up to the dais,
as the wind puts its tail between
the cleft of the mountain, and a wave
coughs once, abruptly.
Who will name this silence
respect? Those forced, hoarse hosannas
awe? That tin-ringing tune
from the pumping, circling horns
the New World? Find a name
for that look on the faces
of the electorate. Tell me
how it all happened, and why
I said nothing.

The Wind in the Dooryard

(for Eric Roach)

I didn't want this poem to come
from the torn mouth,
I didn't want this poem to come
from his salt body,

but I will tell you what he celebrated:

He writes of the wall with spilling coralita
from the rim of the rich garden,

and the clean dirt yard
clean as the parlour table
with a yellow tree
an ackee, an almond
a pomegranate
in the clear vase of sunlight,

sometimes he put his finger
on the pulse of the wind,
when he heard the sea in the cedars.
He went swimming to Africa,
but he felt tired;
he chose that way
to reach his ancestors.

No, I did not want to write this,
but, doesn't the sunrise
force itself through the curtain
of the trembling eyelids?
When the cows are statues in the misting field
that sweats out the dew,
and the horse lifts its iron head
and the jaws of the sugar mules
ruminate and grind like the factory?

I did not want to hear it again,
the echo of broken windmills,
the mutter of the wild yams creeping
over the broken palings,
the noise of the moss
stitching the stone barracoons,

but the rain breaks
on the foreheads of the wild yams,
the dooryard opens the voice
of his rusty theme,

and the first quick drops of the drizzle
the libations to Shango
dry fast as sweat on the forehead
and our tears also.

The peasant reeks sweetly of bush,
he smells the same as his donkey –
they smell of the high, high country
of clouds and stunted pine –
the man wipes his hand
that is large as a yam
and as crusty with dirt
across the tobacco-stained
paling stumps of his torn mouth,
he rinses with the mountain dew,
and he spits out pity.

I did not want it to come,
but sometimes, under the armpit
of the hot sky over the country
the wind smells of salt
and a certain breeze lifts
the sprigs of the coralita
as if, like us,
lifting our heads, at our happiest,
it too smells the freshness of life.

The Bright Field

My nerves steeled against the power of London,
I hurried home that evening, with the sense
we all have, of the crowd's hypocrisy,

to feel my rage, turned on in self-defence,
bear mercy for the anonymity
of every self humbled by massive places,
and I, who moved against a bitter sea,
was moved by the light on Underground-bound faces.

Their sun that would not set was going down
on their flushed faces, brickwork like a kiln,
on pillar-box-bright buses between trees,
with the compassion of calendar art;
like walking sheaves of harvest, the quick crowd
thickened in separate blades of cane or wheat
from factories and office doors conveyed
to one end by the loud belt of the street.
And that end brings its sadness, going in
by Underground, by cab, by bullock-cart,
and lances us with punctual, maudlin
pity down lanes or cane-fields, till the heart,
seeing, like dark canes, the river-spires sharpen,
feels an involuntary bell begin
to toll for everything, even in London,
heart of our history, original sin.

The vision that brought Samuel Palmer peace,
that stoked Blake's fury at her furnaces,
flashes from doormen's buttons and the rocks
around Balandra. These slow belfry-strokes –
cast in the pool of London, from which swallows
rise in wide rings, and from their bright field, rooks –
mark the same beat by which a pelican goes
across Salybia as the tide lowers.

Dark August

So much rain, so much life like the swollen sky
of this black August. My sister, the sun,
broods in her yellow room and won't come out.

Everything goes to hell; the mountains fume
like a kettle, rivers overrun; still,
she will not rise and turn off the rain.

She's in her room, fondling old things,
my poems, turning her album. Even if thunder falls
like a crash of plates from the sky,

she does not come out.
Don't you know I love you but am hopeless
at fixing the rain? But I am learning slowly

to love the dark days, the steaming hills,
the air with gossiping mosquitoes,
and to sip the medicine of bitterness,

so that when you emerge, my sister,
parting the beads of the rain,
with your forehead of flowers and eyes of forgiveness,

all will not be as it was, but it will be true
(you see they will not let me love
as I want), because, my sister, then

I would have learnt to love black days like bright ones,
the black rain, the white hills, when once
I loved only my happiness and you.

Sea Canes

Half my friends are dead.
I will make you new ones, said earth.
No, give me them back, as they were, instead,
with faults and all, I cried.

Tonight I can snatch their talk
from the faint surf's drone
through the canes, but I cannot walk

on the moonlit leaves of ocean
down that white road alone,
or float with the dreaming motion

of owls leaving earth's load.
O earth, the number of friends you keep
exceeds those left to be loved.

The sea-canes by the cliff flash green and silver
they were the seraph lances of my faith,
but out of what is lost grows something stronger

that has the rational radiance of stone,
enduring moonlight, further than despair,
strong as the wind, that through dividing canes

brings those we love before us, as they were,
with faults and all, not nobler, just there.

Oddjob, a Bull Terrier

You prepare for one sorrow,
but another comes.
It is not like the weather,
you cannot brace yourself,
the unreadiness is all.
Your companion, the woman,
the friend next to you,
the child at your side,
and the dog,
we tremble for them,
we look seaward and muse
it will rain.
We shall get ready for rain;
you do not connect
the sunlight altering
the darkening oleanders
in the sea-garden,
the gold going out of the palms.
You do not connect this,
the fleck of the drizzle
on your flesh
with the dog's whimper,
the thunder doesn't frighten,
the readiness is all;
what follows at your feet
is trying to tell you
the silence is all:
it is deeper than the readiness,
it is sea-deep,
earth-deep,
love-deep.

The silence
is stronger than thunder,
we are stricken dumb and deep
as the animals who never utter love
as we do, except
it becomes unutterable
and must be said,
in a whimper,
in tears,
in the drizzle that comes to our eyes
not uttering the loved thing's name,
the silence of the dead,
the silence of the deepest buried love is
the one silence,
and whether we bear it for beast,
for child, for woman, or friend,
it is the one love, it is the same,.
and it is blest
deepest by loss
it is blest, it is blest.

Earth

Let the day grow on you upward
through your feet,
the vegetal knuckles,

to your knees of stone,
until by evening you are a black tree;
feel, with evening,

the swifts thicken your hair,
the new moon rising out of your forehead,
and the moonlit veins of silver

running from your armpits
like rivulets under white leaves.
Sleep, as ants

cross over your eyelids.
You have never possessed anything
as deeply as this.

This is all you have owned
from the first outcry
through forever;

you can never be dispossessed.

To Return to the Trees

(for John Figueroa)

Senex, an oak.
Senex, this old sea-almond
unwincing in spray

in this geriatric grove
on the sea-road to Cumana.
To return to the trees,

to decline like this tree,
the burly oak
of Boanerges Ben Jonson!

Or, am I lying
like this felled almond
when I write I look forward to age –

a gnarled poet
bearded with the whirlwind,
his metres like thunder?

It is not only the sea,
no, for on windy, green mornings
I read the changes on Morne Coco Mountain,

from flagrant sunrise
to its ashen end;
grey has grown strong to me,

it's no longer neutral,
no longer the dirty flag
of courage going under,

it is speckled with hues
like quartz, it's as
various as boredom,

grey now is a crystal
haze, a dull diamond,
stone-dusted and stoic,

grey is the heart at peace,
tougher than the warrior
as it bestrides factions,

it is the great pause
when the pillars of the temple
rest on Samson's palms

and are held, held,
that moment
when the heavy rock of the world

like a child sleeps
on the trembling shoulders of Atlas
and his own eyes close,

the toil that is balance.
Seneca, that fabled bore,
and his gnarled, laborious Latin

I can read only in fragments
of broken bark, his
heroes tempered by whirlwinds,

who see with the word
senex, with its two eyes,
through the boles of this tree,

beyond joy,
beyond lyrical utterance,
this obdurate almond

going under the sand
with this language, slowly,
by sand grains, by centuries.

Selections from

*The Star-Apple
Kingdom*

Sabbaths, WI

Those villages stricken with the melancholia of Sunday,
in all of whose ochre streets one dog is sleeping

those volcanoes like ashen roses, or the incurable sore
of poverty, around whose puckered mouth thin boys are
selling yellow sulphur stone

the burnt banana leaves that used to dance
the river whose bed is made of broken bottles
the cocoa grove where a bird whose cry sounds green and
yellow and in the lights under the leaves crested with
orange flame has forgotten its flute

gommiers peeling from sunburn still wrestling to escape the
    sea

the dead lizard turning blue as stone

those rivers, threads of spittle, that forgot the old music

that dry, brief esplanade under the drier sea almonds
where the dry old men sat

watching a white schooner stuck in the branches
and playing draughts with the moving frigate birds

those hillsides like broken pots
those ferns that stamped their skeletons on the skin

and those roads that begin reciting their names at vespers

mention them and they will stop
those crabs that were willing to let an epoch pass
those herons like spinsters that doubted their reflections
inquiring, inquiring

those nettles that waited
those Sundays, those Sundays

those Sundays when the lights at the road's end were an
    occasion

those Sundays when my mother lay on her back
those Sundays when the sisters gathered like white moths
round their street lantern

and cities passed us by on the horizon

Forest of Europe

(for Joseph Brodsky)

The last leaves fell like notes from a piano
and left their ovals echoing in the ear;
with gawky music stands, the winter forest
looks like an empty orchestra, its lines
ruled on these scattered manuscripts of snow.

The inlaid copper laurel of an oak
shines through the brown-bricked glass above your head
as bright as whisky, while the wintry breath
of lines from Mandelstam, which you recite,
uncoils as visibly as cigarette smoke.

'The rustling of rouble notes by the lemon Neva.'
Under your exile's tongue, crisp under heel,
the gutturals crackle like decaying leaves,
the phrase from Mandelstam circles with light
in a brown room, in barren Oklahoma.

There is a Gulag Archipelago
under this ice, where the salt, mineral spring
of the long Trail of Tears runnels these plains
as hard and open as a herdsman's face
sun-cracked and stubbled with unshaven snow.

Growing in whispers from the Writers' Congress,
the snow circles like cossacks round the corpse
of a tired Choctaw till it is a blizzard
of treaties and white papers as we lose
sight of the single human through the cause.

So every spring these branches load their shelves,
like libraries with newly published leaves,
till waste recycles them – paper to snow –
but, at zero of suffering, one mind
lasts like this oak with a few brazen leaves.

As the train passed the forest's tortured icons,
the floes clanging like freight yards, then the spires
of frozen tears, the stations screeching steam,
he drew them in a single winter's breath
whose freezing consonants turned into stones.

He saw the poetry in forlorn stations
under clouds vast as Asia, through districts
that could gulp Oklahoma like a grape,
not these tree-shaded prairie halts but space
so desolate it mocked destinations.

88

Who is that dark child on the parapets
of Europe, watching the evening river mint
its sovereigns stamped with power, not with poets,
the Thames and the Neva rustling like banknotes,
then, black on gold, the Hudson's silhouettes?

From frozen Neva to the Hudson pours,
under the airport domes, the echoing stations,
the tributary of emigrants whom exile
has made as classless as the common cold,
citizens of a language that is now yours,

and every February, every 'last autumn',
you write far from the threshing harvesters
folding wheat like a girl plaiting her hair,
far from Russia's canals quivered with sunstroke,
a man living with English in one room.

The tourist archipelagos of my South
are prisons too, corruptible, and though
there is no harder prison than writing verse,
what's poetry, if it is worth its salt,
but a phrase men can pass from hand to mouth?

From hand to mouth, across the centuries,
the bread that lasts when systems have decayed,
when, in his forest of barbed-wire branches,
a prisoner circles, chewing the one phrase
whose music will last longer than the leaves,

whose condensation is the marble sweat
of angels' foreheads, which will never dry
till Borealis shuts the peacock lights
of its slow fan from L.A. to Archangel,
and memory needs nothing to repeat.

Frightened and starved, with divine fever
Osip Mandelstam shook, and every
metaphor shuddered him with ague,
each vowel heavier than a boundary stone,
'to the rustling of rouble notes by the lemon Neva',

but now that fever is a fire whose glow
warms our hands, Joseph, as we grunt like primates
exchanging gutturals in this winter cave
of a brown cottage, while in drifts outside
mastodons force their systems through the snow.

The Schooner Flight

Chapter 11: After the Storm

There's a fresh light that follows a storm
while the whole sea still havoc; in its bright wake
I saw the veiled face of Maria Concepcion
marrying the ocean, then drifting away
in the widening lace of her bridal train
with white gulls her bridesmaids, till she was gone.
I wanted nothing after that day.
Across my own face, like the face of the sun,
a light rain was falling, with the sea calm.

Fall gently, rain, on the sea's upturned face
like a girl showering; make these islands fresh
as Shabine once knew them! Let every trace,
every hot road, smell like clothes she just press
and sprinkle with drizzle. I finish dream;
whatever the rain wash and the sun iron:
the white clouds, the sea and sky with one seam,

is clothes enough for my nakedness.
Though my *Flight* never pass the incoming tide
of this inland sea beyond the loud reefs
of the final Bahamas, I am satisfied
if my hand gave voice to one people's grief.
Open the map. More islands there, man,
than peas on a tin plate, all different size,
one thousand in the Bahamas alone,
from mountains to low scrub with coral keys,
and from this bowsprit, I bless every town,
the blue smell of smoke in hills behind them,
and the one small road winding down them like twine
to the roofs below; I have only one theme:

The bowsprit, the arrow, the longing, the lunging heart—
the flight to a target whose aim we'll never know,
vain search for one island that heals with its harbour
and a guiltless horizon, where the almond's shadow
doesn't injure the sand. There are so many islands!
As many islands as the stars at night
on that branched tree from which meteors are shaken
like falling fruit around the schooner *Flight*.
But things must fall, and so it always was,
on the one hand Venus, on the other Mars;
fall, and are one, just as this earth is one
island in archipelagos of stars.
My first friend was the sea. Now, is my last.
I stop talking now. I work, then I read,
cotching under a lantern hooked to the mast.
I try to forget what happiness was,
and when that don't work, I study the stars.
Sometimes is just me, and the soft-scissored foam
as the deck turn white and the moon open
a cloud like a door, and the light over me
is a road in white moonlight taking me home.
Shabine sang to you from the depths of the sea.

Notes to the Poems

Notes to the Poems

The Harbour

A young poet's meditation on his choice of sacred over profane love, 'The Harbour' contrasts the lonely, imperilled journeying of a soul seeking illumination through art with the 'safe twilight' available to one content with human love – though that love obfuscates vision ('raises.walls') and is subject moreover to Time. The poem proceeds via ironic parallels. The 'old lies' of the lover are 'bitter and sly' but the poet too is engaged in 'an antique hoax' (since illumination is ultimately inaccessible?) and therefore drowning, though a different drowning, awaits each, the lover sinking into bemusement ('since feelings drown'), the poet (l. 14) into madness, perhaps; and while the poem plainly proffers a view of the poet's heroism, the lover also has his 'secret faring-forth'. None of this quite saves the young Walcott from self-dramatization, or from a certain smugness in that dismissal of 'the secure from thinking' – but the tone of the poem is melancholy rather than assertive, and its last, withdrawing image gives a scale: in comparison with the immensity of Life the poet is himself a mere paddler.

The theme of 'The Harbour' is archetypal (read, for instance, the short chapter, 'The Lee Shore', from Melville's *Moby Dick*) and the religious significance, for the poet, of the initial image is elsewhere made explicit, in the line (from 'Sainte Lucie', published a quarter of a century later) 'your faith like a canoe at evening coming in'. But its chief delights lie elsewhere: in the voluptuous sibilance (characteristic of serpents and seas) which pervades the whole poem; in the dynamism of the fifth line, its lurch, pause, surge and collapse mimetic of a wave of the sea; in the languor of all those long vowels. Notice also how nearly physical is that difficult spondee 'humped hills' (in its context, a sexual image); how the sunny certainties of the traditional sonnet's rhyme scheme are first darkened by half-rhymes (dusk/ask, move/gave) and then abandoned altogether; how the preponderance of heavy stresses in the last line brings the poem to its 'dying fall' – and how, amid the calm vowels of that line, the diphthong denotes the horror.

94

To a Painter in England

The poem begins by contrasting 'cities of fog' with 'personal islands' (consider the aptness of the rhyme: industry/I). In the succeeding verses, however, the poet's attitudes to the English city and the Caribbean are abruptly reversed – so much so that 'sicken' (l. 4), for which 'yearn' might have appeared a synonym, virtually reverts, after the nervous exhaustion of v. 3, to its literal meaning. With v. 4 it becomes apparent that what has prompted this turnabout – as it stands, a confusion in the poem – is the writer's sense of his own inadequacy as a painter (which the young Walcott had hoped to be). Thus the island is 'virginal', the trees 'spinsterish', because they remain 'unpossessed' by the artist. None the less, the poet affirms, there survives in him an impulse to bless – a specifically religious impulse, though Walcott is at pains to dissociate it from the 'Sabbath logic' of Christianity and to assert the 'decision' of the individual soul. 'Silence' (v. 5, l. 6) in that state of grace is brimful: the womb of speech (cf. 'And the Word was made flesh, and the Word *was* flesh').

An enduring strength of Walcott's poetry has been its author's mastery of the iambic pentameter. Notice with what apparent effortlessness the elegant, mannered speech of the first four verses accommodates itself to that line. How does Walcott achieve, in the last verse, the change of tone which lifts it to declamation and dénouement?

Gauguins (v. 1, l. 4): Paul Gauguin, French post-impressionist painter (1848–1903), who, seduced by their beauty and the apparent wholeness of their (pre-industrial) cultures, lived and painted in both Martinique and Tahiti.

Discloses around corners an architecture (v. 5, l. 2): The image is of turning a corner and coming into sight of a church.

Ruins of a Great House

Descriptive, narrative and meditative by turn, 'Ruins of a Great House' conveys the experience of having one's conventional responses to the iniquities of West Indian history subverted: first, by perplexity at the evident coexistence of beauty and evil – yoked also in the phrase 'murderers and poets' – and secondly, by a sense of the impermanence of all human achievement. Images of death predominate: limes, ash. Empires rise only to fall, and in the end it is always the crow, the worm and the mouse which are the victors. It occurs to Walcott that the gulf between slaveowner and slave is not so great as to obscure their essential brotherhood and common destiny in time – the grave. Time, furthermore, may heal – 'The river flows, obliterating hurt' – and thus the attempt at rage rings false; consider that voluptuous 'manorial' in the penultimate verse. In the last verse the poem reclaims a response appropriate to its central lament: 'Deciduous beauty prospered and is gone'.

disjecta membra (v. 1, l. 1): Scattered components. From Horace's 'disjecti membra poetae'.

Great House (v. 1, l. 1): The principal and most ostentatious dwelling-place on a plantation, usually occupied by the owner or manager.

Marble as Greece (v. 4, l. 1): Marble is limestone in a crystalline state. It was extensively used by the Greeks in architecture and sculpture in the time of the Grecian Empire.

Faulkner's (v. 4, l. 1): William Faulkner (1897–1962). American novelist and recipient of the Nobel Prize for Literature (1949), Faulkner saw the American South as condemned by its sinful exploitation of land and man. In his novels he explored the phenomenon of personal and social disintegration, charted the persistence of the past into the present, and affirmed the virtue of endurance.

Kipling (v. 6, l. 6): Rudyard Kipling (1865–1936). English writer, famous for his poems and stories set in India – the country of his birth, and at that time part of the British Empire.

Hawkins, Walter Raleigh, Drake (v. 7, l. 3): English adventurers and pirates who operated in the West Indies and the Spanish Main during and just after the reign of Elizabeth I, when England was the dominant maritime power in Europe. Raleigh was also a poet.

The rot remains with us, the men are gone (v. 7, l. 8): Cf. Shakespeare's *Julius Caesar*: 'The evil that men do lives after them.'

Donne (v. 7, l. 11): John Donne (1572–1631). English metaphysical poet and author of the famous passage beginning: 'No man is an island, entire of itself; every man is a part of the continent, a part of the main. If a clod be washed away, Europe is the less, as well as if a manor of thy friend's or thine own were . . .'

Albion (v. 8, l. 4): Old poetic name for Britain, perhaps derived from its white (Latin: *albus*) cliffs visible from the coast of Gaul (France).

Tales of the Islands: Chapter III

One of a sequence of sonnets in which Walcott departs from the conventional form by largely eschewing rhyme. Chapter III nonetheless falls naturally into the Petrarchan sonnet's division into octet and sestet. The theme ('la belle qui fut') is similar to that of 'Ruins...' ('Deciduous beauty prospered and is gone') but its treatment here is both funnier and more horrific. The poem should be read in a tone of exaggerated wonder, a burlesque of wonder – the tone of a parent reading a bedtime story to a small enthralled child. The technique is ironic; the effect depends on the dissociation between what is being said and how it is being said.

lazaretto (l. 1): A hospital for the diseased poor, especially lepers.

Magdalen of Donatello (l. 5): Donatello (diminutive of Donato) was a Florentine sculptor (1386–1466), one of the founders of Renaissance art. The 'Magdalen' belongs to his final creative phase, which was marked by a new depth of psychological insight, and in which the powerful torsos found in his earlier work became withered and spidery – overwhelmed, as it were, by tremendous emotional tensions.

Tales of the Islands: Chapter X

The last of the sonnet sequence, it is also the one in which rhyme reappears. (To what effect, do you think?) The scenario is one of departure; the repeated 'I watched' evokes the young man's nostalgia for his receding island, as do the lovingly observed details (with perhaps one lapse: difficult to see the fuselage from inside the plane). The poem is placed in its autobiographical context in Chapter 17 of Walcott's later book, *Another Life*. Account, if you can, for the peculiar, cathartic power of the last line.

A Careful Passion

'A Careful Passion' (and as the poem unfolds the title is seen to be self-accusing rather than paradoxical) evokes the sensations of a man engaged in quitting an adulterous affair – like that 'old Greek freighter quitting port'. Bored and disaffected, he allows his mind to wander back to another past love (v. 2, ll. 3–5) and is in consequence disturbed by a sense of life as meaninglessly repetitive: a succession of waves on

97

sand, or an old windmill vacantly turning – the latter the hidden image underlying 'the rusty cries/Of gulls revolving in the wind'. His attempt at stoicism (v. 3, l. 4) fails – the line discloses instead sententiousness and self-pity – and, failing, releases an image of death, in particular of spiritual death: 'eyes full of sand'. Dissociation (v. 3, l. 8) and self-mockery follow.

'A Careful Passion' is less about the death of love than about an inability to love. It is about the way in which 'the self-seeking heart . . . desperate for some mirror', engenders its own alienation, forcing its owner into the role of actor, and thus of cynic. Though the theme is hardly original, the experience comes over as felt, and the poem's near-perfect marriage of subject matter and form makes it almost entirely successful. Consider, for example, how the predominance of end-stopped lines, each reinforced by rhyme, enacts the narrator's ennui and isolation; or how several apparently artless descriptive details (those tables 'fixed like islands', that 'freighter quitting port', those 'coupling flies', the wind playing 'with the corners of her skirt', the street 'brightening', but with sunset, vanguard of night) contribute to the thematic unity of the poem; or the appropriateness of the feminine rhyme with which the poem closes. Notice also how the 'city's edge . . . harbour's edge' are resolved into the thrice-repeated 'water's edge'. (Water: traditionally a symbol of passion, but also the mirror which enticed the 'self-seeking' Narcissus to his death.)

(An amusing insight into the exigencies of metre is provided by that ungrammatical comma near the end of v. 2, l. 6. The lines 'The hand which wears her husband's ring lies on/The table idly, a brown leaf on the sand' are pentameters, and almost certainly existed in this form in an earlier draft of the poem. The poet, however, for the sake of the pun, decided to stop the first line at 'lies' – and then found himself with a problem of scansion. This he 'solved' by inserting the comma, the pause it denotes standing for the initial unstressed syllable of the last foot of that line.)

Castiliane

In 'Castiliane' Walcott attempts to enrich his actual environment – perceived as vaguely sordid, with its heat, flies, and 'odours of the port' – by invoking into it the fabled centuries of Spain, or of Spanish culture as manifested in the Caribbean. As the incarnation of that culture the poet imagines 'a wraith . . . frail Donna'. The vision is tenuous; reality (section II, v. 2) keeps breaking in, and even when it doesn't the poet is forced wryly to admit that his wraith would probably have ended up married to some 'goldtoothed' merchant, 'a man who hawks and profits in this heat', since 'whoever lived by verse?' 'Castiliane' is escapism consciously indulged in; yet in the final verse (in which the tone of the poem grows serious) the poet affirms the endurance of the wraith as the 'ancient, simple spirit' of a traditional – if now debased – culture.

A lighter look at love than 'A Careful Passion' affords, 'Castiliane' strikes a note of idle fancy uncharacteristic of Walcott's poetry (though frequently in evidence in his plays). There is a sense of the poet at his ease, allowing imagination the range of its whimsy, and indulging in the music of words – the latter to effects at times both gorgeous and funny, as in the first five lines of the last verse of section II. The product of this playfulness is none the less impressive; the poem seems effortlessly accomplished.

Golondrina (v. 1, l. 1): Spanish for 'swallow' (the bird).

noon's despair (v. 1, l. 10): T. S. Eliot quotes Emerson as saying that 'the lengthened shadow of a man is history'. Noon, the shadowless time, may represent the poet's sense of the absence of history, of connection.

fin de siècle (v. 3, l. 4): Invoking characteristics of the late nineteenth century, the phrase has connotations of decadence.

Alhambras (v. 3, l. 6): The Alhambra was the fortress of the Moorish monarchs of Granada, built in the Middle Ages.

da Falla (v. 5, l. 2): Manuel de Falla (1876–1946), a Spanish nationalist composer, born in Cadiz, whose compositions include music for the bullring.

A Lesson for this Sunday

In another poem Walcott writes of travelling by train through an idyllic landscape, then concludes sadly: 'Why feel that had we found them earlier some good/Could come out of a country change? We would/have spoiled such places too . . .' The theme of 'A Lesson for this Sunday' is, likewise, man's irruption into Paradise. Since the butterfly's tormentors are small children, the liberal argument – that it is our upbringing which warps us away from a predisposition to good – cannot hold; the poet is forced to recognize '*Heredity* of cruelty everywhere', and thus to reconsider the meaning of free will.

Because it does not go beyond stating that dismaying realization, 'A Lesson for this Sunday' remains a minor poem. None the less it exhibits the density and unity of a little masterpiece. Consider the relationships between 'simple praise' and 'mantis prays'; between 'lemon frock' and 'the frocks of summer'; between 'my hammock swings' and 'the mind swings'; between 'Crouched on plump haunches' and 'shrieks to eviscerate its abdomen'. Notice how in the first verse the absence of punctuation and the sibilant, regular lines suggest a dreaming, undisturbed world – until, with its abrupt parenthesis (v. 2, l. 1) the human voice arrives.

The last line both echoes and modifies the first: to what effect? How would the poem have differed if the poet had carried the ironic approach (begun at v. 2, l. 4 and abandoned seven lines later) through to the conclusion of the poem? At several places in the poem Walcott suggests an identification between the girl and the butterfly; can you identify these? How does this identification modify the meaning of the poem? What is implied by reference to the scythe's 'design'?

Allegre

One of the few free verse poems in *In a Green Night*, 'Allegre' seems written rather for the West Indian conversational voice, which favours the anapaest, than for the slowed and heightened speech characteristic of the iambic pentameter. The effect of spontaneity is reinforced by the 'artless' piling on of details – 'And the sunward sides ... And the slopes' – and is as appropriate here, given the poem's theme, as it would have been incongruous in, say, a ruminative poem like 'Ruins of a Great House'.

Elsewhere Walcott has written: 'I may have many sorrows, /Dawn is not one of them'. 'Allegre' is for the most part a celebration of dawn, of youth. The day, the poet and the country are young and the morning is 'full of elation'. But Walcott is essentially a meditative poet, so it is not surprising that towards the end of the poem the mood changes. (Consider also the remark of the American poet Robert Frost, that a poem 'should begin in delight and end in wisdom'.) Two of the three lines beginning with 'No temples ...' state what seem to

Walcott to be paradoxes (which are they?) and the poet is moved to caution: as the sky is loveliest when the earth is barren, so the elation may be 'useless and empty' so long as the 'true self' remains undiscovered.

The last eight lines of 'Allegre' seem to invite discussions of an historical and philosophical nature. Are West Indians rootless? In what sense can elation be 'useless' – or, for that matter, useful? It may be a flaw of the poem that the assertions these lines contain are contradicted by an earlier image, 'The roots of delight growing downward', which suggests that it is possible to *put down* roots (as well as to emerge from them) and that delight (elation) can achieve this. It may also be mentioned that an older Walcott in several of his later poems implicitly disavows the doubts at the end of 'Allegre' – consider, for example, 'Names' (for Edward Brathwaite), or the fact that in 'Commune' it is the snake which hisses 'this is not enough,/ neither the love nor the work of love enough'.

The roots of delight growing downward, /As the singer in his prime (v. 3, ll. 2–3): An image, presumably, of the way that a baritone at the crescendo of his song seems increasingly 'rooted' at his hands, palm upward, rise. Cf. Ezra Pound: 'What thou lovest well is thy true country'.

The stream keeps its edges, wind-honed (v. 5, l. 1): Obscure, since it is difficult to imagine the wind 'honing' either a stream or its edges. The remainder of the verse claims the detachment of the intellect from the affective life, and thus prepares us for the intrusion of intellectual concerns upon the pastoral scene.

Conqueror

The obdurate consonants of the opening line aptly introduce the conqueror: an 'Iron deliverer' (a comprehensive pun) with 'the wet-metal blaze/Of the sun in his sunken eye'. (Why 'sunken', do you think?) We are not prepared for his appearance; like a creation of the 'still, directionless hour' itself he is suddenly there, immobile.

We are familiar with this figure. His latter-day counterpart is the lone cowboy silhouetted on the ridge at dusk, overlooking the unsuspecting town. Both are 'men of iron', transformed by some purpose which overrides the natural man, and it is this aspect of the conqueror, the violence which the god or purpose in him enacts against his 'human' nature, which engages Walcott's imagination. In v. 2 he states the conqueror's predicament; in v. 3, with the description of the ongoing rural life of the valley, he further implies it – from that idyll the man of iron is excluded. Furthermore, his conquests must necessarily be incomplete (consider the function in the poem of 'those unconquered peaks').

Yet for all that, the conqueror is the embodiment of one of 'nature's laws', which the rhyme identifies. (Look again at 'A Lesson for this Sunday'.) In a diversion constituted by the last eight lines of v. 3, Walcott, as in 'A Lesson' and 'Allegre', questions the validity of the pastoral dream, 'the quiet of unknowing'. The 'small, furred beast' (which reappears many years later – see 'Mass Man') frighteningly dramatizes the conqueror's work; the sparrows, 'Fables of innocence ... Or natural thoughts', are poignantly contrasted with 'that armed mass quiet on [the hidden side of] the hill'.

Where in the poem, and why, is the conqueror referred to as 'it'? How effective is the description of the soldiers' lances as 'iron sheaves'? Why should 'joy remembered make rage the more'? And, assuming that the rhythm of the poem's last five lines constitute an attempt to mime the actions they describe or imply (including the conqueror's horse moving joltingly off downhill) how would you react to the suggestion that the penultimate line should be made into a regular pentameter by removing the word 'sighing'?

'Conqueror' describes an imaginary painting. Does this information help you to understand or appreciate the poem? In what way(s)?

The Castaway

In another Walcott poem, 'Crusoe's Island', the 'bearded hermit' succeeds in stocking his 'Eden' with 'all the joys/But one/Which sent him howling for a human voice'. 'The Castaway', likewise, delineates an experience of isolation. The castaway's hunger for human company ('a sail') brings him close to hysteria – to a state in which any action would quickly become frenzied. Even lying still he hallucinates, perceiving himself as 'sailing' – i.e. piloting – the 'ribbed shadow' of a palm frond stirring above him (an echo perhaps of Coleridge's 'The Ancient Mariner', in which a vessel approaching the doomed ship of the mariner turns out to be a 'spectre-ship' with

102

'naked ribs' through which the low sun peers. A comparable hallucination afflicts the sailor-narrator of Walcott's 'The Schooner *Flight*').

Verses 4–7 evoke the natural world, engaged in its unhurried, aimless, eternal routines. In this world, only the castaway is capable of giving a scale; and when, 'cracking a sea-louse', he declares that he has made 'thunder split' (and is thus 'Godlike') the reader is prepared for the gesture of despair with which the poem closes, the renunciation of both selfhood and the world.

You should recognize, however, that Walcott is not the castaway but the castaway's creator – and thus capable of commenting (implicitly) on the behaviour of his creature. With this in mind, look again at the last three verses. Notice that while the catalogue of 'dead metaphors' is ostensibly there to tell us what the castaway is renouncing, our final experience of the poem is not of his renunciation but of the metaphors themselves. Is it possible, do you think, that while establishing the fact of the castaway's despair Walcott means us to take a very different impression from these lines? What do you make of that oblique reference to the crucifixion of Christ (the Redeemer) with which the poem ends?

In formal terms, a defining characteristic of *The Castaway* (the collection which takes its title from the present poem) is Walcott's struggle against his own predisposition towards the iambic pentameter – a struggle evident in the fact that many lines which were obviously composed as pentameters to begin with, are broken up or run on in the final version (e.g. 'Blowing sand, thin as smoke,/Bored, shifts its dunes', or 'the rage with which the sandfly's head is filled'). And to students coming to 'The Castaway' from the poems of *In a Green Night* it may also be evident that the texture of the poems has changed. (Can you say in what ways?) Do you see any connection between the two developments – the formal and the textural? (What would you make of the charge that 'The Castaway', while more immediately effective than, say, 'The Harbour', is also less 'resonant'?)

The Swamp
Here are three interpretations of 'The Swamp':

(1) The historical: The consciousness behind 'The Swamp' is that of a white American from the Deep South of slavery ('cracker convicts, Negroes'). He senses that the 'black mouth[s]' threaten the

103

civilization ('highway') he has erected among them; that his culture is progressively enervated by their 'black mood'; and that somewhere along 'the road ahead' – i.e. in the future – he will lose his racial memory ('go black with widening amnesia'), whereupon their 'chaos' will overrun everything. The poem thus presents that familiar historical phenomenon, the colonizer's fear and loathing, born of guilt, of those whom he has colonized.

(2) The psychological: 'The Swamp' presents in metaphorical terms a struggle between the ego and the id, and premonishes the eventual triumph of the latter. In it, as in one of Tennessee Williams's fantastical gardens, the denizens of the unconscious press forward, suffocating the ego ('highway') – that is, the individual's sense of selfhood – with images of an infernal and promiscuous paradise (vv. 6–7). Even while the ego protests (v. 8), it is drowning in the 'fast-filling night'. Soon, the last bird 'drinks darkness', amnesia encroaches upon the ego, and in the orgiastic image with which the final verse opens we perceive the triumph of the id: the confusion of different parts of the body into a 'knot' implying the breakdown of self-awareness, and thus the advent of 'chaos'.

(3) The philosophical: The affirmation latent in 'The Swamp' is that there exists an indissoluble relationship between order and life: death, it is argued, may be less cessation than a kind of biological insanity – a return to the primordial 'knot'. In equating a swamp's teeming confusion with 'limbo' and the void (by which 'nothing', v. 4, l. 1, is translatable) the poet implies the primacy of the quiddity of things, thus adding a spiritual dimension to life.

Which interpretation do you prefer? (Why?) Is it possible that all three are valid? If so, what does this tell you about (1) the nature of poetry; (2) the pitfalls of criticism? Notice, however, that we cannot adequately describe the achievement or effect of the poem without also considering its language – e.g. the part played by those horrific aspirates (ll. 2 and 8) and dark vowels (in: home, growth, hero, shallows, mangrove, toad, road, throat) in *creating* the 'black mood' of 'The Swamp'.

Hemingway's hero (v. 3, l. 3): From Ernest Hemingway's story, 'Big Two-Hearted River': 'He did not feel like going on into the swamp . . . In the swamp fishing was a tragic adventure. Nick did not want it.'

The Flock

In 'The Flock' Walcott invokes the virtues of stoicism: austerity, fortitude and constancy ('fixity'). 'The Flock' is a tragic poem, since Walcott realizes (as Shakespeare's Caesar does not) that 'fixity' cannot save a man from 'annihilation' (remember how Shakespeare, with heavy irony, has Caesar killed within twenty lines of proclaiming himself 'constant as the northern star'), and since Walcott also recognizes the existence of a greater 'stoic': Arctic Earth, which – impartial, glacial, and capable of freezing 'giant minds in marble attitudes' – revolves 'with tireless, determined grace/upon an iron axle'. Yet in the final verse the poem achieves a saving balance, an ennobling compromise between the ideal of absolute stoicism – which approaches stoneheartedness – and the enthralled acquiescence of those who, like migratory birds, are prepared to 'blow with the wind'.

'The Flock' opens with an ingenious metaphor out of archery. Notice that the birds – those 'arrows of yearning' – exist at the whim of the seasons. Winter produces their flight, as the mind of the poet produces its own migrating images. (What qualities of the mind do you think the poet means to establish by linking it thus with winter?)

Next, Walcott introduces into that hostile landscape a lone horseman, a 'sepulchral knight'. (Why 'sepulchral'? What similarities do you find between him and the Conqueror of Walcott's earlier poem?) The poet's technique here is cinematic: the knight appears first in close-up ('hooves cannonading snow') and then is rendered from such a distance as to seem 'antlike [on] the forehead of an alp'. (What do you think of the view that, as images of the stature of man, both perspectives may be valid – as in Walcott's witty line, from 'Guyana': 'Ant-sized to God, god to an ant's eyes'?) Is it the horseman or the alp that is crouched 'in iron contradiction' to the weather, or both? Why do you think Walcott renders the alp in anthropomorphic terms?

The knight is both less and more than human: less, in that he is 'Vizor'd with blind defiance' ('Vizor'd': helmeted; but also, in conjunction with 'blind', blinkered); and more, in that his quest is superhuman: what he seeks is nothing less than the source of life itself: a 'yearly divination of the spring'.

In the final lines of the verse Walcott likens the activity of the poet to that of the knight. Both 'travel through . . . silence, making dark/

symbols ... across snow [in the poet's case, the white and lifeless page] measuring winter's augury'; and thus, by extension, the poet is also 'sepulchral' (read, in connection with this notion of a poet, W. B. Yeats's 'The Leaders of the Crowd') and his quest is, likewise, to 'claim the centre of life' (Walcott: 'Force').

In the wake of such monumental concerns, and the epic imagery in which they are expressed, the second verse of 'The Flock' comes as a chastening corrective. By comparison with the 'inflexible' grandeur of the world 'as it revolves upon its centuries', man seems transient and inconstant (v. 2, l. 4), prepossessed with images of escape, both his judgements ('condemnation') and his imaginings ('the sun's/exultant larks') ineffectual. The verse thus implies the pathetic diminution of human nature ('antlike' as the knight) when viewed against the backdrop of the cosmos. The question is again one of perspective. Here, as elsewhere, Walcott seems bewitched by the question: since we are human, yet capable at times of seeing through God's eyes, to which perspective should we strive to be true?

The final verse asserts a compromise: a worldview which incorporates elements of both. Thus, while Walcott prays that his mind may reflect the 'fixity' of the world, he rejects its indifference (to the howling of seals and the torn birds), acknowledging instead his human need to 'greet the black wings ... as a blessing', and for a 'sense of season'. The poem ends in a quietude of acceptance (note that its three feminine line-endings all occur in the last six lines) which tempers, without wholly disowning, the iron argument of its first verse.

'The Flock' is a major poem, and the most accomplished poem in *The Castaway*. It turns upon a balancing of perspectives, and upon wittily established identifications between (1) migratory birds and poetic images; (2) winter and the mind; and (3) knight and poet. Consider the function of metaphor in suggesting these identifications. (In what sense can the 'Arctic' freeze 'minds'?)

Compare the first four lines of 'The Flock' with those of 'The Harbour'. Would you agree with the view that the lines from 'The Flock' seem tauter, yet at the same time more 'arbitrary' than those of the earlier poem? What would you make of the remark that in 'The Flock' Walcott moves away from the poetry of Earth, and into the mansions of the mind?

The Whale, His Bulwark

This is a wry poem (but for one flash of anger at those 'derisive, antlike villagers') about the growth of a negative aspect of egalitarianism: the resentful urge to 'humble the high'. Walcott is not interested in anything so banal as 'high society'; his concern, which he later states (in 'Volcano'), is that the capacity for awe, without which people 'are no more than erect ash', has been 'lost to our time': we deride not only grandeur ('majesty') but also the possibility of mystery ('the unfathomable').

In 'The Whale, His Bulwark', as increasingly in his later work, Walcott writes out of the knowledge that in essential concerns he is out of step with his age; and while in some of the later poems his reaction is angry or bitter, in the present poem it is, rather, one of quiet (and embattled: cf. the final line) affirmation. The nostalgia which the poem exhibits in that thrice-repeated 'Once' derives from the poet's memory that not so long ago 'God and a foundered whale were [still] possible' – in the title, 'His' means God's – and his awareness that in the eyes of some readers he will appear to be being perverse is rendered in the ironic repetition of 'yet' (ll. 4 and 18).

Note the aptness of the rhymes to the poem's theme. Verse is cursed; what the Lord raises to our eyes we reduce to pigmy-size; the unfathomable becomes the unfashionable. Consider also the further diminution from the ironic 'mythological' to 'apocryphal' in the light of the references to belief in the first two lines of the last verse. The clause, 'Though the boy may be dead' has at least two meanings; what are they?

Missing the Sea

Imagine living near to a waterfall or wave-breaking beach and waking one morning to discover that its accustomed roar has inexplicably ceased. Your first perception will be of a wrong stillness, a 'deafening absence'; and for some hours perhaps you will have the sensation of walking through 'a thick nothing now' – i.e. a present ('now') which feels oppressively empty, lacking the pressure upon it of the past, and thus any connection to a conceivable future. That sense of being 'estranged' from time – and thus from life – is the state of mind which Walcott evokes in 'Missing the Sea' – most tellingly in the image of the newly bereaved unwilling to go on, to accept the onward flow of time, since to do so would be to acquiesce in being carried away (by time) from the beloved, for whom time has stopped.

'Missing the Sea' relies entirely on imagery. Can you think of other images (e.g. the dead hush that comes over trees before rain) that might have found a place in the poem? Without resorting to imagery, attempt to describe the state of mind with which this poem deals. Compare Walcott's poem with what you have written in a brief essay entitled 'The function of imagery'.

The Almond Trees

'The Almond Trees' is an extended metaphor for the enslavement, suffering, endurance, and finally the triumphant 'metamorphosis' into daughters of the grove (i.e. women of the islands) of West Indian women of African descent. In the main successful, it is marred by its one-line verse (heavily redundant, since the identification between woman and tree has already been wittily established by the reference to 'Daphnes', and further realized in vv. 6 and 7) and also – and more damagingly – by the poet in the penultimate verse ascribing to fire a mutilating function, in contradiction to the rest of the poem wherein fire is presented as a curing or refining element: an ambivalence which weakens the triumphant claims of vv. 6 and 7. Notice though how the horrific image of v. 12 (wherein 'holes' means lipless mouths) is defeated in the imagination by the grievous beauty of the last verse.

its spinning rays ... amaze the sun (v. 3, ll. 3–5): Cf. T. S. Eliot: 'The lengthened shadow of a man/is history, said Emerson'.

the forked limbs of girls toasting their flesh (v. 4, l. 3): The image is of girls sunbathing with legs splayed. It includes connotations of a barbeque – and a satanic pun on 'forked'.

Pompeian bikinis (v. 4, l. 4): In AD 79 several thousand Pompeians living at the foot of Vesuvius perished when that volcano erupted. In many cases the bodies left perfect moulds in the ash. The bikinis may resemble (obscurely?) such moulds. The phrase strengthens the relationship between fire and sexuality latent in the previous line and variously suggested elsewhere in the poem.

brown daphnes (v. 5, l. 1): In classical mythology, Daphne was the daughter of a river-god. Pursued by Apollo, she prayed for help and was turned into a tree.

their furnace (v. 7, l. 5): In the case of the trees, the sun and seablast. In the case of the women, the inferno of forced migration and slavery.

hamadryad's (v. 11, l. 1): In classical mythology, a hamadryad was a nymph living and dying with the tree she inhabited. Walcott may have introduced her (and the pastoral world to which she belonged) in order to destroy, with an emphatic negative ('Not as . . .') the rather too idyllic connotations of the earlier phrase 'brown daphnes'.

Veranda

A poem about the 'unguessed' continuities of life, 'Veranda' falls thematically into three parts. In the first (vv. 1–5) Walcott conjures up the ghosts of representatives of the British Empire – planters, colonels, middlemen and usurers – in the late nineteenth century, when the Empire was 'a fading world' ('flamingo colours': in certain circumstances, e.g. captivity, flamingos fade from their original bright red colour. The quote is from a review by Ronald Bryden of a novel about India). See how many images, all dealing with death, you can unravel and develop from that compressed sentence: 'the sunset furled/round the last post' ('last post' has three meanings).

In the second part (vv. 6–9) the poet recognizes – stepping forth from those 'grey apparitions' – his grandfather's ghost, and the language of the poem changes. Whereas till now it has been dispassionate and ironic ('Planters whose tears were marketable gum', 'usurers whose art/kept an empire in the red'), now, impelled by the poet's memory of his grandfather's migration and death, it moves towards the reverence of cadence ('Sire', and later, 'sir', 'father') and to the consonants of love, those liquid els and esses which lift v. 9 into lyricism. The section ends with the poet's affirmation to his ancestor that 'your genealogical roof tree, fallen, survives . . .' Notice the pathos of the question in v. 8: the ghost cannot speak, the poet must interpret its question, repeat it to be sure.

The final section is dominated by consoling images. Death is but a dream, a sea-crossing, a migration of the soul. The ancestors are sacred (earth, the grave, both enshrines and pardons them), and furthermore the living may redeem the dead. And in a lovely image (v. 11, l. 2) the poet develops the affirmation of continuity made in v. 9. In the light of all this, Walcott asserts his identity with his father and is able to countenance, with calm, the prospect of his own death.

Note that the poet's hand is 'darkening' because (1) he is stepping out of the sun into the shade of the veranda; (2) he is nearing the 'twilight' of the ancestors (i.e. death); and (3) the generations of West Indian Walcotts are each progressively darker-skinned than the last (cf. the reference to his father: 'your mixed son'). Why, and to what effect, does the poem end with a variation (i.e. a varied continuation) of its first line?

In 'Between the Porch and Altar', the American poet Robert Lowell writes: 'The twinkling steel above me is a star;/I am a fallen Christmas tree.' Find in 'Veranda' a pair of lines that echo these, and see if you can demonstrate the similarities in rhythm and cadence between them.

Lampfall

In *Another Life* Walcott writes of being 'balanced at [the] edge by the weight of two dear daughters'. 'Lampfall' likewise re-creates that perilous state of mind in which the impulse to die is held in check – but only just – by love for one's family and friends. Thus the celebration of life encouraged by the 'windy leaves' near the end of v. 1 is at once countered by 'But'; and thenceforth images of alienation predominate. Under the sway of the 'monster' (the deathwish) Walcott perceives himself as being drawn through the inhuman void of deep space, where 'no lights flash ... but the plankton's drifting, phosphorescent stars'. From there he can observe, but can neither be observed (his gaze, 'dead green [and] glaucous', contains no self-reflection) nor be communicated with (his ear is a 'shell'). He feels cut off, far; and in the image of the sea-rock 'Shuttling its white wool' like Penelope, boredom and meaninglessness threaten.

The poem gains in poignancy from certain echoes of Wordsworth's 'Tintern Abbey' (e.g. the lines 'And I'm elsewhere, far as/I shall ever be from you whom I behold now/Dear family, dear friends' recall the earlier poem's 'Oh! yet a little while/May I behold in thee what I was once,/My dear, dear Sister!'). And there are attempts at affirmation: the 'lantern's ring that the sea's/Never extinguished', or the last line of the penultimate verse, wherein Venus is (1) the planet, by which it is possible to navigate; and (2) the goddess of love, the emotion which alone can save us from being lost.

There is, however, an odd change of tone in the final verse. (In fact, it seems less to emerge from the rest of the poem than to undercut it.) Like the desperate, short sentences (and in particular that 'yet') of the penultimate verse, the shift to the past tense is ominous; and in the secondary image of the last line the poem tips towards death. (Note that while the primary image of that line is of technology overrunning everything – beetles=Volkswagens=cars – its secondary meaning is that, as in 'The Swamp' the road ahead threatened to 'merge/Limb, tongue and sinew into a knot', so now the road ahead is increasingly inhabited by beetles. Walcott has also written, in *Another Life*, of 'the path increas[ing] with snakes'.)

the moth-flame metaphor (v. 1, l. 2): Moths are often attracted to (and incinerated by) the heat of lamps, candles, etc. The metaphor is of being drawn to that which kills.

Coleman's (v. 1, l. 3): A Coleman is a lamp whose pressurized fuel emits a steady hum as the mantle burns. The line is probably a metaphor for the human heart poised on the edge of nothingness.

Joseph Wright (v. 1, l. 5): An eighteenth-century American portrait painter who studied in England, his work includes a painting of someone explaining the astrolabe, a graduated circle for taking altitudes at sea. An image of a huddled, lamplit group, the line also prepares us for the later reference to celestial navigation.

Penelope (v. 4, l. 3): In mythology, Penelope, the wife of Odysseus, was often courted by local nobles while her husband was away. She put them off by pretending that she could not remarry until she had finished weaving a shroud for Laertes, Odysseus' father. Every night she unravelled her day's work, so that the shroud was never finished.

This is the fire . . . door of heaven (v. 4, ll. 7–8): Roughly: 'Our dread of losing the warmth of human company prevents us from committing suicide, an act which in Christian religions is punishable by hellfire. Thus to accept human love is to pass through the furnace door into heaven.'

111

Like you (v. 6, l. 1): Presumably a relative or friend; although the person referred to may be Sylvia Plath, an American poet whose posthumously published collection, *Ariel*, was reviewed by Walcott around the same time that 'Lampfall' was written. (Walcott singled out for praise Miss Plath's description of an evening sky 'palely and flamily igniting its carbon monoxide'.) Sylvia Plath committed suicide in 1964. Her poems are generally thought of as bearing witness to the ways in which technology oppresses people.

Ebb

'Ebb' may be read as a poem about alienation and its essential consequence: the erosion of our sense of 'the freshness of life' (Walcott: 'The Wind in the Dooryard') by an unfocused anxiety which sees 'terror in the habitual, miracle . . . in the familiar'. Technology is identified as the enemy of nature (including human nature), and in the first half of the poem Walcott chronicles its assault in these islands. Note the pun on 'fretted'; how an oil slick confounds 'rainbow' with 'muck'; and the connection between 'littered' and 'afterbirth'. The poet is aware that while that 'dark aisle/of fountaining, gold coconuts . . . the last sacred wood' may be an 'oasis' (how rhymed?) or source of spiritual nourishment (cf. 'aisle', 'sacred') it too is marked for demolition. Yet while it survives it contains, 'netted in its weave' (like a ship in a bottle?), the image of an island schooner. An emblem of the spirit of adventure, the 'crippled' survivor of an older, pre-industrial world, the schooner has also been condemned, to irrelevance: 'like the washed-up moon/to circle her lost zone'. (Consider the slang meaning of 'washed-up'.) Walcott disclaims, as inaccessible, the schooner and its world: 'The schooner's out too far,/too far that boyhood'.

Yet in preferring 'safety' to the possibilities of adventure which the schooner represents, Walcott is aware of choosing ignobly: the penultimate verse exhibits a self-accusation sharpened rather than tempered by the claim that 'each sunfall,/the wildest of us all' makes the same choice, and by the guilty belligerence of the ensuing question. The final word of 'Ebb' should therefore be interpreted not as a corroboration of the rest of the verse but rather, in its colloquial sense, as a sardonic expression of disbelief: the disclaimer of a disclaimer. The poem ends in irresolution and self-disgust.

In a sense 'Ebb' continues the theme of 'Lampfall'. As an image of meaninglessness, of action which achieves nothing, its 'treadmill' resembles the Penelope of 'Lampfall'; the word 'elsewhere' echoes as sinisterly in the latter poem as in the former; and of course the world of 'Lampfall's last line holds the poet's dismayed attention throughout the first half of 'Ebb'. Where 'Ebb' differs, however, is in the poet's attitude to his choice; the wryness of his observation, in 'Lampfall', of 'the fire that draws us by our dread/Of loss' gives way to the bitter accusation that in choosing 'safety' we 'mortgage life to fear'.

The moon is a traditional symbol of the creative imagination. And elsewhere in the same volume (*The Gulf*) Walcott writes of 'measuring how imagination/ebbs'. Can you substantiate a reading of the poem which suggests it is 'really' about the decline of the creative imagination? How might the advance of industry, which makes obsolete the schooner and her world, endanger the creative imagination itself? What is the function of the punctuation with which the poem ends?

Hawk

In an essay entitled 'On Choosing Port-of-Spain' Walcott writes of Trinidad's Carnival ('a Creole bacchanal') as an 'exultation of the mass will', and describes the Creole mentality as 'the shrillest kind of hedonism, asserting with almost hysterical self-assurance that Trinidad is a paradise', and as 'a particular boastfulness, passing for panache or a sense of the good life...'

The boldfaced trochees of 'Hawk' (in Spanish, *gabilan*) mime both the cuatros' 'treng-ka-treng' and the stamping euphoria of Carnival. In all but six lines of the poem Walcott re-creates that gloating spirit; then, in the remaining lines (three each at the end of the penultimate and last verses) he deftly destroys it. Notice that the undercutting of that fantastical world (which the poet sees as sentimental and cruel – how do we know?) is achieved not merely by referring to the hawk by its English name, but by abrupt changes in the rhythm and tone of the poem. Attempt to analyse these.

Why (in v. 3) are the mouths 'slack'? What or whose 'limbs' are left shaking? Give two meanings of the first line of v. 4; what view of West Indian history is Walcott offering in 'Hawk'?

Consider that shadowy figure to which the hawk is compared: a grandee with extended hands 'waltzing alone,/alone, to the old parang'. Does he escape the poet's condemnation? (Would you like him to? Why?)

Mass Man

In 'Hawk' Walcott indicts the Creole mentality and its revellers; in 'Mass Man' he defends (against their counterattack?) the role in society of the meditative man.

The poem opens with images of Carnival. Notice how, by describing the man-inhabited costumes as 'metaphors', the poet cannily implies a parallel between the masqueraders' activity and his own. Furthermore, 'coruscating' means glittering, but also 'brilliant in intelligence or wit'. Likewise, 'making style' (v. 2), a colloquialism translatable as 'showing off', has as its secondary meaning 'creating a style' or cultural mode (see also below). The revellers, whose 'hedonism is so sacred that to withdraw from it, not to jump up, to be a contemplative outside of its frenzy is a heresy' (Walcott, in 'On Choosing Port-of-Spain'), challenge the poet-heretic to join them. The poet's defence of his role as spectator-witness is threefold. He points to the existence of suffering in the midst of the carnival (that child who 'collapses, sobbing'); he claims identity with the revellers, reminding them of their common history of slavery and acknowledging his own 'mania' (as history's creation? Cf. *Another Life*: 'The dream/of reason had produced its monster:/a prodigy of the wrong age and colour'); and he asserts that 'someone' must bear witness to the tragic dimensions of life, must link the dancers to their past and inescapable future ('dust to dust'), and in this way give them back to themselves.

Mass Man: A pun. Carnival masqueraders are termed 'mas men'; but see also Walcott's description of Carnival as 'an exultation of the mass will'.

barges (v. 2, l. 2): Another pun. Cleopatra travelled down the Nile on a ceremonial barge.

making style (v. 2, l. 3): For Walcott's views on the function of mimicry in the creation of a culture, see his essay, 'The Caribbean: Culture or Mimicry?' or these lines, from 'The Schooner *Flight'*: '. . . and we,/if we live like the names our masters please,/by careful mimicry might become men'.

114

'Join us,' they shout, 'O God, child, you can't dance?' (v. 2, l. 4): What gods and children share is an untrammelled capacity for joy. But the line is also an exact reproduction of colloquial Trinidadian. (Notice how 'dance', in dragging the last syllable of 'radiance' towards rhyme, ensures a Trinidadian pronunciation of the latter word.)

your penitential morning (v. 4, l. 1): Ash Wednesday, the first day of the Roman Catholic season of Lent. It follows immediately upon the two days of Carnival.

Landfall, Grenada

In 'Nearing Forty' Walcott relates how, as a poet, his 'life bled for/the household truth, the style past metaphor/that finds its parallels, however wretched,/in simple, shining lines . . .' 'Landfall, Grenada', in itself a minor elegy, exhibits that movement away from rhetoric (both verbal and emotional) and towards the age-old simplicities of 'true feeling' (Walcott: 'Winding Up'). Appropriately, the poem extols the virtue of reticence, and its language approaches that of prose. The rhymes are unobtrusive: either unstressed (heard/lowered, stars/mariners), or internal (ocean/motion, those/impose, ease/elegies), or the rhyme words are widely separated (place/race, offend/end). The syntax is straightforward, the cadences calm. Indeed, the poem tends towards silence – itself identified by the poet as a circumstance of death ('cannot be heard', 'climbs out of sound'). The exhortation of the last five lines may constitute an unwitting irony (the poem is itself a neat, gravestone elegy rhyming the dead man's end), and the odd surge of gallows humour ('rigidly anchored', 'Deep friend') threatens the tone of steady acceptance which the poet seeks and, in the main, achieves. The canes 'surging to cumuli' are presumably burning (though 'cumulus' has another, esoteric meaning, viz. accumulation). The line, 'your death was a log's entry', is prose. Consider the implications of 'tiered sea', 'ruled stars'.

Homecoming: Anse La Raye

And so one summer after I returned, we arranged
to stay in the old village, and we spent
two days and one night there, but except

115

for the first few hours it was somehow different,
as if either the island or myself had changed ...
and I left there that morning with a last look
at things that would not say what they once meant.

WALCOTT: Another Life

'Homecoming: Anse La Raye' re-creates that experience, of the loss of one's sense of home. The poet, visiting the island of his birth, discovers that 'there are no rites/for those who have returned'. The landscape strikes him as desultory and as though war-torn; the children, like the stunted survivors of a war, reveal the symptoms of malnutrition. He finds that they mistake him for a tourist, a potential source of money, and sees his earlier hope that 'it would mean something to declare/today, I am your poet, yours', as having been futile. The reference to 'homecomings without home' is of course ironic; the actual experience is of arriving nowhere. Thus in the final verse the poet feels 'dazed', and the real world seems forbidding, alien. Ghosts occupy the shade under the palm trees.

Helen (v. 1, l. 3): Helen of Troy, in the *Iliad* and *Odyssey* the wife of Menelaus. Her abduction by the Trojan Paris, who marries her, causes war between the Trojans and the Greeks. After the war she is successfully reconciled with her first husband and homeland. The parallel lies in the notion of the poet also being married twice: first to the island of his birth, and later to the muse of poetry, who leads him abroad. The reference to Helen also prepares us for the battlefield imagery of the succeeding lines.

the shades /of borrowed ancestors (v. 1, ll. 3–4): Anticipates the 'dead fishermen' of the final verse, in a sense the poet's 'real' ancestors.

her looms (v. 1, l. 7): The overzealous listener may hear 'heirlooms', but the phrase is obscure, unless Walcott is now referring to Penelope, another of the *Odyssey*'s embattled wives, and a tireless weaver – see note to 'Lampfall'.

drilled in our skulls (v. 1, l. 8): Force-fed us at school. But 'drilled' also sustains the loom image.

Suffer them to come (v. 2, l.1): Cf. Christ: 'Suffer little children to come unto Me.' How appropriate is the poet's likening of his relationship with the children to that of Christ's? (Is it ironic, do you think?)

your needle's eye (v. 2, l. 2): Christ taught that it was easier for a camel to pass through the eye of a needle than for a rich man to enter heaven.

reflecting nothing (v. 3, l. 8): (1) unthinking; (2) manifesting emptiness; (3) having no relationship with the environment. The phrase also echoes the earlier 'You give them nothing'. (Is the poet referring only to money, do you think?)

dead /fishermen . . . eating their islands (v. 3, ll. 14–16): An hallucination. The 'dazed' poet sees ghosts playing draughts with the West Indian islands, 'eating' them. The vision reflects the 'disappearance' of his sense of home. The reference to politicians is probably meant to direct our minds to the disintegration of the West Indies Federation, a collapse now widely attributed to self-seeking politicians 'playing politics' with the islands.

Cold Spring Harbour

'Cold Spring Harbour' evokes simultaneously two kinds of death. There is psychic death, the loss of hope: that 'dark child's' dreaming preparation for 'the white world of men' is shown to have been misconceived; the child's expectation of what lies beyond the 'door' (l. 10) is confounded in the man ('dumbstruck') when the door opens. And there is the poet's intimation of actual death: 'the strange violation . . . of perfect snow'. In the poem the two themes are interwoven and cannot really with coherence be unravelled (a triumph or weakness of the poem?); none the less, think if you can of two meanings of 'the white world of men', one applicable to each kind of death.

The poem develops between the poles of its parentheses (of which the first – syntactically implied – is, 'did/he know it was dark then'). Notice how our sense of the child's wonder, evoked mainly by the *w* sounds of ll. 7–9, gives way, with successive repetitions of the word 'white', to intimations of a blanker silence; and that 'What urges [him] towards this white,/snow-whipped wood' is – ominously – left unsaid. Consider also how resistant to true cadence (i.e. to respite) is the run-on tetrameter, the poem's main line.

Cold Spring Harbour is on Long Island, off the north-eastern seaboard of the United States. Given the poem's theme, however, what is the significance of the name itself? Is the poet missing his children

117

because they are not with him in the flesh? Or because they too are lost, as he was, in a dream of 'old Christmas card[s]?'.

'Cold Spring Harbour' is one of a number of poems in which Walcott refers to himself in the second person singular, in effect addressing himself. While this mannerism (which first appears in *The Gulf*) may be taken as symptomatic of the poet's loss of faith in the existence of an audience for his poetry, the impression on the reader is rather of a division, or gulf, arising between Walcott-the-poet and Walcott-the-man. The latter listens – and, presumably, obeys – as the former guides, admonishes, explains. In the present poem there is a third Walcott: the 'dark child' referred to as 'he'. Consider how much of its tension, its shrouded sense of disturbance and danger – which converges upon the lure of that 'white, snow-whipped wood' – 'Cold Spring Harbour' owes to the impression of dissociation which the existence of these three Walcotts conveys.

Love in the Valley

Though it may shine, bemuse or enchant, art is not life. What is living moves and changes; art stays still; and like memory it glazes its object. The world of art is a dream-world, its creatures spectral, its light winterish or submarine or stilly gold; and in that sense it is deathly: as silent – and as eternal – as death. 'Love in the Valley' re-creates the experience of entering the world of art (in this case, of literature): its wonder and drifting, dreamlike sequences, and also its silence.

Notice how Walcott persuades language into creating that aura of silence. While others have used the iambic trimeter to hurry a poem along (the hallmarks of this line are briskness and a clipped concision), Walcott uses it here to quite different effect. This he does (1) by allowing the line to dictate the cadence. Notice that virtually all the lines (with the exception of the last verse – why?) end either with unstressed syllables or with monosyllabic nouns, in each case causing the auditory imagination momentarily to linger. Thus the poem is full of – at times, barely perceptible – pauses, even where no punctuation occurs. (2) By *not* allowing (except, for dramatic reasons, 'heavy', v. 8, and 'literature', v. 16) any cadence to be too pronounced. There is a deliberate dearth of full stops, and in most cases the word upon which the period falls is soon picked up by rhyme. The combined effect of (1) and (2) is to defeat the speaking voice, which moves normally in broad sweeps between pronounced cadences, and to cause the poem to be read either silently, or in a voice of quiet incantation; and this, given its theme, is also its main, and major, achievement.

The sun goes slowly blind (v. 1, l. 1): i.e. the material world fades.

the valley of the shadow (v. 1, l. 3): Cf. 'Yea, though I walk through the valley of the shadow of death, I will fear no evil, for Thou art with me ...'

evening dims the mind (v. 2, l. 2): A variation of the first line, it indicates that while the journey about to be made may be rendered metaphorically in terms of the material world, it is in fact to be a journey of the imagination.

I shake my head in darkness (v. 2, l. 3): Secreting the image of a horse, this line prepares us for the head of Pasternak 'like a thaw-sniffing stallion' (v. 7).

leaden as eyes (v. 4, l. 1): In what state do eyes become leaden?

a skein of drifting hair (v. 4, l. 2): Appearing from nowhere, as things do in dreams? Or from the shaken head? Follow the path of that skein of hair; under what guises does it reappear?

the blank pages (v. 5, l. 1): Of the poet's workbook.

vertiginous (v. 5, l. 3): Causing dizziness and a sense of falling. Here, falling out of the material world and into the world of imagination, of art.

drift (v. 6, l. 1): Since the narrator is now disembodied. The 'I' is thus his imagination, not his corporeal self, and therefore ...

through hostile images /of white and black, and look (v. 6, ll. 2–3): ... the world becomes a child's wonderland ('and look').

thaw-sniffing (v. 7, l. 1): i.e. sensing the moment when winter breaks, and life resumes.

Pasternak (v. 7, l. 2): Boris Pasternak (1890–1960), Russian poet and novelist, awarded the Nobel Prize (which he refused) for his novel *Dr Zhivago* – a love story (whose heroine is called Lara, see v. 15, l. 3) set against the turmoil of revolutionary Russia.

the frozen spring (v. 8, l. 1): ... of passional life in post-revolutionary Russia. Pasternak was expelled from the Union of Soviet Writers for criticizing the Soviet system. The succeeding lines symbolize his death.

a white childhood (v. 9, l. 1): Because the world of imagination is conceived here as white? Or because the children's stories were usually set in a world of white people and of winter?

bracelets (v. 9, l. 2): Of frost.

Hawthorne's fairy book (v. 10, l. 3): Nathaniel Hawthorne (1804–64) was an American novelist who published a volume of stories for children entitled *The Tanglewood Tales*.

Hardy's (v. 12, l. 2): Thomas Hardy (1840–1928), English poet and novelist. His novels include *Tess of the D'Urbervilles* and *Far from the Madding Crowd*, in which the heroine is called Bathsheba (see v. 15).

hailstorms (v. 12, l. 3): Possibly a reference to the First World War. Hardy's work revealed a premonition of doom such as was realized by that war.

the depth of whiteness (v. 14, l. 3): Silence and death – see introductory paragraph to this note.

the numbing kiss (v. 15, l. 1): Their kiss is 'deathly' (cf. above) ...

whose tragedy ... love of literature (v. 16): ... and yet their fictional tragedies make real life by comparison seem mundane, and their love seems more vital than (my) love of fiction.

Nearing Forty

Two impulses contend in 'Nearing Forty'. There is the poet's lament for what he perceives as his failing powers, and there is his (compensatory?) affirmation – in support of which the quote from Johnson has clearly been adduced – of 'the household truth'.

The affirmation, to begin with, is tenuous. Bitterness and disgust threaten (consider the tone of 'which would be just', or the emphatic rhymes, 'wretched/stretched', 'gutter/sputter') and the poet becomes aware of the temptation to succumb to these, and thus to wind up sounding like 'the dry wheezing of a dented kettle'. Another approach occurs to him, however: to 'rise and set your lines to work/with sadder joy but steadier elation'; and though the poem announces no choice, its movement implies that Walcott will embrace the latter alternative, of acceptance and duty.

Thematically, 'Nearing Forty' is reminiscent of Wordsworth's 'Intimations of Immortality'. In particular, its final eight lines recall these of the latter poem:

> Though nothing can bring back the hour
> Of splendour in the grass, of glory in the flower,
> We will grieve not, rather find
> Strength in what remains behind ...
> In the faith that looks through death,
> In years that bring the philosophic mind.

And, like Wordsworth's poem, 'Nearing Forty' is 'rigidly-metred' and rhymed – an appropriate approach for a professional poet, one who feels his 'imagination ebb[ing]' but who is none the less determined to 'rise and set [his] lines to work'.

Is there a problem with all this, though? Does Walcott in fact view his work as 'a false dawn, fireless and average'? Does the fact that 'Nearing Forty' runs on, without losing coherence, for 32 lines without a full stop – except at the end – suggest the effort of a failing poet, or some kind of *tour de force*? (Look again at 'seems' in the final line.)

The Walk
Predominantly an evocation of the nervous exhaustion – like 'cold sweat fil[ing] from high tension wires' – which can afflict a writer after a hard day's work, 'The Walk' nonetheless attempts to affirm the bulwarks, of heart and home, which may restrain a man in such a state from an act of despair.

Under the influence of the poet's 'doubt' – really a malaise whose symptom is the 'brain that tires,/and loses faith' in the worth of its effort – the religious imagery of the opening lines gives way to images of illness. The poet sees himself as a patient who has spent the day 'prone, haemorrhaging' poems. Taking a stroll (like a convalescent?), he is struck by the way people ('cats') with the capacity to be free-ranging souls ('lions') none the less seem to prefer the boredom

('yawn') of being caged; then, finding himself instinctively turning
back at the end of the street, he acknowledges his own heart's attach-
ment, and finds awesome ('terrible') its fidelity, not only to home, but
to life, i.e. its capacity to endure – which is why the poet praises it as a
'rose of iron'.

In a vacant lot the poet comes upon a bamboo grove through which
a path 'hisses' – like a serpent (a visual image), but perhaps also like
the tempter in paradise. The temptation, since 'Only the pain . . . is
real', is to commit suicide; but in a startling image (final line), in which
the houses are portrayed as having acquired the leonine qualities
surrendered to them by their tenants, the poet discovers himself
implacably restrained.

'The Walk' however achieves at best an inconclusive statement.
The experience it imparts is of despair only tenuously held in check by
the heart's capacity to endure and by the gravitational pull of home. In
'The Chelsea', written a decade later, when Walcott, in his late forties,
had begun to wander the world, he writes of 'Happier lives, /settled
in ruts, and great for wanting less'. On the evidence of 'The Walk', do
you think he really believes this? In what tone would you declaim the
exhortation, 'arise, stroll on . . .'? Do you find anything melodramatic
about the utterance, 'Only the pain, /the pain is real' (and if so, what
does this suggest about the pain?). How central to the poet's mood is
the belief stated in ll. 17–19, and is this belief a cause or effect of that
mood?

Re-read 'The Walk', interpreting 'you/your' as the poet's spirit, and
the house as a house of flesh, i.e. his body. Can this interpretation be
sustained? Does it enrich the poem?

Another Life, Extract A

The opening movement, it introduces the poem's main themes: West
Indian history and the poet's own cultural ambivalence; the nature of
imagination; the author's apprenticeship as a painter; and a landscape
awaiting 'verification'. The extract also introduces two of the poem's
three main characters (apart from the poet himself). The girl is 'Anna'
(see Extracts F and G), the poet's first love; the master is Harold
Simmons, the young Walcott's artistic guide, and the subject of the
moving elegy which comprises Extract H.

Another Life, Extract B

Death, physical or psychic, shadows *Another Life* in many guises. The extract describes the child's first experience of death. The lantern-jawed gravekeeper will reappear, with the impact of a mythic character, at the end of the poem.

Another Life, Extract C

The 'heroes' are St Lucia's cast of 'characters', many of them eccentrics, described in previous chapters. The extract advances the notion of the identity of the religious and artistic impulses; describes a crucial experience in the adolescent's life; recalls the attraction for the young poet of the retreating 'ordered, colonial world'; declares that, for him, (another?) 'life began' when he fell in love with art – and then immediately brings nearer the figure of Anna, thus suggesting connections (though the poet also warns of contradictions) between the love of art and sexual love. The departure of the 'moonlit' liner, with which the chapter ends, premonishes other journeys – including the journey into the realm of imagination – and intimates also the poet's own eventual death.

Another Life, Extract D

Introduces 'Gregorias' – the St Lucian painter Dunstan St Omer – the third major character of the poem, and describes the awakening 'golden' year of the two young painters, 'drunk' on their love of art and determined to chart, in paintings, the 'several postures' of their 'virginal' island. The extract captures the idealism, elation, wonder and self-assurance of late adolescence. The 'finished soldier' is St Omer's widowed father.

Another Life, Extract E

Forewarning of a later, darker stage in the life of the artist, his youthful euphoria gone and nervous exhaustion threatening, the extract is informed by the mature Walcott's experience of subsequent 'deaths': the suicide of Simmons, the failure of Gregorias, the near-breakdown of the poet himself. It ends with a dramatic evocation of the great fire that razed most of Castries, the capital of St Lucia, in 1948.

Another Life, Extract F
Following Anna's soliloquy, that of a girl awaking to young woman-hood, the chapter moves swiftly to an intimation of eventual separa-tion and its recurring motifs: the walk/journey/voyage. It ends with a majestic sonnet exploring the contradictory demands of spirit and flesh, divine and human love ('in time' means in due course; but also 'in the temporal world' – which art transcends).

Another Life, Extract G
Describes the merging, in the young poet's imagination, of 'his' Anna with the Annas of literature (in particular, the heroine of Pasternak's *Dr Zhivago*) – an act of possession which none the less constitutes an unwitting denial of the uniqueness of the real Anna, who (partly in consequence?) soon leaves the island to study nursing in England. The extract represents a feat of sustained and passionate lyricism without parallel (to this annotator's knowledge) in English language twentieth-century poetry.

Another Life, Extract H
Following the poet's discovery that Harold Simmons has killed him-self, this extract comprises Walcott's elegy for his former tutor. It expresses a reverential notion of the relationship between the artist and his community: Simmons becomes 'a man no more/but the fer-vour and intelligence/of a whole country'.

Another Life, Extract I
Argues the primacy of the creative imagination, and its capacity both to possess and to transcend the events of history. (See Walcott's essay: 'The Muse of History'.)

Another Life, Extract J
The conclusion of the poem. In it Walcott asserts, with a rather forlorn defiance ('And what if . . .?'), the enduring power of Imagination ('the moon/will always swing its lantern') in the face of general destruction

(specifically, of the island's landscape, but one recalls the poem's other 'deaths'); asks forgiveness of the folk; confronts again the spectre of the old gravekeeper; bids farewell to Gregorias and Anna – and then, as if reluctant to let the poem end here, resurrects Gregorias to recall (as Othello, at the last, recalls his greatest triumphs) the mood and achievements of their 'golden year'. The gesture seems one of defiance. The last line of the poem is disturbingly private. (In fact, both names were the poet's nicknames for St Omer.)

The Virgins

Though Frederiksted is in the Virgin Islands, the title is of course ironic; the poem is a wry, and in places bitter reflection on the ways in which tourism can destroy the culture of a small and predominantly rural community. Its chief delights are to be found in its compression of meaning, its controlled and certain tone, its relentless evocation of vacuity, and – assaulting this last – the ingenious and 'vigorous' metaphor with which it ends.

the dead streets (l. 1): Dead because (1) it is the hottest time of day; (2) some rumour of impending civil unrest has driven the tourists away for the time being; (3) tourism has 'killed' the island's culture.

sun-stoned (l.1): (1) pelted by the sun; (2) dazed, as with sunstroke.

free port (l. 2): Where certain taxes have been lifted in order to attract commerce. But in context the term also refers to the original port (i.e. harbour or home) of the island's once 'free' inhabitants.

at funeral pace (l. 3): Why?

of life not lost to the American dream (l. 4): i.e. 'of a time when life in the islands had not yet been corrupted by the American dream of affluence'. Likewise, ll. 6–8.

civilized (l. 6): Ironically contrasted with 'simplicities'. Walcott is of course upholding the latter against the former.

for the good life . . . on the rise (ll. 8–9): Meaning (roughly): these islands sell their few assets (of climate and coast) so cheaply that their economies remain stagnant, increasing the numbers of the unemployed, who in desperation turn to crime.

125

blighted (l. 10): The sun brings the tourists and tourism destroys; thus the sun is a blight.

blown dry by the hysteria (l. 11): Notice the cry of the wind in *'hysteria'*.

A condominium drowns/in vacancy (ll. 12–13): Try to imagine *how* that condominium 'drowns' in 'vacancy'.

jewelled (l. 14): Descriptive of a housefly in the sun. But Walcott also intends us to think of the stereotype of the bejewelled American matron.

by revving up . . . banks of silver thresh (ll. 18–19): The image is of local craft collecting and ferrying tourists to the casinos and banks. But of course those 'banks of silver' are not only the commercial banks 'thresh[ing]' their harvests of profits, but also underwater banks of fish. Walcott thus manages to suggest the past and present in a phrase, and to imply the destruction of the livelihood of the locals (fishing) by the advent of tourism.

Adam's Song

The notion behind 'Adam's Song' is that the Word made Flesh ceases to be the Word – that while divine love assures immortality, profane love humanizes us and, thus, commits us eventually to die. So, when Adam sings 'the song to Eve' he does so 'at the price/of his own death' and in fear 'of the jealousy of God'. Yet the poet clearly sides with Adam, whom he presents as a brave, doomed – but above all, human – figure. 'Adam's Song' asserts the essential tragedy (but also the poignancy – witness the ineffable tenderness of the song) of the human condition.

The adulteress stoned to death (v. 1, l. 1): Christ halted a mob intent on stoning an adulteress to death by insisting that the first stone should be thrown by someone 'without sin'.

that films her flesh with slime (v. 1, l. 4): Both the imagery and the sound of the line recall the serpent. The implication is that malicious gossips are like the devil.

horned God (v. 2, l. 2): Horned means betrayed. But the devil is also popularly depicted with horns, i.e. as 'a horned God'. In this sense 'for' means 'for an image of'.

the song to Eve/against his own damnation (v. 4, ll. 1–2): 'Against': (1) 'in defiance of', i.e. even at the price of; (2) 'as proof against'. The lines thus compose this paradox: that human love, which condemns us to die, is also our salvation. (Do you see any connection between this and the American poet Robert Lowell's affirmation of 'man's lovely/peculiar power to choose life and die'?)

with the lights . . . kingdom (v. 5, ll. 1–2): The lights are coming on in the panthers' eyes because darkness is falling (and cats can see in the dark). But the image is also of an incipient attack. The panthers are in this sense God's avengers, 'coming out of the trees' towards Adam.

the jealousy of God (v. 6, l. 2): Like that of a jilted lover. In fact the Old Testament God is often portrayed as jealous, temperamental and wrathful.

The song ascends to God, who wipes his eyes (v. 7): God hears Adam's song, and stops weeping. Why, do you think?

Heart . . . the dew is (v. 8, ll. 1–3): The word 'Heart' at the beginning of each of these lines is Adam's term of endearment for Eve.

Parades, Parades

In this poem Walcott scathingly indicts one of the post-Independence West Indian governments – a government which he views as uncreative and gluttonous, and thus inherently totalitarian.

'Parades, Parades' opens in a tone of mixed bemusement and indignation. (Notice that the opening line seems to fade into air, suggesting: tiredness? bewilderment? vacancy? How is this effect achieved?) Independence has opened up horizons – desert, ocean, sky – but the old iniquities remain, while the politicians 'plod/without imagination', so that the fountain of creative action remains dry. (Lines 5–7 are imprecise: their meaning seems to be that the jets scratch the same lines, or trails, in the blue sky above the mountains.) In the repetition of 'same' – 'the same lines . . . the same steps' – Walcott's bemusement gives way to irritation, and he declares the Governor-General a 'fool'. (Why, do you think?)

In the second verse the poet describes a more sinister aspect of the Independence Day parades. He watches the 'eyes of the beautiful/and unmarked children' from the countryside 'widen in terror' of the nationalistic sentiments being thundered at them, and is moved to consider the heretical notion that nationalism may be evil – that perhaps life was 'truer' in the colonial days, when 'the law lived far away' (and, being remote, might also have been impersonal?). In fact, the impulse behind these lines is the conservative belief that the people of a country have a right not to be harangued by the State.

In the final verse the political circus appears: Papa (Papa Doc was the nickname of the despotic ruler of Haiti) and his 'sleek, waddling seals ... trundling up to the dais'. (Notice how 'sleek' suggests slyness, and 'waddling' both gluttony and gracelessness. Is there a sense, do you think, in which contemptuous laughter, like Walcott's here, can destroy its object?) The wind, symbol of 'inspiration', puts its tail between its legs. Note how, as the crowd falls suddenly silent, the poem itself stops 'abruptly'. (How does Walcott create that decisive cadence?)

The ensuing questions are rhetorical. We know that the silence is not one of respect but of unease; that the 'hoarse hosannas' (why the religious term, do you think?) represent 'awe' only in its debased sense of fear (they were 'forced'); and that the poet's conception of a 'New World' of the spirit is a far cry from the 'tin-ringing tune' of those 'pumping, circling horns'.

To whom is the poet speaking in the last five lines of the poem? Is his demand, 'Tell me ... why I said nothing', really a confession of complicity, that he remained silent when he should have spoken up in protest? Or a further indictment of the regime, that in its presence (from which even the wind flees) poetry is not possible? (Cf. W. B. Yeats, in 'A Model for the Laureate': 'The muse is mute when public men/Applaud a modern throne:/Those cheers that can be bought or sold,/That office fools have run...') What name would you be inclined to give to 'that look on the faces/of the electorate'?

The Wind in the Dooryard

Eric Roach, to whom this poem is dedicated, was a Tobagonian poet (b. 1914) who committed suicide in 1974. In his poetry he celebrated the life of the village, those rural communities of peasants and fishermen of African origin now modishly referred to as 'the folk'. He is reported to have been deeply disillusioned by the break-up of the West Indies Federation, which, like Walcott (see 'Homecoming: Anse

La Raye') he attributed to the ambitions of individual politicians – and which appears to have coincided with the beginning of Roach's preoccupation with his own death, a preoccupation which progressively became obsessive. In his last years he waged a brief but bitter (if eventually futile) battle against the breakdown of literary standards in the islands, as evinced by a rash of publications of mostly worthless verse – publications which were nonetheless championed by certain academics as heralding a breakthrough of the oral tradition into scribal literature, and as sociologically relevant. Roach was for many years Agriculture Reporter for the *Trinidad Guardian*.

'The Wind in the Dooryard' shares with 'Parades, Parades' a certain informality of construction. In both Walcott eschews metre, and the tingling near-approach to metre which characterizes some of his most successful poems, and relies instead upon his ear for the natural cadences of the speaking voice. This is of course the method of *vers libre*, but without a sure organic movement of the whole poem it becomes an alibi for the inclusion of anything. 'The Wind in the Dooryard' seems – as 'Parades, Parades' does not – to transgress the boundary between flexibility and formlessness. (One suspects, for example, that the shape of the poem would be modified hardly at all by omitting the whole of the eighth verse – or by adding, here and there, a number of one-line descriptive clauses.) The student of poetry might do well to consider here the air of *inevitability* which characterizes a good poem. To what extent does the repetition of 'I didn't want . . . I did not want' temper the sensation of arbitrariness which the form of the poem exudes?

Dooryard: The (often dirt) yard outside the door of a house or shack. But the term is almost certainly meant to bring to mind Walt Whitman's great elegy for the assassinated American President, Abraham Lincoln: 'When Lilacs Last in the Dooryard Bloom'd'.

salt (v. 1, l. 4): Embittered; but also, 'salted by the sea'. While it was later discovered that Roach had taken poison and thrown himself from a cliff, the news that his body had been found at Quinan Bay (on the south-east coast of Trinidad) led most people initially to believe that he had drowned himself by swimming out to sea. 'The Wind in the Dooryard' (see also ll. 17–20) exhibits this misapprehension – as does at least one other poem on the subject written soon after Roach's death.

129

what he celebrated (v. 2): Notice that Walcott's poem, while dedicated to a man who finally turned his back on life, is itself a celebration of life – an implicit disavowal of Roach's last action. Thus, rather than being a lament about death, the poem is, rather, a testament to the implacable surge of life (note that the sunrise, v. 5, 'force[s]' the sleeper to awake); a lifeforce which, Walcott asserts, Roach once recognized, and affirmed, in the rhythms and activities of the country.

his rusty theme (v. 7. l. 4): Can you think of three reasons (apart from the suggestion of 'rustic') why Walcott refers to Roach's theme as 'rusty'?

Shango (v. 7, l. 6): Yoruba god of thunder and fertility.

The Bright Field

In 'The Bright Field' Walcott returns to and develops the theme of the much earlier 'Ruins of a Great House', the common destiny of colonist and colonized. The poems are also worth comparing in terms of language. Notice how, in the fifteen or more years which separate them, the voice inhabiting the pentameter has grown markedly less mellifluous, less declamatory, and more flexible: in short, more open to the movement of intelligence. Analyse the ways in which the two poems employ metre and rhyme. To what extent does your analysis throw light upon the ways in which this change of tone has been achieved?

the sense/we all have (v. 1, ll. 2–3): The first gesture of inclusion. London and the Caribbean are further linked, both explicitly (in 'cane or wheat', 'cab [and] bullock-cart', 'lanes or cane fields') and by simile ('like dark canes, the river spires') and metaphor (the 'pool of London', [The Thames] i.e. like the bay of Salybia). See also the parallel between swallows and pelicans in the final verse.

self-defence (v. 1, l. 4): Against the civilization of the former colonists. But they also, living in London, must employ self-defence, since 'selves' (l. 6) are 'humbled [i.e. feel threatened] by massive places'.

who moved . . . was moved (v. 1, ll. 7–8): Who once moved in anger . . . was moved to pity. (Cf. 'Ruins of a Great House': 'All in compassion ends'. Also, 'The Harbour': 'Time knows that bitter and sly sea'.)

Underground-bound (v. 1, l. 8): Headed for (1) the subway, (2) the grave.

Their sun that would not set was going down (v. 2, l. 1): Like other imperial nations, Britain once harboured the hope that 'the sun would never set' on its empire; i.e. that the empire would endure for ever. Walcott's line is an ironic comment on that hope; but in the context of the poem it is also a reminder of mortality.

with the compassion of calendar art (v. 2, l. 4): Art may conceivably be termed compassionate because it immobilizes scenes, preserving them from time, and thus from death. Calendar art, however, is meant to endure for a specific time only, before the page is turned. It is unclear whether Walcott means us to see compassion in the fact that the depicted scene is preserved at all, even for a short time, or in the swiftness and painlessness with which it is banished.

like walking sheaves of harvest (v. 2, l. 5): Night is the harvester. It gains support as a metaphor for death from that antithetical 'quick' in the same line.

the loud belt (v. 2, l. 8): Walcott likens the street to a conveyor belt. The implication is that the inhabitants of great cities are reduced by them to component parts in a factory (see note on 'self-defence').

feels . . . everything (v. 2, ll. 14–15): The passage from Donne quoted in the notes to 'Ruins of a Great House' ends: 'And therefore never send to know for whom the bell tolls; it tolls for thee.'

original sin (v. 2, l. 16): In Christian religions original sin brought the knowledge of good and evil into the world, destroying Paradise and initiating history. London (i.e. the British) is here credited with (or accused of) having destroyed the 'paradisal' islands, and initiating West Indian history.

Samuel Palmer (v. 3, l. 1): English eighteenth-century engraver. In *Another Life* Walcott quotes Yeats's reference to twilight as 'the lonely light that Samuel Palmer engraved'.

Blake's (v. 3, l. 2): William Blake, English poet, painter and prophetic visionary, was a contemporary of Palmer's. Believing in the possibility of building a new 'Jerusalem' in 'England's green and pleasant land', he was enraged by the sordid effects of the early industrial revolution on the English people and landscape. Why do you think Walcott focuses here on that pivotal moment in English culture?

These slow ... rooks (v. 3, ll. 4–6): The belfry-strokes are imagined as stones thrown into a pool, the swallows as their concentric ripples. They function also as concretizations of that 'involuntary bell' which the heart feels.

across Salybia as the tide lowers (v. 3, l. 8): Notice how, like the poem and the belfry-strokes themselves, 'lowers' dies away.

Dark August

'Dark August' turns on its parenthetical lament (penultimate verse), in which 'they' refers to society – cf. those 'gossiping mosquitoes'. The poet's love is adulterous or in some other way considered anti-social. On account of it 'Everything goes to hell'.

'Dark August' thus belongs to that most populous family of poems – added to by every age, in every nation – singing of love embattled or thwarted. Where it differs from most of its companion pieces is in its conclusion; in the poet's determination to 'learn to love black days like bright ones'. (Does 'to love' have here any more emphatic meaning than 'to accept'? Can you think of a sense in which it is possible to love sorrow?)

Notice that while 'the dark days, the steaming hills' (echoed later by 'the black rain, the white hills') is an evocation of grief, the word 'rain', wherever in the poem it appears, stands rather for passion. ('Fixing', v. 4, is in this sense a veterinary term, meaning 'de-sexing'.) What connections does the poet suggest between passion and grief? How successful do you find the personification, 'My sister, the sun'? (Do you find daunting, for example, the leap of imagination necessary to conceive of the sun as having a 'forehead of flowers and eyes of forgiveness'?)

In this poem, only two words fully rhyme. Which are they? What term describes the relationship between 'ones' and 'once'?

Sea Canes

In 'Frederiksted, Dusk', Walcott writes of the existence of 'something between life/and death' (notice, incidentally, the artful delineation –

as if that 'something's habitat was the small pause between the lines).

This 'something' is not identified. In fact it seems to be as mysterious, as ultimately unnameable, as Wordsworth's 'something far more deeply interfused ... a motion ... a spirit ...', though Walcott appears to conceive of it rather as a species of light. (In 'Frederiksted, Dusk' he refers to it as 'Whatever it is/that leaves bright flesh like sand and turns it chill', and observes that it 'would shine in them'.)

In 'Sea Canes' this 'something' is again alluded to. We learn that it is 'stronger' than lost love; that it has 'the rational radiance of stone'; that it goes (or lies) 'further than [or beyond] despair'; that it is 'strong as the wind' – and that it is capable of bringing 'those we love before us [just] as they were'. Its main attribute thus seems an ability to create an intense, emotionless realism, in defiance of time and death. Since the poet himself cannot name this 'something' (whatever it is) it is unlikely that we, his readers, should be able to. None the less, the student who is prepared to say something like 'I feel I know what he means but I can't describe it', should attempt to go further. (Is it an objective phenomenon? A state of mind? Imagination? Memory? Then, what is it?)

'Sea Canes' employs two distinct metres. The first four verses are predominantly trimetrical (producing an effect of – sadness? terseness? barely controlled emotion?) after which the lines lengthen into pentameters (suggesting – resignation? comprehension? peace?). Notice that the sixth line, rewritten as 'from the surf's faint drone', loses in effect – why? 'Green and silver' (l. 14) may imply daylight and moonlight (i.e. life and death) but as a visual image in the setting of the poem it is problematic (is the colour green discernible by moonlight?).

with faults and all, I cried (v. 1, l. 4): Do you find jarring the dissonance (after 'dead', 'earth', 'instead') of 'cried'? If so, do you think the dissonance was intended, or is a flaw of the poem?

snatch their talk (v. 2, l. 1): Assume that the poet began the line with the phrase 'snatches of conversation' in mind, then changed the first noun into a verb. What light does this throw on the nature of the poetic imagination?

surf's (v. 2, l. 2): What 'surf', precisely?

I cannot walk ... earth's load (v. 2, l. 3 – v. 4, l. 1): These lines describe the disembodied souls of the dead in the act of leaving earth.

The sea-canes by the cliff flash green and silver (v. 5, l. 1): Look up, in connection with this line, the meaning of 'animism'.

enduring moonlight (v. 6, l. 2): Capable of enduring the light (or presence) of death (see note to 'The Schooner *Flight*').

Oddjob, a Bull Terrier

'Oddjob' was the name of a dog belonging to friends of Walcott. The poem describes the day of its dying: a darkening day, with rain coming and 'the gold [of sunlight] going out of the palms'. (Cf. Walcott's reference, in 'Frederiksted, Dusk', to 'Whatever it is/that leaves bright flesh like sand and turns it chill'.) The fading of light from the external world thus parallels (or is an 'objective correlative' of) the fading of life in the dog. The poet is struck by the owners' unpreparedness for their pet's death – by the fact that no one connected 'the fleck of the drizzle ... with the dog's whimper' – an unpreparedness which, Walcott reflects, was in part due to the animal's inability to communicate: 'what follows at your feet/is trying to tell you/the silence is all'. (But consider that 'what follows' is not merely the dying dog but, in a wider, human sense, death itself.) With this reflection the poem arrives at its theme, which is silence; not only 'the silence of the dead' but also 'the silence of the deepest buried love' (a pun on 'buried'). The poet affirms that to be 'stricken dumb' is to be stricken 'deep' – that the profoundest emotions are 'unutterable/[yet] must be said'.

This reverence for silence, on the part of one whose preoccupation as a poet is first and foremost with language, is not paradoxical. Rather, Walcott is here acknowledging silence as the matrix of poetry, the brimming hinterland of emotion from which poetry issues. Can you think of a sense in which the silence of love – i.e. a love endured in silence – is 'blest/deepest by loss'? Is the tone of the last line one of grief, or wonder, or affirmation – or a combination of these?

One often comes across poems whose language overreaches their emotional content. 'Oddjob, A Bull Terrier' is the converse: a moving poem of great simplicity of expression. Consider the predominance of short or end-stopped lines, and the appropriateness of this to a poem

134

whose theme is silence, or the power of silence. Is there a causal connection between the poem's ability to move us and the simplicity of its language?

Earth
It has been said – usually as a warning or rallying cry in a political context – that those who have nothing have nothing to lose. In 'Earth' Walcott takes this maxim and offers it as a source of solace and strength to someone in danger of emotional or psychic destitution. The poet, however, modifies the maxim. Those who have nothing else, he implies, still retain their connection with the earth, and, in an act of imitation so fervent that the poem describes it as a metamorphosis, can learn earth's stoicism (see, in connection, 'The Flock' – or, for a contrary view, the narrator's lament, in Chapter 5 of V. S. Naipaul's *The Mimic Men*, at 'the lack of sympathy between man and the earth he walks on').

'Earth' exhibits an intensity and a spareness which together convey the impression of urgency, turning the reader's concerned attention to the (unnamed) imperilled man or woman whom the poet is addressing, and giving the poem its dramatic force. As contributing to that air of urgency, consider (1) the poem's monolithic imagery; (2) its emphatic (because they begin their lines) exhortations: 'Let', 'feel', 'Sleep'; (3) the slow-burning hypnotist's voice behind the repeated 'You have never possessed anything . . . This is all you have owned . . .'

In the volume *Sea Grapes* 'Earth' follows immediately upon 'Odd-job, a Bull Terrier'. Does this fact seem significant?

To Return to the Trees
A poem concerned with the approach of old age, and the spectre of death which it brings, 'To Return to the Trees' affirms the need for a stoicism 'beyond joy [or] lyrical utterance'. Its heart lies in the significances imparted to the colour grey, in lines which constitute the poem's main achievement, since we are persuaded by them (and by that lovely easing of pace in the last verse) that the poet – and thus, by extension, the reader – is capable of confronting death with 'a heart at peace'.

135

Senex (v. 1, l. 1): Latin for 'old man'.

unwincing (v. 1, l. 3): Sounds the key note of the poem, and looks forward to 'stoic' and 'obdurate'.

geriatric (v. 2, l. 1): Ageing, or aged.

Cumana (v. 2, l. 2): A small town on the north-east coast of Trinidad.

To return to the trees (v. 2, l. 3): (1) To seek solace in the trees' capacity to endure; (2) to die, be buried, decompose, and thus become one with the tree-producing soil.

to decline (v. 3, l. 1): To fall. But the term also registers a schoolboy's 'laborious' declensions of Seneca's Latin (v. 15).

Ben Jonson (v. 3, l. 3): Elizabethan poet and playwright. Boanerges was his nickname.

lying (v. 4, l. 1): A (rather heavy-handed) pun: lying down/telling a lie.

gnarled (v. 5, l. 1): Like Seneca's 'gnarled' Latin, and (implicitly) the gnarled trunk of the 'felled almond'.

bearded with the whirlwind (v. 5, l. 2): Like certain pictorial representations (e.g. Blake's) of the Old Testament God (?).

flagrant (v. 7, l. 1): Flaming. Note that the meditation on grey grows out of the poet's observation of the day's 'ashen end'.

as it bestrides factions (v. 11, l. 3): Since it embraces both sides of a dispute. The notion is of an infinite capacity for acceptance.

Samson's (v. 12, l. 3): In the Bible, Samson was a judge of Israel famed for his strength. After many tribulations (he was seduced and betrayed by Delilah to the Philistines, who put out his eyes), he destroyed his captors' temple by pushing over its supporting pillars.

Atlas (v. 14, l. 2): In Greek mythology the Titan responsible for guarding the pillars of heaven (notice the train of thought *en route* from Samson), he was originally credited with holding up the sky (not 'the world', as in later representations, including Walcott's).

Seneca (v. 15, l. 2): Roman contemporary of Christ's, he was, among many things (orator, diplomat, financier), a playwright whose

136

tragedies tended to suffer from verbosity – hence, 'that fabled bore'.

its two eyes (v. 17, l. 2): The pair of 'e's in 'eye', each of which contains an aperture or 'eye'.

this obdurate . . . slowly (v. 18, l. 3 – v. 19, l. 2): In another poem Walcott writes of the poet sinking 'to lose [his]name', and becoming the 'muscle shouldering the grass/through ordinary earth'.

Sabbaths, WI

'Sabbaths, WI' is an evocation of the 'melancholia' of small-island Sundays, thirty or forty years ago: the empty streets, the silent landscape, the old men playing draughts under the sea-almonds, the adults 'resting' after lunch, the revivalists gathering at dusk, on the horizon the tourist ships passing . . .

Comprised wholly of introductory clauses, the poem depends upon repetition and intonation to complete the sense of the sentence which it withholds (something like: 'pass before the mind's eye now'). Notice how the whole poem converges upon the line 'Those Sundays, those Sundays' – a line which composes its strenuous rhythms and webs its disparate images. After it, 'the engine of the sea' (*Another Life*) only seems to begin again; in fact the poem musingly dies away.

What is the effect of the lack of punctuation? The emotion concentrated in the line quoted above? The significance of the last line?

Forest of Europe

Joseph Brodsky, to whom the poem is dedicated, is an exiled poet from Soviet Europe living in the United States. 'Forest of Europe' has as its main setting the 'brown cottage' which Walcott, while teaching poetry in the USA (and thus a temporary 'exile' himself) shared with him for part of an Oklahoman winter.

The poem begins (and ends) with evocations of a winter forest whose location, appropriately, might equally be America or Europe. Winter has traditionally appeared in literature as a metaphor for exile (why, do you think?) and, between its opening and closing stanzas, 'Forest of Europe' explores that condition. The poem moves from the memory of Osip Mandelstam (see below) to the parallel experience of the American Indian (vv. 4–5) and then, via a reflection upon the cyclical nature of life (v. 6) to the great migrations of refugees from Soviet Europe and their archetypal experience: the journey of departure. With the reference to Brodsky's exiled compatriots as 'citizens of a language that is now yours', 'Forest of Europe' begins its own (counter-) movement, of affirmation. Poetry will survive persecution (v. 13, l. 2) as it survives the seasonal changes of earth (v. 13, l. 5), since it is the language of God (v. 15) – or of the indestructible urge towards self-expression (even the primates 'grunt').

Not the least of Walcott's claims upon our attention is this fact: that in an age that treats poetry as marginal, tolerating it (more or less) as a series of whimsical footnotes to a dour text co-authored by technologists and ideologues, he remains one of a very few poets writing in English who have steadfastly refused that trivializing notion of their function, insisting rather that the writing of poetry is a serious (not 'solemn') and ennobling exercise, calling for long, ardent apprenticeship, engaging the whole man, and capable of dealing with any aspect of human experience. 'Forest of Europe' is a major (arguably, a great) poem – multi-layered, unified, unclouded in perception, thematically epic and sure of tone – which could not have been composed by a poet used to approaching his task in any other spirit.

The last leaves . . . ear (v. 1, ll. 1–2): Can you imagine a sense in which the notes from a piano might resemble 'ovals' (or vowels)? The falling leaves are likened to musical notes; but in v. 13 the poet asserts that the 'music [of poetry] will last longer than the leaves'.

gawky music stands (v. 1, l. 3): The trees resemble music stands (1) visually, since their branches are bare; (2) because their leaves fell like musical notes ('notes' having in the meantime taken on the meaning of annotated music sheets).

manuscripts of snow (v. 1, l. 5): Pages of writing are throughout the poem likened to snow – cf. vv. 5 and 6. The snow is 'scattered' like the music sheets/musical notes/leaves.

the wintry breath (v. 2, l. 3): (1) because Brodsky is reciting the poem in winter; (2) because Mandelstam was deported by the Soviets to the frozen wastes of Asia, where he died; (3) because the lines themselves premonish (see note to v. 3, l. 1) the winter of exile.

Mandelstam (v. 2, l. 4): Osip Mandelstam was a lyric poet, born in Poland, who lived and published in the Soviet Union. For maintaining his independence from Stalinism he was persecuted and driven into exile. The date of his death has been kept secret by the Soviets, but is believed to be in 1940.

The rustling ... Neva (v. 3, l. 1): actually, 'The rustling of hundred-rouble notes above the lemon Neva.' The line is from Mandelstam's 'I Was Like a Child', which begins: 'I was like a child in that world of sovereign power/... and spiritually owe nothing to that world,/save that I may have suffered in the semblance of others.' The river Neva emerges into the sea at what is now Leningrad. Notice the evolution of the poem's opening image into that of Mandelstam's.

barren Oklahoma (v. 3, l. 5): Oklahoma, one of the American States, is described as barren because (1) it is in fact largely so, containing part of the eastern slope of the Rocky Mountains; (2) the time is winter; (3) to the two exiles it is not home.

Gulag Archipelago (v. 4, l. 1): Alexander Solzhenitsyn, a dissident Russian writer, was imprisoned and later expelled by the Soviets. (His fate thus resembles Mandelstam's.) In *The Gulag Archipelago* he describes the vast system of concentration camps for political dissidents which grew up under Stalin, and has survived him.

under this ice (v. 4, l. 2): i.e. buried in the American past.

the long Trail of Tears (v. 4, l. 3): Refers to the forced migrations of American Indians before the waves of colonists of European ancestry.

Choctaw ... treaties and white papers (v. 5, ll. 3–4): The Choctaw, an Indian tribe, signed treaties with the American Government but were none the less cheated out of their ancestral lands in present-day Alabama and Louisiana (white papers: Government edicts). The verse indicts the tendency of Movements (even those which begin with good intentions) to sacrifice, as they gather momentum, the 'single human' in the name of the Cause. Its placement in the poem implies that it is this tendency which is responsible for the creation of refugees and exiles.

one mind (v. 6, l. 4): Mandelstam's/Brodsky's.

the forest's tortured icons (v. 7, l. 1): In terms of the train journey, the winter trees. In terms of a journey of the imagination, artists incarcerated in 'forests' of concentration camps by totalitarian States. (Icons are sacred images of Eastern Christianity.)

the spires /of frozen tears (v. 7, ll. 2–3): Like stalagmites (?); cf. the 'salt, mineral spring' (v. 4, l. 2).

space /so desolate it mocked destinations (v. 8, ll. 4–5): Consider 'Forest of Europe' as a parable of the human condition – of the soul's journey through life. How is the phrase illumined by this interpretation of the poem?

that dark child (v. 9, l. 1): The young Brodsky. What is the expression on his face as he watches the river mint 'sovereigns stamped with power, not with poets'?

sovereigns (v. 9, l. 3): Coins – a visual image of light on unstill water; (2) rulers. In this sense the line refers to the growth of totalitarian regimes.

tributary (v. 10, l. 3): A branch of a river; but note the echoes of 'tribute' and 'tribulation'.

my South (v. 12, l. 1): The Caribbean.

there is no harder prison than writing verse (v. 12, l. 3): Because the writing of poetry (including 'free verse') involves submission to the dictates of form. The line, though it may be heartfelt, is of course an overstatement.

when, in his forest of barbed-wire branches (v. 13, l. 3): Notice that the forest of Europe has evolved from stands of trees to concentration camps.

Borealis . . . Archangel (v. 14, ll. 3–4): The Aurora Borealis is a luminous atmospheric phenomenon occurring near the earth's magnetic poles and visible from time to time by night. The image is of a peacock's tail, the extremities of its fan extending like callipers from Los Angeles in the USA to Archangel in the USSR. The verse affirms that poetry will live as long as earth itself. There is a secondary meaning, however. Boreas was the Greek god of the north wind, and 'boreal' means frosty or wintry. Borealis may thus be rendered as 'the hand of winter' – in the context of the poem, the creators of exile (i.e. totalitarian governments). Thus memory will need 'nothing to repeat', since exiles live on memories, and there will be then no exiles.

heavier than a boundary stone (v. 15, l. 4): Echoes v. 7, l. 5. The verse affirms the heroism of Mandelstam, who imprisoned, frightened, starved (and ill?), none the less went on writing poetry, itself an exhausting occupation.

as we grunt . . . cave (v. 16, ll. 2–3): Walcott affirms the identity of impulse which lies behind the poetry of modern writers like Brodsky and himself, and the first grunting approximate speech of man's ancestors. The implication is that speech as self-expression has always existed in human history and (by extension) always will. Note that Mandelstam's 'divine fever' produced a poem which, like an eternal flame, 'warms' (i.e. keeps alive the spirit of) other, latter-day exiles.

mastodons (v. 16, l. 5): The giant ancestors (now extinct) of the elephant. Walcott uses them here as a metaphor of States enforcing their ideological systems; the image contains the parallel prophecy of the eventual extinction of such regimes.

The Schooner *Flight*, Chapter 11 (After the Storm)

In 'The Harbour' the young poet/navigator began his 'progress outward/on a sea which is crueller than any word/of love'. Three decades on, 'The Schooner *Flight*' describes the experience of that voyage.

The poem's narrator and central character is Shabine ('the patois for/any red nigger'), a poet and occasional seaman. In the opening chapters he gives his reasons for quitting Trinidad, his homeland: (1) he was broke; (2) the corruption and materialism all around him had begun to 'poison [his] soul'; (3) he had been used (and then discarded) by a 'big government man' to smuggle Scotch – and now a Commission of Inquiry into smuggling was being set up; (4) he was quarrelling with his mistress, Maria Concepcion – quarrels which were 'mashing up my house and my family'. To escape all these (and after a mental breakdown which lands him in the lunatic asylum), he decides to enlist as a seaman on the inter-island schooner, *Flight*. This movement of the poem ends with Shabine's lament: 'Where is my rest place, Jesus? Where is my harbour?'

The ensuing chapters describe his real and imagined experiences

141

(including an hallucination of the fleets and slaveships of history, and the *Flight*'s survival of a primal storm) on the voyage north.

Initially a simple narrative, 'The Schooner *Flight*' progressively and subtly emerges as an allegory of the journey of the poet's soul through life. That journey begins with the poet turning his back upon the loves and griefs of human society (though the memory of Maria Concepcion continues to haunt him like the ever-sought, never-possessed Muse of poetry – notice that her name echoes Catholicism's 'Muse': Mary of the Immaculate Conception). It leads him through the triumphs and travails of a life dedicated to poetry; until, in the final chapter (which comprises the present extract) he is granted a premonition of his own eventual end, as the light of literature merges with that of death to become 'a road in white moonlight taking me home'.

Though Walcott has not quite been able to overcome a certain tension inherent between Shabine the narrator (poet and contemplative) and Shabine the dramatic character (smuggler and brawler), 'The Schooner *Flight*' remains a major poem, containing virtually all the main themes of literature: imagination, history, exile, love and death. Below the engaging narrative it is philosophically profound – consider, for example, that unforgettable couplet: 'I try to forget what happiness was/and when that don't work, I study the stars.'

In it Walcott forges, from the diverse strands of his region's history – from the rhythms, intonations and syntax of West Indian dialect and the vocabulary and syntactical possibilities of Standard English – a poetic language that is musical, compressed and subtle.

THE CARIBBEAN WRITERS SERIES

The book you have been reading is part of Heinemann's long-established Caribbean Writers Series. Details of some of the other titles available are given below, but for a catalogue giving information on all the titles, and on the African Writers Series write to:
Heinemann Educational Publishers,
Halley Court, Jordan Hill, Oxford OX2 8EJ
United States customers should write to:
Heinemann Inc., 361 Hanover Street,
Portsmouth, NH 03801-3912, USA.

CLEM MAHARAJ
The Dispossessed

The history of Highlands, a sugar estate,
is bound up with the lives of the poor people who live and labour on it. Clem Maharaj brings a delicate clarity
to his heartfelt description of these workers.

IAN McDONALD
The Humming-Bird Tree

Alan lives with his parents in 1940s Trinidad.
When he becomes friends with the East Indian servants,
his parents intervene.
The Humming-Bird Tree is now a BBC film.

IAN McDONALD & STEWART BROWN (EDS)
The Heinemann Book of Caribbean Poetry

In a collection that celebrates the richness of the Caribbean,
editors Stewart Brown and Ian McDonald offer the best
of the new work being produced in English in the region,
together with the finest poetry of
an earlier generation of Caribbean writers.
The anthology features such well-known names as Derek Walcott, Louise Bennett and Andrew Salkey, as well as younger poets such as David Dabydeen and Jean Binta Breeze.

FRANK COLLYMORE

The Man Who Loved Attending Funerals and Other Stories
(With an afterword by Harold Barratt)

An engaging collection of shorter fiction by this multi-talented Barbadian. The title story depicts a man who revels in ritual at the burials of acquaintances, but has to recognise his own mortality.

LAWRENCE SCOTT

Witchbroom

Lavren Monagas de los Macajuelos pours forth epic and intimate tales of conquest, crime and passion. As this extraordinary hermaphrodite character both observes and acts in the unfolding drama, we are drawn into his/her account of the quest for El Dorado. The stories are told in the traditional Caribbean style of irony – *mamaguy*.